Understanding childhood:
a cross-disciplinary approach

This book is part of the series *Childhood* published by The Policy Press in association with The Open University. The four books in the series are:

Understanding childhood: a cross-disciplinary approach (edited by Mary Jane Kehily)

ISBN 978-1-447-30580-4 (paperback)

ISBN 978-1-447-30927-7 (ebook)

Children and young people's cultural worlds (edited by Sara Bragg and Mary Jane Kehily)

ISBN 978-1-447-30582-8 (paperback)

ISBN 978-1-447-30925-3 (ebook)

Childhoods in context (edited by Alison Clark)

ISBN 978-1-447-30581-1 (paperback)

ISBN 978-1-447-30924-6 (ebook)

Local childhoods, global issues (edited by Heather Montgomery)

ISBN 978-1-447-30583-5 (paperback)

ISBN 978-1-447-30926-0 (ebook)

This publication forms part of the Open University module E212 Childhood. Details of this and other Open University modules can be obtained from the Student Registration and Enquiry Service, The Open University, PO Box 197, Milton Keynes, MK7 6BJ, United Kingdom (Tel. +44 (0845 300 60 90, email general-enquiries @open.ac.uk).

www.open.ac.uk

Understanding childhood:
a cross-disciplinary approach

Edited by Mary Jane Kehily

Published by
The Policy Press
University of Bristol
Fourth Floor, Beacon House
Queen's Road, Clifton
Bristol BS8 1QU
United Kingdom
www.policypress.co.uk

in association with
The Open University
Walton Hall
Milton Keynes MK7 6AA
United Kingdom

First published 2003. Second edition published 2013

Edited and designed by The Open University.

Typeset by The Open University.

Printed in the United Kingdom by Bell & Bain Ltd, Glasgow.

British Library Cataloguing in Publication Data:
A catalogue record for this book is available from the British Library.

Library of Congress Cataloging-in-Publication Data

A catalog record for this book has been requested

ISBN 978-1-447-30580-4 (paperback)

ISBN 978-1-447-30927-7 (ebook)

2.1

Contents

Series preface

The books in this series provide an introduction to the study of childhood. They provide a cross-disciplinary and international perspective which develops theoretical knowledge about children and young people, both in the UK and overseas. They are core texts for the Open University module E212 *Childhood*. The series is designed for students working with or for children and young people, in a wide range of settings, and for those who have more general interests in the interdisciplinary field of childhood and youth studies.

The series aims to provide students with:

- the necessary concepts, theories, knowledge and skills base to understand the lives of children and young people

- relevant skills of critical analysis

- critical reflection on and analysis of practices affecting children and young people

- an understanding of the links between children's experiences on a global and local level

- an understanding of the analytical, research and conceptual skills needed to link theory, practice and experience.

The readings which accompany each chapter have been chosen to exemplify key points made in the chapters, often by exploring related data, or experiences and practices involving children in different parts of the world. The readings also represent an additional 'voice' or viewpoint on key themes or issues raised in the chapter.

The books include:

- **activities** to stimulate further understanding or analysis of the material

- **illustrations** to support the teaching material

- **summaries** of key teaching points at appropriate places in the chapter.

The other books in this series are:

Bragg, S. and Kehily, M. J. (eds) (2013) *Children and Young People's Cultural Worlds*, Bristol, Policy Press/Milton Keynes, The Open University.

Clark, A. (ed) (2013) *Childhoods in Context*, Bristol, Policy Press/Milton Keynes, The Open University.

Montgomery, H. (ed) (2013) *Local Childhoods, Global Issues*, Bristol, Policy Press/Milton Keynes, The Open University.

Professor Mary Jane Kehily

Series Editor

Contributors

Mary Jane Kehily

Mary Jane Kehily is Professor of Childhood and Youth Studies at The Open University, UK. She has a background in cultural studies and education, and research interests in gender and sexuality, narrative and identity and popular culture. She has published widely on these themes.

Heather Montgomery

Heather Montgomery is a Reader in the Anthropology of Childhood at The Open University, UK. She has carried out research with young sex workers in Thailand and written extensively on issues of children's rights, global childhoods and representations of childhood.

Laurence Brockliss

Laurence Brockliss is Lecturer (CUF) in Modern History and Professor of Early Modern French History at Magdalen College, University of Oxford. He works on the history of education, science and medicine in early modern France and Britain and has a general interest in the history of European ideas.

Lesley Gallacher

Lesley Gallacher is a lecturer based in the Moray House School of Education at the University of Edinburgh. She has a background in human geography. Her research interests fall broadly into two categories: materials, bodies and spaces in early childhood; and the international reception of Japanese popular culture. Lesley has published on socio-spatial relations in childcare settings, the practices of reading manga and methodological issues in childhood research.

Martyn Hammersley

Martyn Hammersley is Professor of Education and Social Research at The Open University. His early research was in the sociology of education. Later work has been concerned with the methodological issues surrounding social and educational enquiry. These include objectivity, partisanship and bias, and the role of research in relation to policymaking and practice. More recently he has investigated ethical issues in social research and how the news media represent social science research findings.

Martin Woodhead

Martin Woodhead is Professor of Childhood Studies at The Open University. With a background in psychology, sociology and educational research, his research, teaching and publications are wide-ranging, including early child development, education and care, as well as theoretical and methodological contributions to child research and interdisciplinary childhood studies. He pioneered undergraduate teaching in childhood and youth studies at The Open University and in recent years has concentrated on policy-focused international research. He has also carried out studies on child labour, and children's rights, including consultancy work for Save the Children, Council of Europe, OECD, UNICEF, and UNESCO.

Introduction

What does it mean to be a child in today's world? Do popular images of childhood match the reality of young people's lives? How is childhood affected by poverty, ill-health and adversity? Do children have different rights from adults and, if so, why? How are modern lifestyles and technologies changing children's relationships and identities? What part does a child play in shaping their childhood? Such questions inform this cross-disciplinary introduction to childhood and youth studies, covering the age range 0–18 and including case studies from three contrasting parts of the world: Cape Town (South Africa), Chittagong (Bangladesh) and Oakland (USA).

The anthropologist Margaret Mead referred to children as:

> pygmies among giants, ignorant among the knowledgeable, wordless among the articulate ... to the adults, children everywhere represent something weak and helpless, in need of protection, supervision, training, models, skills, beliefs, education.

(Mead, 1955, p. 7)

Over 55 years later, the idea of a universal prescription for young humanity is much challenged. Children share the biological process of development, growth and learning, which, viewed globally, is as diverse as children themselves. The idea that childhood is differently viewed and differently experienced across time and place is now a commonplace view central to childhood studies. Childhood is not one thing but many. This book explores the many facets of childhood, how it can be understood and how it can be studied. Since the systematic study of childhood began in Europe and North America in the nineteenth century, numerous disciplines have contributed to the field, each with its own set of theoretical assumptions, research questions, methodologies and internal debates. Childhood is also a major area of applied study, evident in fields such as medicine, law, social policy and education. Recent developments in education and the social sciences have seen the further growth of childhood studies as an academic field. In recent years childhood studies has become a recognised area of research and analysis. A growing body of literature points to the importance of childhood as a conceptual category and as a social status for the study of a previously overlooked or marginalised group –

children. Childhood studies offers the potential for cross-disciplinary research that can contribute to an emergent paradigm, wherein new ways of looking at children can be researched and theorised.

This book encourages critical engagement with the cultural beliefs and representations generated by such a diverse body of work. This broad approach to childhood inevitably leads to collisions between sets of ideas and practices. Ideas about childhood are contested and struggled over at many levels. This volume introduces readers to the cross-disciplinary field of childhood studies, covering a range of themes as seen from the different research perspectives and academic traditions of history, anthropology, developmental psychology and the sociocultural. The book builds upon the success of the first edition and the growing interest in childhood studies as an academic endeavour. The range and scope of the content extends our understanding of childhood in ways that will appeal to a new generation of childhood scholars. Collectively, the chapters discuss and respond to changes that have an impact on children's lives – from the local to the global. Throughout the volume we use the term 'minority world' to refer to the West and 'majority world' to refer to the geographically larger non-West. The two areas are not separate; they are connected through processes of globalisation.

Since the publication of Woodhead and Montgomery's *Understanding Childhood* in 2003, concerns about children and young people have become central to sociopolitical initiatives nationally and internationally. Despite the privileges afforded to children in the minority world, minority-world childhoods are no longer seen as the 'ideal' to which all should aspire. Recent reports and policy concerns focus on how growing up in the minority world may be marked by the commercialisation of childhood, producing unhappiness, poor health, loss of innocence and a general lack of well-being among children themselves. Additionally, parenting practices are subject to increased scrutiny and surveillance as the family is positioned as the locus of parent–child conflict and disharmony. The new volume considers these and other key changes that shape the experience of being a child in the context of global processes that create diverse and unequal childhoods.

Chapter 1 poses the question 'Is childhood in crisis?' At the beginning of the twenty-first century, media commentary and public discourses on childhood commonly invoke a notion of 'crisis'. This chapter asks, 'What is new about the current invocation of crisis and how does it manifest itself?' Specifically, the chapter explores the ways in which media texts, cultural commentary and policy documents/initiatives collectively produce a dominant discourse of childhood in crisis. It aims to trace the anatomy of this so-called 'crisis' in childhood, to examine how far it exists and what the main features of such a crisis may look like from different perspectives. In doing so, it considers and comments upon the relationship between the past and the present, and the ways in which a historical perspective can be instructive in understanding how concerns about childhood are conceptualised and given meaning. Based on an analysis of cultural texts that promote or collude in the normative idea of a crisis in childhood, the chapter provides alternative ways of conceptualising prevailing ideas and assumptions of crisis and calamity. The chapter draws upon a textual analysis of pregnancy magazines to examine the ways in which parents may be responding to the idea of a crisis in childhood and the impact this has on their parenting practices. Finally, the chapter argues that contemporary meanings of childhood are shaped by the links between the past and the present, to be found in residual notions of childhood in the popular imagination, and contemporary accounts of risk and crisis. In the context of contemporary child-rearing, childhood is reconfigured as a generative mixture of Romantic, late-modern and scientific identifications.

The following chapters in the book introduce different disciplinary perspectives for understanding childhood, beginning with historical approaches. Chapter 2 traces the development of adult ideas about childhood and considers the ways in which historical representations of childhood come into being through the dominant discourses of a particular time and space. The chapter draws upon a range of historical sources to unpack our common assumptions about 'the child' and 'childhood', and explores the meanings and values that are commonly attributed to them. The chapter argues that while there continue to exist substantial differences and inequalities that affect real children in material and often harmful ways, 'the child' also acts as an important cultural construct at both a symbolic and a psychological level. It is in the blurring and overlapping of adults' multiple and diverse notions of what 'the child' is and should be, that confusions and contradictions arise.

Chapter 3 explores the meanings of childhood through the lens of developmental psychology. It introduces students to childhood as a biological and psychological life-phase. The key concept of development is explored chronologically, tracing the emergence of this research field as a powerful voice in defining what childhood is and how it can be understood. The chapter draws on a range of rich research examples to illustrate respects in which development is both natural and social/cultural.

In Chapter 4, Heather Montgomery invites us to concentrate on social anthropology's contribution to childhood, especially in its focus on children outside the minority world. The chapter emphasises the diversity of children's lives and the diversity of ideas about childhood, and the implications this might have for the ways in which children are treated. It looks at the methods used by social anthropologists to study childhood, especially their use of ethnography, participant observation and thick description, as well as key theories such as cultural relativism and social constructionism. Through the use of global case studies and examples, this chapter traces anthropology's involvement with children's lives and ideas about childhood from Margaret Mead's pioneering work in Samoa through to the rise of child-centred or child-focused anthropology. It considers the specific contribution that anthropologists have made to the study of childhood while also drawing links between anthropology and other social sciences.

In Chapter 5, Lesley Gallacher and Mary Jane Kehily outline and bring sociocultural approaches to the concept of childhood, considering the social implications of these for the ways in which children are perceived and positioned in contemporary societies. The discussion outlines how the social sciences have previously handled childhood either through theories of socialisation or through developmental psychology – both of which have led to children being considered as a natural rather than a social phenomenon. The chapter offers a greater appreciation of the sociocultural perspectives that make up our knowledge of children and childhood. It provides a critical framework through which to understand the child and childhood, mapping the field, as well as commenting upon the influence of contemporary work in the burgeoning field of children's geography.

In the final chapter of the book, Martyn Hammersley reviews a variety of methodological approaches and sources of data used by the disciplines discussed in Chapters 2–5. He considers the theoretical approaches used to investigate children's lives and the factors that shape them. There is discussion of historical research and of the analysis of textual data more generally. This leads into questions about the nature and role of science, and there is a discussion of experimentation as a means of understanding children's capacities and behaviour. The use of official statistics and social survey data follows on from this. Attention then switches to ethnography. There is a brief history of this approach in general terms, detailing how its character differs somewhat between disciplines and how it has changed over time. From here the discussion widens into the broader range of approaches used in sociocultural studies and social geography, such as participatory methods. Some of the political and ethical issues surrounding research on childhood are then considered. Throughout the chapter, examples mentioned earlier in the book are used as illustration, and methodological aspects of these are examined in more detail.

To summarise, this broad-based text is:

Introductory – childhood has a place in everyone's lives, but recent commentary suggests that childhood is in crisis. The idea of childhood as lost or in decline is one of the starting points for the module, which will be equally relevant whether you are a parent or work with children, or are simply interested in how children and young people are treated and understood.

Cross-disciplinary – the book introduces a range of perspectives on childhood, drawing on recent research and theories from sociology, anthropology, psychology, cultural studies, geography, social history, philosophy, social policy and children's rights.

International – there is an exploration of childhood (and cultural beliefs on the subject) in different societies and at different periods in history, with modern minority-world childhood as one among many examples. Diversity and inequality are central themes, as are the ways in which childhood is becoming globalised and regulated by universal standards.

We would like to thank the people who contributed to the preparation of this book, particularly Professor Chris Philo (University of Glasgow) for his insightful comments on draft chapters in his role as external assessor, and Professor David Messer (The Open University) for his support throughout.

Mary Jane Kehily,

The Open University, 2012

References

Mead, M. (1955) 'Theoretical setting – 1954', in Mead, M. and Wolfenstein, M. (eds) *Childhood in Contemporary Cultures*, Chicago, IL, University of Chicago Press.

Woodhead, M. and Montgomery, H. (eds) (2003) *Understanding Childhood: An Interdisciplinary Approach*, Chichester, Wiley/Milton Keynes, The Open University.

Chapter 1

Childhood in crisis? An introduction to contemporary Western childhood

Mary Jane Kehily

Contents

In this chapter, you will:

- explore the concept of childhood and the ways in which the notion of crisis may shape how children in the minority world are seen
- consider some of the different ways in which the idea of childhood in crisis is constructed and reproduced
- develop your own ideas on how childhood may be constructed
- develop an awareness of the ways in which the notion of crisis may have practical consequences for children's lives, identities and experiences.

1   Introduction

Since the beginning of the twenty-first century, media commentary and public discourses on childhood have commonly invoked a notion of 'crisis' (Furedi, 2001; Palmer, 2006; Hardyment, 2007). The idea that childhood is currently in crisis appears to be *everywhere*. A general assumption that childhood is not what it used to be and that this, in itself, signals catastrophe appears to saturate our social worlds. It is a cliché of adulthood that childhood is not what it used to be. In this sense, nostalgia and loss appear as familiar features in conversations that reflect upon the past.

Remembering childhood, for some, may call to mind benignly romantic fantasies of play and adventure, the polite and deliciously well-ordered escapades of fictional children of the 1950s conjured up by Enid Blyton in *The Famous Five*, or a looser version of magical freedom that bespeaks how things ought to be. Childhood as an idealised state of innocence and purity has a long trajectory that can be traced to the Romantic movement of eighteenth-century Europe and particularly the work of Rousseau. Believing that children came from God, the figure of the child came to embody a spiritual dimension, placing children close to nature as blessed creatures unsullied by the adult world. Concerns were expressed over children who 'lost' their innocence; most commonly looking upon them as prematurely or unnecessarily contaminated by exposure to the adult world. This chapter illustrates how Romantic ideals still influence the way we think about childhood. It discusses the way traces of Romantic ideas resonate with contemporary concerns about childhood in order to consider the idea that childhood is in crisis. It may be pertinent to ask 'What is new about the current invocation of crisis?' The chapter explores the ways in which the media, cultural commentary and policy documents/initiatives collectively promote the idea of childhood in crisis. It aims to trace the anatomy of this so-called 'crisis' in childhood, to examine how far there is really a crisis and what the main features of such a crisis may look like from different perspectives. In doing so, the chapter considers and comments upon the relationship between the past and the present, and the ways in which a historical perspective can be instructive in understanding how versions of childhood are shaped and given meaning. Based on an analysis of reports and newspaper coverage that promote or collude in the idea of a crisis in childhood, the chapter provides alternative ways of conceptualising prevailing ideas and assumptions of childhood as a site of crisis and calamity. The chapter draws upon pregnancy magazines to examine the ways in which parents may be responding to the idea of a crisis in childhood and the impact this has on their parenting practices. Finally, the chapter argues that contemporary meanings of childhood are shaped by the past and the present, located in residual notions of childhood in the popular imagination and in contemporary accounts of risk and crisis.

The approach adopted in the chapter draws upon and takes inspiration from the 'new sociology of childhood' (Jenks, 1996; James and Prout, 1997; James et al., 1998). This approach views childhood as a social construction that is brought into being by the discourses that name and shape it. In keeping with this framework, the chapter places emphasis on understanding how the idea of a crisis in childhood is constituted and ascribed meaning within particular contexts. The argument presented in this chapter is based upon analysis of a range of sources: media reports, policy documents, commissioned research and popular commentaries on childhood, and content analysis of pregnancy magazines. The chapter covers five themes. The first two outline the ways in which the notion of crisis in invoked and how it can be understood historically, while the third and fourth themes offer ways of interpreting the 'crisis' through recourse to cultural studies and late-modern perspectives. The final theme turns to an analysis of pregnancy magazines to consider the ways in which contemporary discussions of childhood may have some implications for child-rearing practice.

Figure 1   Is childhood in crisis?

2 Contours of a 'crisis'

Outlining the features that may contribute to the idea that childhood is in crisis prompts me to consider ways of documenting how the experience of being a child may have changed over time. Personal reflection may provide some insight into changes across generations, highlighting some of the differences and points of continuity between childhoods past and present. In the following activity you are encouraged to use your own childhood experience as a resource to reflect upon childhoods past and present.

Activity 1   Memories of childhood past
Allow about 30 minutes

Reflecting on your own childhood, consider and make a note of some of the ways you spent your leisure time.

- Roughly how much leisure time did you have (a) during school term time and (b) during school holidays?
- Were you free to do whatever you wanted? What did you do? Did it involve siblings, friends or adults?

- How do your think your use of leisure time compares with that of children today? How would you describe and account for the main points of difference?

Comment

Growing up in a small spa town in the English Midlands in the 1960s, my memory of childhood is temporally marked by the feeling of having acres of leisure time. Time seemed to stretch out before me as an endless and unbounded dimension that I struggled to make sense of. Homework was never insisted upon, there were no structured activities and I was allowed to play outside from an early age, about four or five. Filling time was a freewheeling and haphazard affair. I can recall playing with siblings, friends and other children I met in the fields across the road from where I lived and in the local park. Adult intervention was unknown. During summer holidays my five siblings and I were encouraged/told to vacate the house as soon as possible for as long as possible, only to return for a snack to keep us going. Moving in and out of different friendship groups, we made dens on the riverbank, created alternative homes and knew all the local characters, including the older 'bad' boys, one of whom was famously arrested by the police before our very eyes while in the middle of a game of rounders. Our favourite spot was the 'broken brook' where a group of us built a raft that looked good but was a miserable failure on the water. We laughed at our efforts to keep afloat on it before falling in brought events to an inevitably wet and muddy conclusion.

Before I'm overcome with the joy of remembering, I should say that this was far removed from *The Famous Five* or literary accounts of feral middle-class fun that defined who you were forever, as in the filmic *Stand by Me* mode. There were no lashings of lemonade, no character-making incidents and no big adventures. Just a bunch of working-class kids with time on their hands. It was largely unspectacular but, in retrospect, not without its excitement and dangers. What parent today would let their children play unsupervised for hours by a river? And if they did, what would they be called by the tabloid press? Other childhood memories recall a couple of family holidays spent with relatives in Ireland. Staying on farms in rural Mayo – the bit without electricity, gas or running water – we children could do whatever we liked from morning until night, free from the usual strictures applied at home. We didn't even have to wash. We could ride the pig, collect eggs, cut up peat and fetch water from the well all before breakfast. In contrast to what I observe of children in my circle of family and friends, I had a great deal of freedom and some responsibility for household chores and the care of younger siblings.

Noticeably absent from my childhood was the whole idea of adult-organised, extra-curricular activities and supervised play. Going to school was enough and I walked there on my own as soon as I started infant school. A couple of years later my younger sister came with me and it was my job to see she arrived safely. Children I know get ferried to school by their parents and many of them follow a packed programme of after-school activities, again enabled by parents. As a local and very personal snapshot, the differences I observe suggest that children today may have less unsupervised time and parents have more responsibility to organise and facilitate children's out-of-school activities.

2.1   Mapping the crisis

In minority-world contexts, focusing particularly on the UK, public commentary on childhood appears to be haunted by the spectre of darkness and danger. On 13 September 2006 a national newspaper in the UK, *The Daily Telegraph*, launched a campaign to halt the death of childhood. Warming up Postman's (1982) lament that childhood was being eroded by the modern world, 'Hold on to Childhood' called for a public examination of children's lives. Supported by 110 academics, writers and medical experts, the much publicised letter in the *Telegraph* asserted that children have been 'tainted' by overexposure to electronic media, lack of space to play and an overemphasis on academic testing in schools. A UNICEF report (2007), on the well-being of children and young people in 21 industrialised countries, ranked the UK at the bottom of the table in their assessment of child well-being and the USA as second from bottom. The report focused on six areas: material well-being; health and safety; educational well-being; family and peer relationships; behaviours and risks; and young people's own perceptions of well-being. It placed The Netherlands at the top of the table, followed by Sweden, Denmark and Finland. The report offers an economic account of the findings, powerfully suggesting that despite the UK's national wealth, children who grow up in poverty are more vulnerable and their experiences of childhood more difficult: findings that led the UK Children's Commissioner to comment, 'There is a crisis at the heart of our society' (quoted in *The Guardian*, 14 February 2007).

The notion of childhood in crisis has been amplified by contemporary commentators. Sue Palmer's (2006) text, *Toxic Childhood: How the Modern World is Damaging our Children and What We Can Do About It*, has received extensive media coverage in the UK, consolidating her status as an authoritative critic on all that is wrong with modern childhood. This position is substantiated by her profile as an educator with a long career in primary education. Palmer suggests that technological change over the last 25 years has had a big impact on modern life. The side effects of cultural change have produced a toxic cocktail that is damaging the social, emotional and cognitive development of children. Palmer asserts that consumerism constitutes a key ingredient of the cocktail. Children have come to associate happiness with the 'stuff' of consumer culture and the desirous nature of consumption patterns; wanting things, buying things and having things bought for you have acquired misplaced prominence in children's lives, distorting notions of what happiness really is and how it can be achieved. Other ingredients of the toxic cocktail include the denigration of play and places to play, and the stress of exams and academic achievement. Modern childhood puts children under increased surveillance and excessive pressure, producing anxiety and contaminating children's experience of childhood. In a somewhat hackneyed metaphor drawn from the less than glamorous world of agricultural production, Palmer proposes that today's children are 'battery reared' rather than 'free range'.

Taking a different approach but anticipating many of Palmer's concerns, Frank Furedi (2001) locates the trouble spots of contemporary childhood within the family. Furedi asserts that parenting magazines and other media sources indicate that the family is in crisis. He suggests that the idea of the family in crisis has had a destabilising impact on parents, creating a loss of confidence in their abilities to parent and a pervasive sense of being under threat and out of control. Parenting in contemporary times, according to Furedi, is imbued with feelings of fear and paranoia. An obvious manifestation of paranoid parenting can be seen in parents' approach to child safety, a matter that has escalated from a concern to a national obsession. Furedi cites the example of a mother who drove behind the school coach to ensure that her son arrived safely at his destination. Parental fear for their children's safety may be out of proportion to the risks posed; however, it does not stop parents playing an overactive role in all aspects of child-rearing to the point where households appear to function as autonomous entities with little connection to neighbourhood or even extended family.

Furedi's account of the changes in the way parents care for children can be explained by what he terms a 'breakdown in adult solidarity' (Furedi, 2001, p. 33). Adults no longer look out for each other or regard themselves as having a duty of care to *all* children. Rather, a distrust of adults in general has emerged in a climate where *all* adults, including parents, could be potential child abusers. Furedi suggests that the widespread distrust of adults is acknowledged and acted upon by children who may be keen to exploit adult insecurities in order to exercise power for their own ends. Furedi's views on the media and consumerism contrast with Palmer's in that he considers them as scapegoats for parents who feel powerless and, in their paranoid state, may be all too ready to castigate outside influences as a threat to their authority. Ultimately, Furedi concludes that child-rearing practices are linked to and reflect the parenting style that is encouraged by the culture.

2.2 Reports of crisis

Concern over children and the protection of childhood has been a persistent refrain in recent government documents, legislative approaches and official reports in the UK. *Every Child Matters* (2004), the government Green Paper prompted by the death of Victoria Climbié in London four years earlier, opened up a dialogue aimed at improving services that focused on the needs of children, young people and families. At the heart of this initiative was the desire to promote 'joined-up services' to prevent the abuse, neglect and premature death of children through ill-treatment. In consultation with children and young people, *Every Child Matters* summarised their needs as requiring help and support to: be healthy; stay safe; enjoy and achieve; make a positive contribution; achieve economic well-being. These five aims formed the basis of the Children Act 2004, legislation focused upon developing more effective and accessible services for children and young people. A further outcome of the consultation process was the recognition that children need to be represented at a national level and their voices need to be heard. In March 2005 the UK government appointed Professor Al Aynsley-Green as England's first Children's Commissioner. The Commissioner's main responsibility is to promote awareness of the views and interests of children. Children themselves indicated that they are concerned about bullying, personal safety and the pressure of educational work. The Commissioner has a brief to work independently of government in ways that complement the United Nations Convention on the Rights of the Child.

A further voice to join the chorus of childhood in crisis came from The Children's Society, a UK-based charity which, in 2007, published the findings of its *Good Childhood Inquiry*, an independent survey commissioned to explore adult perspectives on children and childhood. The inquiry aimed to examine society's understanding of childhood for the twenty-first century in order to improve relationships with children. Key findings of the survey critically comment on the place of play and the role of consumption in children's lives. Despite the recognition that having friends and being able to spend time with them was regarded as central to a good childhood, 43 per cent of 1148 adults said that children should not be allowed out with friends until they were 14. Wanting children to have their freedom appears to be equally matched by the fear of letting them move freely outside the home without adult supervision. A pessimistic picture also emerges in relation to consumerism and material culture. Of the 1255 people surveyed, nine out of ten felt that children are more materialistic now than in previous generations and that advertising at Christmas puts pressure on parents to spend more than they can afford. In a culture where the children's market is estimated to be worth £30bn a year, Bob Reitemeier, Chief Executive of The Children's Society, called for adults to take stock, 'Unless we question our own behaviour we risk creating a generation who are left unfulfilled through chasing unattainable lifestyles' (BBC News 24, 2008). A majority of the sample also agreed that children's television and computer time should be restricted, and that violent video games make children more violent. Other contributors to the childhood debate include the Primary Review's *Community Soundings* (2007), an independent inquiry into the condition and future of primary education in England. Summarising the findings of 87 regionally based witness sessions, authors Alexander and Hargreaves note:

> we were frequently told children are under intense and perhaps excessive pressure from the policy-driven demands of their schools and the commercially-driven values of the wider society; that family life and community are breaking down; that there is a pervasive loss of respect and empathy both within and between generations; that life outside the school gates is increasingly insecure and dangerous; that the wider world is changing, rapidly and in ways which it is not always easy to comprehend ...
>
> (Alexander and Hargreaves, 2007, p. 1)

Finally, in the litany of grievances that constitute a crisis, the latest 'trouble' with children is that they are too fat. Concerns over rising levels of childhood obesity has led the British Medical Association into a debate to determine whether overfeeding children should be regarded as parental neglect. While official and policy-orientated sources present a more muted version of childhood than Palmer or Furedi, they nevertheless draw upon a compelling notion of childhood in crisis and children at risk.

Figure 2   Parental fears prevent children from playing outside (Source: Thomson and Kehily, 2008)

Activity 2   Responding to a national survey

Allow about 35 minutes

If you were to participate in a survey such as the *Good Childhood Inquiry,* how would you respond to the following questions?

- Do children today play with friends more, less or about the same as children in previous generations?
- At what age do you think children can be allowed to go out on their own, unsupervised by adults? Age 5 / 7 / 9 / 11 / 13 / 15 / 17?
- Are children more materialistic, less materialistic or about the same as children in previous generations?
- Advertising puts pressure on parents to spend more than they can afford on Christmas presents for their children. Do you agree strongly, agree, disagree or disagree strongly?

Comment

Despite disagreeing with the general flavour of the Children's Society report, I found myself answering questions in ways that largely concurred with their findings. My responses: children play with friends less; can go out alone from age 11; are more materialistic; and I agree that advertising puts pressure on parents to spend more than they can afford. Each question, however, prompted me to ask more questions: play with friends in what context; go where on their own; what advertising and which parents spend more? As a loose simulation of some of the questions that researchers may have asked on behalf of The Children's Society, this activity points to some of the difficulties generated by surveys of this kind. As a respondent I felt frustrated that the structure of the questions left little scope for nuanced responses, layers of detail or moments of ambivalence. I felt shoehorned into a set of responses that appear to support the general findings rather than reflect what I think.

Summary of Section 2

Memories of childhood can be evocative and powerful and may raise a range of emotions that have a bearing on how we think childhood should be.

The idea that childhood is in crisis is developed across a range of sites: media texts, cultural commentary and policy documents/ initiatives.

Concerns over children's happiness and well-being have been expressed in policy documents commissioned by the UK government.

3 Crisis in context

So is the crisis in childhood, as presented in so many contemporary accounts, real or is it more indicative of a media-fuelled panic about the state of the nation? And if we assume that some features of the crisis present an accurate portrayal of children's lives, does that necessarily signal the calamitous end of childhood and the despoilment of future generations?

In order to look into the future it may be helpful to cast an eye back over the past. In response to contemporary articulations of crisis and anxiety, historian Hugh Cunningham suggests that these ideas are far from new. Rather, Cunningham (1995) argues that since the year 1500, patterns of change in the experience of childhood across Europe and North America have been similar and, furthermore, the antecedents of the present 'crisis' can be found in familiar echoes of the past, as expressed in the early twentieth century. Following Elias (1969), Cunningham notes that the process of civilisation creates greater distance between children and adults, with childhood being seen as a special state requiring special status. The defining spirit of the age at the beginning of the twentieth century held that the future would be determined by the way children were treated. Children were conceptualised as an asset of the state and childhood became a site for the intervention of the state. In order to reduce infant mortality, for example, mothers must be educated in matters of hygiene and duties of care. Maternal instinct was no longer enough. Children's health was a matter of public concern, monitored through weight, as it is now; the present preoccupation with overweight children has a parallel with past concerns about underweight children. Then as now, policies on children were dependent upon medical and scientific knowledge – indicating that state intervention is justified by evidence that overshadows the views of parents. As successive governments revised and refined their vision for childhood, increased state intervention inevitably entailed increased surveillance of families, particularly the children of the poor. Tensions between families and the state in all matters concerning the care and responsibility of children exist as recognisable fault lines in the present landscape. Cunningham suggests that the big changes to impact upon children's lives – compulsory schooling and a reduction in infant mortality – were accompanied by a significant change in the way adults thought about children. The transition from valuing children for economic reasons and their ability to contribute to the family income to valuing children for emotional reasons was 'probably the most important [change] to have occurred in the history of childhood' (Cunningham, 1995, p. 177). Investing in children emotionally can be regarded as the pre-eminent approach to twenty-first century childhoods, assumed in a range of cultural texts and policy-orientated approaches.

The fissure marking contemporary approaches to childhood begin to appear, according to Cunningham, in the second half of the twentieth century. Children's exposure to visual culture, commercialism and new technologies fragment the possibilities of preserving an idealised childhood in the Romantic sense. During this period children began to have enhanced rights, firstly to a childhood but subsequently as individuals, demanding to be treated more like adults with access to the privileges and pleasures of the adult world – though not the world of employment. Cunningham notes a significant shift in the balance of

Figure 3 Compulsory schooling marks a shift in the way adults think about children

power within families, with child-rearing becoming a matter of negotiation between parent and child, a process that is monitored by the state and other agencies. Cunningham concludes with the insightful comment that present tensions lie in the struggle between the idea of the child as a person with rights and the legacy of Romanticism which asserts that the right of a child is to be a child. From this perspective the contemporary 'crisis' in childhood can be productively understood as the collision between competing and contradictory versions of childhood. The powerful pull of the Romantic ideal and the pragmatism of contemporary child-rearing practices appear to create an incongruous space, giving rise to a range of discordant voices and harbingers of doom.

3.1 Moral panic and the construction of crisis

The insights gleaned from historical approaches to childhood can be complemented by the perspectives of cultural studies, particularly those studies concerned with examining the power of dominant constructions. Cultural studies analyses of the notion of 'crisis' have commonly cast the phenomenon in terms of 'moral panic'. The concept of moral panic points to the ways in which some events acquire the status of symbolic acts of deviance through inflated media reports that exaggerate and distort the threat posed. The concept draws upon the work of Cohen (1973) whose study of mods and rockers in south-east England focused on the role of the media as instrumental in portraying young people as 'folk devils' in reports that generated moral panic among its readership. For our purposes it is possible to take the concept of moral panic as a term that seeks to explain the way events come to be spoken about and 'known', illustrated here by two examples, the first of which is Geoffrey Pearson's study *Hooligan: A History of Respectable Fears* (1983). Pearson's study presents a carefully worked history of moral panics from the mid-1800s to the 1980s. His argument, based upon textual analysis of historical documents and contemporary representations, suggests that every 20 years or so there is a moral panic about youth. Furthermore, each moral panic repeats the themes of the previous moral panic. Just when the panic is fading from popular memory it re-emerges in a newly configured form to be visited upon the next generation of young people.

The second example is drawn from the work of Martin Barker. Barker (1989) develops a similar analysis in relation to young people and popular culture. Beginning with the *Penny Dreadful* comics of the 1950s, Barker looks at why these comics were considered to be bad for boys and how these arguments (usually concerned with exposure to violence) were mounted in the press, in politics and the law, among professionals, politicians and parents. Barker subsequently argues that these themes are repeated every time a new cultural form comes along. In recent times there have been regular waves of panic focusing upon so-called 'video nasties' – that is, violent videos/DVDs – (implicated in the murder of James Bulger), teenage magazines (blamed for exposing girls to over-sexualised content) and social networking sites (drawn upon to present worries about internet bullying/grooming and happy slapping in the digital age). Both Pearson and Barker comment upon collectively constructed and media-generated moral panics that commonly rest upon fear of change and invocations of the past. Particularly, there is a concern with the power of dominant memories, how they are generated collectively and how they become imbued with ideological content. This approach highlights the ways in which moral panics may also be imaginative projections of one sort or another that articulate an anxiety about change and loss. Seen in these terms the idea of childhood in crisis can be understood as a moral panic that can be seen as a cyclical concern rather than a new phenomenon.

Activity 3 Reading A

Allow about 35–40 minutes

Go to the readings at the end of the chapter and look at Reading A 'Can these be children?', by Geoffrey Pearson.

Geoffrey Pearson invites us to think about the relationship between young people's crime as represented by the Artful Dodger figure and the social change brought about by the Industrial Revolution. After reading the extract, jot down your responses to the following questions:

- How were children and young people identified as a problem in mid-nineteenth-century England?
- How does Pearson suggest that this problem can be understood?
- Do you see any parallels between the recently industrialised period Pearson describes and contemporary British society?
- How can this comparison help us to understand children and young people today?

Comment

Long before the advent of youth culture and the pervasive presence of mass media, Pearson's study presents an eerily familiar portrait of youthful deviance immersed in the nineteenth-century equivalent of sex, drugs and rock 'n' roll. Boys and young men living on their wits and skilled in an elaborate repertoire of criminal activities were characterised by the fictional Artful Dodger of Dickens' imagination. Cohen's (1973) study, discussed above, illustrated how mods and rockers became symbolic representations of all that was wrong with youth in the 1960s–1970s. Pearson suggests an earlier formation of troublesome youth – boys who appeared to be 'diminutive men', having expunged all traces of the child, as undersized adults exercising freedom and agency way beyond their years. For Pearson, concerns over the immorality of the young can be understood in relation to the social change brought about by industrialisation. The idea that social change produces unrest that is acted upon by young people engaging in activities that can be seen as forms of resistance and protest is also a theme running through studies of young people in the twentieth century. In keeping with Cunningham's historical analysis of childhood, Pearson's study also points to the strong links between past and present when looking at the way young people's behaviour is interpreted. Comparison of the past and present leads to an understanding of the way children and young people become a focus for adult fears and concerns as successive generations of adults view them as a 'problem'.

3.2   Late modernity and the notion of crisis

A further way of understanding the idea of childhood in crisis is through the lens of late-modern social theory. Sociologists such as Beck, Giddens and Bauman suggest that late modernity is marked by the emergence of a new relationship between the individual and the social. As the traditions of the industrial order diminish in significance, Giddens argues that self-identity becomes a reflexive project. The 'individualisation thesis' characterising late modernity places the onus upon individuals to take responsibility for producing and maintaining their own biographies:

> What to do? How to act? Who to be? These are focal questions for everyone living in circumstances of late modernity – and ones which, at some level or another, all of us answer, either discursively or through day-to-day social behaviour.
>
> (Giddens, 1991, p. 70)

Through the creation of a set of biographical narratives, individuals tell a story, to themselves and others, of who they are and who they want to be. For Giddens, the reflexive project of self is linked to the sphere of intimacy, 'Romantic love introduced the idea of narrative into an individual's life' (Giddens, 1992, p. 39). Moreover, intimacy has been transformed in late-modern times from a set of social obligations and regulations to a new form of democracy between couples. Giddens suggests that intimate relationships are increasingly based upon personal understandings between two people generated by a bond of trust and emotional communication rather than external norms and values. The changes in intimate relations identified as 'pure relationships' can be viewed as a new and highly personalised form of democracy based upon emotions.

Further commentary on the condition of late modernity is provided by Bauman:

> Everyone has to ask for himself the question 'who am I', 'how should I live', 'who do I want to become' – and, at the end of the day, be prepared to accept responsibility for the answer. In this sense, freedom is for the modern individual the fate he cannot escape, except by retreating into a fantasy world or through mental

disorders. Freedom is, therefore, a mixed blessing. One needs it to be oneself; yet being oneself solely on the strength of one's free choice means a life full of doubts and fears of error ... Self construction of the self is, so to speak, a necessity. Self confirmation of the self is an impossibility.

(Bauman, 1988, p. 62)

Bauman's contribution to the individualisation thesis appears pessimistic in its emphasis on the limitations and inherent uncertainties of individual freedom. The charge of pessimism is further fuelled by Bauman's analysis of consumerism as a form of control that seduces individuals with offers of a 'fantasy community' of freedom and security.

Beck (1992) occupies some of the terrain covered by Giddens in his concern to characterise the late-modern period and articulate the relationship between individuals and society in contexts that have been changed and reshaped by the processes of globalisation and new technologies. Beck suggests that minority-world societies have been reshaped by a process of individualisation marked by three distinctive features: dis-embedding; loss of traditional security; and re-embedding. Dis-embedding refers to the individual's break with traditional ties of family and locality, while loss of security points to a pervasive 'disenchantment', produced by the demise of traditional values associated with the past. Re-embedding, by contrast, indicates the emergence of a new mood found in the creation of reimagined forms of social commitment. For Beck, this is a paradox of the late-modern condition:

On the one hand, men and women are *released* from traditional forms and ascribed roles in the search for a 'life of their own'. On the other hand, in the prevailing diluted social relationships, people are *driven into* bonding in the search for happiness in a partnership. The need for a shared inner life, as expressed in the ideal of marriage and bonding, is not a primeval need. It *grows* with the losses that individualization brings as the obverse of its opportunities.

(Beck, 1992, p. 105)

It is possible to suggest that while the writings of Bauman, Beck and Giddens provide much food for thought, these theories of (post) modern subjects can appear theoretically abstract and cut-off from everyday lives in real contexts.

Extrapolating from late-modern social theory, generatively points to the position of the child as changed and changing within new versions of family. The modern nuclear unit has largely superseded the extended families of previous generations and connections with extended family members may be physically distant as working patterns change and individuals exercise the ability to move. While the nuclear family may still exist as the ideal version of familial relations in the minority world, late-modern social theorists suggest that personal relationships are giving way to 'new practices of intimacy': the move towards 'pure relationships' in which new generations relinquish established practices and develop individualised-choice biographies based on their sole commitment to one another. 'Pure relationships', however, may not reflect the diversity of personal relationships and family forms, and may not be fully accomplished. The break-up of the traditional family unit, or rather its reconfiguration, can be seen in an increase in single-headed households, same-sex couples, unmarried co-habiting parents and post-divorce couples who may each bring children into new relationships. The practice of in vitro-fertilisation (IVF) by which infertile couples, single women, gay and lesbian couples, and mature women can have children, is itself a reproductive technology that is extending the project of self, individualisation and choice in late modernity. Though commonly perceived as a threat to the family, it could be said that this new molecular structure is actually serving to rework what is meant and understood by the term 'family'. As the modern family is restructured in late modernity, work-based relationships and friendship circles can themselves emerge as a new practice of intimacy that, if enduring, may act like a surrogate family, as exemplified by the US comedy series *Friends*.

The emergent social practices of late modernity have many implications for children and childhood. As Jenks (1996) points out, concerns for childhood can be seen as a reflection of broader (adult) concerns for identity and security in changing times. Beck comments on the privileged status of the child in the context of individualisation and new practices of intimacy:

> The child is the last remaining irrevocable, unexchangeable primary relationship. Parents come and go. The child stays. Everything that is not realisable in the relationship is directed towards the child.
>
> (Beck, 1992, p. 18)

The idea of the child as a treasured emotional investment can be seen to suit the contingent nature of the 'pure relationship'. In this context the child becomes the emotional anchor for the couple, the thing that turns choice into permanency and commitment. Wyness (2000) notes that late-modern conceptualisations of the child invoke a Romantic and naive view of children that positions them as dependent upon and subordinate to adults. While late-modern approaches to childhood conjure up the Romantic ideal, children may also exist symbolically as an enhanced fantasy of late-modern coupledom.

Summary of Section 3

A historical perspective can be instructive in understanding how concerns about childhood are conceptualised and given meaning.

Cultural studies, approaches and late-modern social theory offer different perspectives for understanding the idea of childhood in crisis.

Contemporary meanings of childhood are shaped by the links between the past and the present.

Contemporary accounts of risk and crisis draw upon earlier conceptualisations of childhood, particularly Romantic ideals.

---

4 Parenting in late modernity

The legacy of the Romantic movement appears to haunt the late-modern period; however, an analysis of pregnancy magazines suggests that it is combined with an approach to consumerism and science which gives child–parent relationships in late modernity a unique character. As a source of insight into contemporary parenting practices, pregnancy magazines represent child-rearing as a generative combination of romanticism, consumerism and science. These practices can be understood as the 're-embedding' of a reconfigured version of

Figure 4   Pregnancy magazines and popular media suggest that childhood is in crisis

childhood, styled to accommodate changing social relationships. As discussed above, children's relationship to consumption is broadly portrayed as bad news. Within policy-orientated and popular discourses, children are tainted by consumer culture while parents are positioned as the victims of 'pester power', trying in vain to rein in their avaricious offspring. Pregnancy magazines indicate that the consumption practices of parents, however, also point to a desirous and enduring love affair with the fruits of material production. Within post-industrial economies the logic of niche marketing suggests to companies that they pursue an incessant search for ever more specialised and unusual products to appeal to a designated consumer cohort as a necessity for increased profit and economic survival. The baby market – aimed at pregnant women and new parents – provides a rich source of opportunity for the creation and marketing of new products. The range of products and services to aid parenting can be seen in different ways: as labour-saving and supportive or expensive and unnecessary. In the following reading, Alison Clarke focuses on children's birthday parties as an illustration of the interaction between mothers and the commercial world. Her analysis points to the social significance of mothering practices as forms of care in which buying for your children extends beyond the notion of need, and in which ideas of what children 'need' may be flexible.

Activity 4　Reading B

Allow about 35 minutes

Go to the readings at the end of the chapter and look at Reading B 'Making sameness: mothering, commerce and the culture of children's birthday parties', by Alison Clarke.

Clarke develops a beautifully crafted analysis of that seemingly innocuous celebration, the children's birthday party. Consider the following questions after reading the extract:

- How does Clarke suggest that children's birthday parties have changed in recent years?

- How can these changes be explained?

- How do you think children's birthday parties should be celebrated?

Comment

Taking children's birthday parties as an example of the gendered labour that constitutes motherhood, Clarke considers the interface between practices of mothering and the commercial world. The birthday party has been transformed from a small domestic celebration involving home-made jelly and ice cream to a full-blown commercial affair. Children's birthday parties may now involve the hiring of a restaurant, professional caterers and entertainers, themed costumes and the exchange of expensive gifts. Based on an ethnographic study of families in north London, Clarke explores the phenomenon of the birthday party as an event that 'outs' the family, as parenting practices, values and aspirations

Figure 5 Children's birthday parties are a barometer of change

are on show to the peer group of other mothers in the neighbourhood. Clarke documents the ways in which the birthday party becomes a site for the display of certain types of mothering, particularly marked by social class. Clarke notes the subtle cultural and inter-personal processes that provided middle-class mothers with a basis for sociality, while single mothers and those with fewer resources were excluded from the bonding networks. For the in-group of middle-class mothers with cultural capital and material resources, the trick is to host the most spectacular party with the minimum amount of fuss and commercial intervention. Acquiring status in the peer group entails developing a particular aesthetic that eschews 'buying the party' in favour of a personally expressive style of mothering that seeks and achieves the approval of other mothers.

4.1 Parenting and the commercial world

Hardyment (2007) notes the significant increase in the number of books and magazines on parenting since the 1980s, reflecting a burgeoning public awareness of childhood as a newsworthy subject never far from the public eye. In these publications the widely promoted idea that pregnancy is a special time to indulge and be pampered is supplemented by the Romantic notion that children are a gift from God, to be showered with gifts from earth via doting parents, relatives and friends. Parenting magazines amply illustrate the increased commodification of pregnancy, birth and parenting as every aspect of the parental process has a range of products to assist it. The commodities available to parents have extended to areas previously untouched by the commercial sphere. The antenatal scan, for example, once limited to part of the medical assessment process in early pregnancy, has become a commercial venture promoted by several companies as a pre-birth bonding experience for parents-to-be. Widely featured in the classified pages of all the pregnancy magazines, a typical issue will include three to four advertisements from different companies offering 3D and 4D non-diagnostic ultrasound scanning at around £100 per session. The companies' promotional material suggests that they are 'scanning to nurture', offering parents-to-be the opportunity to 'capture precious moments' when their babies may be 'smiling, yawning, blinking, scratching their nose and sucking their fingers' in the womb. One of the largest companies, with branches throughout the UK, provides scans for different stages of pregnancy and claims to be the creator of the 4D scan 'bonding experience' for women in their 24–32 weeks of pregnancy.

Ultrasound scanning companies such as babybond® appear to blend Romanticism with advanced new technology by suggesting that scans are provided for the purposes of 'bonding, reassurance and fetal well-being' (*Mother and Baby*, April 2005). Products from babybond® come as a complete package:

> DVD in sleeve, 1 x A4 colour gloss 3D enlargement in photomount, 6 x A6 colour gloss 3D prints, CD-ROM in white, blue or pink Babybond bag, **to take home: £230**.
>
> (*Mother and Baby*, April 2005)

The experience suggests to new parents that parent–child bonding can be accelerated by pre-birth scanning procedures, giving parents security in insecure times. The success of such products indicates that the link between 'science' and 'baby things' exists as a commercial venture that is popular with parents and lucrative for companies, seductively providing parents with the promise of the best and latest scientific advances.

A further example of the blending between Romanticism and science can be seen in advertisements and features on stem cell research. Though not as prominent or widely available as ultrasound scanning,

Babybond nurtures the parent-to-baby-bond at every scan and is the first Quality Endorsed Ultrasound Company with clinics throughout the UK.

Find your nearest at **babybond.com**

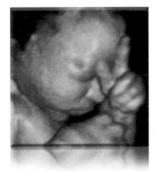

a Babybond® scan is close to you ...

© Babybond Ltd. 2008. Babybond & the Babybond logo are registered trademarks of Babybond Ltd. Company Number 3631645

Figure 6   Pre-birth bonding: blending early nurturing with commercial enterprise?

stem cell retrieval at birth offers parents the hope of being the protectors and saviours of their children. Saving and storing your baby's umbilical cord blood is promoted as a 'natural life insurance' against leukaemia and other related blood diseases. But more than this, stem cell research promises to be a potential panacea for the treatment of many other diseases currently under investigation by leading scientists around the world. Investing in stem cells can be seen as a powerful act of faith, a belief in scientific progress combined with the parental desire to protect children from the foreseen and unforeseeable risks of life. Smart Cells International advertises in pregnancy magazines as the UK's 'leading provider of safe storage of umbilical cord stem cells':

We've got you covered.

Thankfully, the odds of your baby being attacked by a life-threatening disease are small, however, the existing treatments and promising research associated with umbilical cord stem cells, offers families extra peace of mind ... an extra layer of coverage so to speak.

(Pregnancy, September 2004)

Stem cell storage claims to give children a future while also underlining the idea that children *are the future*. A feature on the 'stem cell debate' in *Junior* magazine indicated that the total cost of retrieval and storage of new born stem cells is £1250. One parent had the stem cell from her first child's umbilical cord stored two years ago and is planning to do the same for her second child. She justified her decision as a form of insurance, acting on knowledge that positions herself and her partner as informed and responsible parents:

My husband and I felt that as we knew about it, we couldn't not do it. We just hope it will be a waste of money. The way we looked at it is that the cost is roughly the price of a holiday – I'd rather go without a holiday and be safe in the knowledge that I could be helping my children and possibly other members of the family in the future.

(Junior, February 2005)

The couple's negative premise for stem cell retrieval, 'we couldn't not do it', position them, at least on this matter, as the risk averse subjects of 'new times'. In keeping with Beck's (1992) conceptualisation of late modernity as governed by greater levels of risk, this couple style their identity as parents in relation to a broader culture of risk. In this example the consumption practices of parents can be seen as motivated by the care and protection of children, the avoidance of unnecessary risk and the prioritisation of family needs. It can also be seen as excessive and misplaced. Like buying your way to heaven in the medieval era and cryogenic freezing in the twentieth century, attempts to safeguard the individual in the future appears a worryingly inappropriate endeavour to secure that which can never be known. The need to spend valuable family resources in this way, however, needs to be understood. While it is difficult to offer a full interpretation of emergent parental practices in the here and now, it is possible that babybond® and stem cell retrieval constitute part of a reconfigured approach to child-rearing, informed by modes of consumption and late-modern risk-anxiety, in which the child appears as a late-modern blending of Romantic and scientific identifications.

The following activity invites you to consider some of the more mundane consumption practices faced by new parents. In the reading, Christina Hardyment (2007) notes the ever-increasing consumerism directed at parents of young children before focusing on potentially controversial matters such as disposable nappies and potty training.

Activity 5   Reading C

Allow about 35 minutes

Go to the readings at the end of the chapter and look at Reading C 'Buy a better baby', by Christina Hardyment.

Answer the following questions after you have read the extract:

- How has early childhood become big business?
- Why have disposable nappies become a contested issue?
- What are your views on the issues raised by this reading?

Comment

Hardyment points to changes in the way parents care for children, which are informed by the market and consumer practice. Every aspect of infant development is catered for by an array of products and services. Two generations ago women used terry towelling nappies which, to ensure hygiene, had to be washed at a high temperature. Prior to labour-saving devices such as automatic washing machines and twin tubs, nappies being boiled in a bucket on the stove was a familiar feature in family kitchens. Now most mothers in western Europe use disposable nappies which, aside from convenience, raise environmental issues as landfill sites become overloaded with non-biodegradable plastics largely from nappies. As cloth nappies use hot water, electricity, detergents, physical labour and, often, the fee of signing up to a washing service, the decision over nappies always involves consumption. Like spending on a children's birthday party, preparing for motherhood offers no neutral territory. Attempts to act ethically, do things differently and bypass the market, appear to produce more networks and sites of potential division between women.

Figure 7 Disposable nappies – essential baby product or environmentally unsustainable luxury?

In a study of new mothers (Thomson and Kehily, 2008), we found that asking about their choice of nappy invited them to comment on their relationship to domestic waste, eco-matters and global concerns. Most women positioned themselves as 'green', expressing an interest in responsible consumption and a strong commitment to recycling; however, the practical appeal of disposables was overwhelming. Rather than making a heartfelt decision, women suggested that they were slipping into the idea of using disposables to save time and make life easier. New parenthood was demanding, it was important to be practical and, if necessary, compromise on ideals and personal values. Using cloth nappies was not only less convenient, it involved an ongoing commitment to dealing with urine and faeces, a thought that generated laugher and disgust in equal measures. Women had bought disposable nappies in preparation for the birth even when they expressed a preference for cloth nappies. The introduction of biodegradable disposables provided a compromise position that was readily embraced by women looking for an eco-friendly solution to the nappy dilemma. The constant acts of discernment and interpretive meaning making that accompany maternal practices and consumption practices point to other ways of exploring the idea of childhood in crisis as an unresolved relationship between parents and the market.

Summary of Section 4

Contemporary parenting practices are shaped by prevailing discourses.

The legacy of the Romantic movement can be seen in parent–child relationships in the present.

The commercial world is a feature of family life, extending far beyond the scope of what children need.

Medical procedures, such as ultrasound scanning, and technological advances, such as stem cell retrieval, have been integrated into the range of consumer products available to parents.

5 Conclusion

This chapter has focused on the ways in which media reports and public commentary commonly invoke a notion of childhood in 'crisis'. Media texts, cultural commentary and policy-orientated accounts collectively point to a version of childhood in the popular imagination as despoiled and in crisis. A discussion of these accounts outlines the contours of this crisis, examining its manifestations and boundaries. Texts from a range of different sources suggest a crisis in childhood characterised by a decline in play, over-exposure to consumer culture, the stress of educational testing and a pervasively low sense of confidence in parents. Furedi (2001) and Palmer (2006) elaborate upon the themes inherent to childhood in crisis, locating their accounts, respectively, in 'the breakdown in adult solidarity' and the 'toxic cocktail' of cultural change that has had a detrimental impact upon children's lives.

The chapter has suggested alternative ways of understanding the notion of childhood in crisis: firstly, by placing contemporary accounts within a historical perspective and secondly, by considering cultural studies' approaches to the idea of crisis in studies that explore the concept of 'moral panic'. The chapter has also suggested a further way of understanding the idea of childhood in crisis through the lens of late-modern social theory. Within this body of literature, new practices of intimacy and the increase of risk and uncertainty in minority-world societies play a part in the restructuring of family relationships and child-rearing practices. From this perspective it is possible to suggest that the crisis in childhood exists as a reflection of adult anxiety and insecurity in 'new times'. Late-modern themes have implications for childhood, most noticeable in the way the child is positioned as a treasured emotional investment providing security for couples in an insecure world. This conceptualisation of the child draws upon Romantic ideals of children as innocent and in need of protection. Emergent parent–child relationships gleaned from pregnancy magazines provide an insight into parenthood in late modernity. Consumer practices such as babybond® scanning and stem cell retrieval point to some of the ways in which new parents may be responding to the idea of crisis and risk. Illustrating ways in which practices of consumption can be instrumentally deployed by parents to bond with and protect children, the chapter concludes that these emergent practices may signal a reconfigured approach to child-rearing in late modernity that blends Romantic ideals with technological advances.

References

Alexander, R. J. and Hargreaves, L. (2007) *Community Soundings: The Primary Review Regional Witness Sessions*, Cambridge, University of Cambridge Faculty of Education.

Barker, M. (1989) *Comics: Ideology, Power and the Critics*, Manchester, Manchester University Press.

Bauman, Z. (1988) *Freedom*, Milton Keynes, Open University Press.

Beck, U. (1992) *Risk Society: Towards a New Modernity*, London, Sage.

Cohen, S. (1973) *Folk Devils and Moral Panics*, London, Paladin.

Cunningham, H. (1995) *Children and Childhood in Western Society Since 1500*, London, Longman.

Elias, N. (1969) *The Civilizing Process, Vol.1: The History of Manners*, Oxford, Blackwell.

Furedi, F. (2001) *Paranoid Parenting: Abandon Your Anxieties and Be a Good Parent*, London, Allen Lane.

Giddens, A. (1991) *Modernity and Self-Identity: Self and Society in the Late Modern Age*, Cambridge, Polity Press.

Giddens, A. (1992) *The Transformation of Intimacy: Sexuality, Love, and Eroticism in Modern Societies*, Cambridge, Polity Press.

Hardyment, C. (2007) *Dream Babies: Childcare Advice from John Locke to Gina Ford*, London, Francis Lincoln.

H. M. Government (2004) *Every Child Matters: Change for Children* [online], www.everychildmatters.gov.uk (Accessed 18 June 2007).

James, A. and Prout, A. (eds) (1997) *Constructing and Reconstructing Childhood: Contemporary Issues in the Sociological Study of Childhood*, 2nd edn, London, Falmer Press.

James, A., Jenks, C. and Prout, A. (1998) *Theorising Childhood*, Cambridge, Polity Press.

Jenks, C. (1996) *Childhood*, London, Routledge.

Junior (2005) 'Stem cell debate', Orpington, Kent, Magicalia.

Mother and Baby (2005) 'Babybond, scanning to nurture', London, Emap Esprit.

Palmer, S. (2006) *Toxic Childhood: How the Modern World is Damaging Our Children and What We Can Do About It*, London, Orion.

Pearson, G. (1983) *Hooligan: A History of Respectable Fears*, Basingstoke, Macmillan.

Postman, N. (1982) *The Disappearance of Childhood*, London, W. H. Allen.

Pregnancy (2004), London, Highbury Lifestyle Ltd.

Telegraph Online, *Hold on to Childhood*, www.telegraph.co.uk/news (Accessed 13 September 2006).

The Children's Society (2007) *Good Childhood Inquiry, Reflections on Childhood – Lifestyle*, London, GfK Social Research.

Thomson, R. and Kehily, M. J. (2008) *The Making of Modern Motherhood: Memories, Representations, Practices*, Milton Keynes, The Open University.

UNICEF (2007) *Child Poverty in Perspective: An Overview of Child Well-being in Rich Countries*, Innocenti Report Card 7, Florence, UNICEF Innocenti Research Centre.

Wyness, M. G. (2000) *Contesting Childhood*, London, Falmer Press.

Reading A
Can these be children?

Geoffrey Pearson

Source: *Hooligan: A History of Respectable Fears*, 1983, Basingstoke, Macmillan, pp. 163–7.

The prevailing orthodoxy of mid-nineteenth-century philanthropy which identified the artful Chartist dodger as some kind of embryonic revolutionary cadre, although palpably false as a diagnosis of working-class unrest and political organisation' in the 1840s, nevertheless spoke directly to the central dilemma of this era. If only as a metaphor pointing to another kind of revolution – the Industrial Revolution which had transformed the material basis of life in the space of a few decades – it accurately registered the feared consequences of this great social alteration which, while creating unimaginable wealth, had also upset what was often believed to have been a previously harmonious way of life in pre-industrial Merrie England. For here, in the crucible of the first industrial nation, we see emerging a mature expression of the modernisation thesis which understands crime and violence as a by-product of sweeping social change and the loosening of custom and tradition; a form of understanding which remains with us to this day as a dominant ideological tradition within European and American social thought.

Estimates of the rate of increase in crime varied, although they were in general agreement that the increase was considerable. 'It is too evident that our criminals are steadily increasing,' wrote Thomson, 'not only in absolute numbers, but in relative proportion to the rest of the population', and he estimated that there had been 'an addition of nearly 30 per cent' in the number of committals 'in the last twenty-one years' (Thomson, 1852, p. 1). Beggs reckoned that one out of every 154 of the whole population were in prison, while Samuel Phillips Day arrived at the astonishing conclusion that the prison population had grown by 1,000 per cent since the beginning of the century (Beggs, 1849, p. 287). Worsley calculated that in the same period 'crime generally ... has increased five-fold' (Worsley, 1849, p. 6), drawing attention to the age group from 15 to 20 years who 'form not quite one-tenth of the population, but ... are guilty of nearly one-fourth of its crime' (Worsley, 1849, p. 9) which was 'a feature ... of crime in this country yet more alarming' (Worsley, 1849, p. 10). 'A growing increase in the proportion that juvenile criminals bear to adults' also struck Cornwallis as one of the more frightening aspects of the problem (Cornwallis, 1853, p. 352). Joseph Adshead estimated that 'nearly 7,000 youths are annually added to our criminal population', and working from the same kinds of statistical returns that were available to these native philanthropists Engels calculated a sevenfold increase in crime between 1805 and 1842 (Adshead, 1856, p. 160). It should be said that these early moral statisticians were somewhat cavalier in their use of crime statistics, and that their arithmetic was not always terribly sound, but the numbers only confirmed what the early Victorians already knew in their bones: that crime was advancing at a gallop.

The causes of the problem, as they were understood, were those which have already become wearily familiar. The cheap theatres, penny gaffs and two-penny-hop dancing saloons were regularly identified as incitements to crime and immorality among the young. 'The corruption of youth from spectacles, songs, etc., of an indecent nature' excited Cornwallis no less than others who described how the daring enactments of the outrages of Jack Sheppard, Dick Turpin and Claude Duval 'inculcate the same lesson, exhibit to admiration noted examples of successful crime' and thereby 'attract the attention and the ambition of these boys, and each one endeavours to emulate the conduct of his favourite hero' (Cornwallis, 1853, p. 410).

The breakdown of family life was also described as a consequence of the Industrial Revolution, and working mothers were another source of moral outrage. 'The withdrawal of woman's attention from the care of her offspring, and from domestic duties' was 'an unnatural arrangement' and 'a stigma upon the social state' (Hill, 1853, p. 39). 'Young children are left at home under very inadequate conduct and almost without restraint', wrote Beggs, 'left to play at will, and to expand into every lawless form.' 'Ignorant of cooking and needlework … unacquainted with all that is necessary to promote the comfort and welfare of a home … slatternly and ignorant', Beggs feared that 'the unfortunate man who marries a woman of this class suffers also … there is neither order nor comfort in the home … his meals are irregular and ill-prepared, and his own fireside presents so few attractions that he is tempted to the beer-house' (Beggs, 1849, pp. 72–3). Worsley agreed: the failure 'to discharge the most common duties of a housewife' resulted in 'a house in the grossest disorder, and a home without comfort … another inducement to seek refuge in the exciting pleasures of the theatre, the beer-shop, or gin-palace' (Worsley, 1849, p. 79).

In the minds of so many of these mid-century philanthropists, all roads led back to the beer-house. Drink, as much as ignorance, was held responsible not only for the self-inflicted poverty and wretchedness of the working class, but also in Henry Worsley's words 'leaves them at the mercy of petty orators and selfish demagogues'. Drink was 'the cause of causes ... the arcanum which is at the bottom of the whole superstructure of our national depravity': 'As long as the citadel of crime and iniquity remains fenced with the strong out-works of intemperance, it is impregnable.' Indeed, observing in words that are reminiscent of Karl Marx's judgement on nineteenth-century capitalism that 'All classes are merging in one of two, the indigent and the opulent', Worsley even feared that with the annihilation of the petit-bourgeoisie and small traders, the only small business to survive 'is, it may well be feared, the publican's' (Worsley, quoted in Beggs, 1849, p. 149).

These fears of the demoralisation of the common people were also, quite predictably, gathered around what was seen to be the excessive independence of the young in the manufacturing towns, with the associated feeling of the increasing youthfulness of crime. 'Amid such a state of affairs,' Worsley thought, 'we learn without surprise that crime is precocious in an extraordinary degree'. 'Insubordination to parental authority, leading to insubordination to all authority, is stated to be very general':

> The social evils are aggravated by the independence of the young of both sexes ... the child receives his own wages on his own account. In some cases, he will even remove from the parental roof ... It is palpably a system fraught with innumerable evils ... [especially when] we consider the early direction of the child's mind to the value of money, and the consequent temptation to procure it by illicit means.
>
> (Worsley, 1849, pp. 79–81, 95)

There were complaints in abundance about youths of both sexes mingling promiscuously in the cheap theatres and taverns, sometimes in the company of prostitutes, drinking, singing and swearing in a lewd manner, gambling for pennies in the streets, entertaining themselves with dog-fights, playing dominoes and bagatelle for money or drink, wearing coloured ribbons in their hair, or ganging together to commit robberies. Whereas Worsley had condemned the independence granted to young people through wage labour in the factories and mills, Beggs thought the 'absence of restraint' among street urchins even worse, recounting how 'by the proceeds of their irregular pursuits, they are enabled to lead a life of idleness and licentious freedom' (Beggs, 1849, p. 96). Micaiah Hill was so shocked by the precocity of the young that he posed himself a startling question – 'Can these be *children*?' – arriving at the disturbing conclusion that 'we must regard them as diminutive men' (Hill, 1853, pp. 9, 35). Matthew Davenport Hill was another who was struck by the adult freedom of the young delinquent – 'He knows much and a great deal too much of what is called life ... He is self-reliant ... he submits to no control' – and must be reckoned as 'a little stunted man' (quoted in May, 1973, p. 7).

These worries about the precocity of the young, which perhaps reflected a larger fear of the growing independence of the working class, provided a focal point for the mid-century preoccupation with mounting lawlessness. It may be remembered that this was exactly what struck Oliver Twist when, on arriving in dangerous London, he bumped into a 'strange sort of young gentleman' whom he would come to know as the Artful Dodger. He was 'about his own age', but 'one of the queerest-looking boys that Oliver had ever seen': 'He was a snub-nosed, flat-browed, common-faced boy enough; and as dirty a juvenile as one would wish to see; but he had about him all the airs and manners of a man' (Dickens, 1966, p. 100).

References

Adshead, J. (1856) *On Juvenile Criminals, Reformatories, and the Means of Rendering the Perishing and Dangerous Classes Serviceable to the State*, Manchester, J. Harrison and Son.

Beggs, T. (1849) *An Inquiry Into the Extent and Causes of Juvenile Depravity*, London, Charles Gilpin.

Cornwallis, C. F. (1853) *On the Treatment of the Dangerous and Perishing Classes of Society*, London, Smith, Elder and Co.

Dickens, C. (1966) *Oliver Twist*, Harmondsworth, Penguin.

Hill, M. (1853) *Juvenile Delinquency*, London, Smith, Elder and Co.

May, M. (1973) 'Innocence and experience: the evolution of the concept of juvenile delinquency', *Victorian Studies*, vol. 17, no. 1, p. 7.

Thomson, A. (1852) *Social Evils: Their Causes and Their Cure*, London, James Nisbet and Co.

Worsley, H. (1849) *Juvenile Depravity*, London, Charles Gilpin.

Reading B
Making sameness: mothering, commerce and the culture of children's birthday parties

Alison J. Clarke

Source: 'Making sameness: mothering, commerce and the culture of children's birthday parties', 2007, in Casey, E. and Martens, L. (eds) *Gender and Consumption*, Farnham, Ashgate, pp. 79–92.

> There it was, in the middle of a table strewn with fresh rose petals; a home-made birthday cake in the shape of a Romany caravan. I mean, I'm not joking! It had coloured icing curtains and chocolate Flake wheels. The gift bags, napkins and plates and everything … everything was co-ordinated with the 'folky Gypsy' theme. … all for a bunch of three year olds who'd rather have been stuffing their faces at McDonalds anyway!
>
> Jenny (38), mother in North London

Children's birthday parties, their organisation, design and orchestration might simply be viewed as the epitome of the 'invisible labour' of the gendered work of caring (DeVault 1991); for, as highly valorised spectacles, parties reveal the otherwise unseen consumptive and aesthetic skills of everyday nurturance. For the typical contemporary child's home-birthday party commonly involves the careful selection of a theme (Barbie, Harry Potter, wizards and dragons, fairies and queens, etc.); the making or buying of the ideal cake; the choice of miniature items for the guests' 'gift-bags'; the co-ordination of age-appropriate games and activities; the purchasing or making of party clothes or fancy dress outfits; the selection of party plates, cups, hats and tablecloths; the making or shopping for desirable party treats and snacks and, most importantly, the careful selection of just the right number and range of party guests.

Not only are children's parties becoming more elaborate, they are becoming more commercialised. Enterprises such as McDonalds fast-food outlets, Kid Zone play activity areas and Party Pieces catalogue (selling ephemeral wares exclusively for children's parties) are widely incorporated into children's party planning across Britain. Smaller scale enterprises, such as one-off 'bouncy castle' rentals, and the 'Paint Your

Own Pottery' party shops that have sprung up in street corners of densely child-populated neighbourhoods, are also testament to the enormous economic and social significance of the birthday party. Given the enormous amount of work and social anxiety generated by the typical infant's birthday party in recent years, it is perhaps not surprising that such parties have become increasingly commercialised affairs incorporating the paid services or venues of external companies or 'specialists'. As cultural geographers, sociologists and cultural economists (McKendrick, Bradford and Fielder 2000; Otnes, Nelson, McGrath 1995; Zelizer 2002) have identified, the children's birthday, either commercial or home-based, is a social ritual that is gaining, rather than waning, in significance in contemporary consumer society. Does the burgeoning culture of children's parties signal the vibrancy of neighbourly relations and friendships? Or is this commercialisation of an idealised facet of domestic work, the preparing for and shepherding of a child through the symbolically pertinent social ritual of the birthday, yet more evidence of the penetration of market forces into the sacrosanct non-economic worlds of children and motherly love?

Using excerpts from a broader ethnography of household consumption in north London, this [reading] explores the intersection of commerce and mothering and argues that birthday parties are rarely organised as singular expressions of parental/child relations but rather as part of a broader gendered sociality in which networks of gifts and children are circulated in rounds of reciprocity. The increasingly aestheticised and elaborated nature of children's parties and their intertwining of material culture, social relations and commerce is a form of consumption that is not merely an extension of women's domestic work, but is rather a testament to the ways in which mothering and consumption have become a mutually constitutive phenomenon (see Clarke 2004). It might be convenient to represent the careful preparation of the party event, and the sophisticated gift-giving culture negotiated between mother and child in the attendance of rounds of reciprocal birthday parties, as being redolent of a social anthropologist's classic model of 'authentic' feminised non-market sociality. On the contrary, however, this [reading] suggests that it is through (rather than despite) the appropriation of the market, in the form of mass-produced food, decorations and material culture, commercially hired venues that women as mothers attempt to subvert the tyranny of idealised roles as carers and find alternative renditions of being a 'mother'.

Potlatch and lucky bags: Making the perfect party

On Jay Road, an ordinary street in North London, Julie, the mother of a six-year-old girl, laments that a mother 'unfortunate' enough to have their child's birthday fall in August (between school in-take years) might have attended over twenty parties since the previous September due to the number of friends her child has accumulated. The sheer financial and organisational labour led many mothers to be increasingly ambivalent about 'the snowball effect' of arranging and attending party after party, and buying a seemingly endless round of suitable birthday presents.

Belinda, a mother of three children living in a street adjacent to Jay Road, observes that the 'party circuit' seems to have expanded in size, and lavishness since she was a child brought up in the same neighbourhood. Her own children expect birthday parties at commercial venues (such as a paint-gun play centre or water-world theme park) at enormous cost, and Belinda wonders whether this signals a shift in her own class mobility or a general boom due to increased consumerism and the increasing 'pester power' of children:

> It's just a different world to the one I was brought up in. I think they just make life so difficult for people these days – all this …
> we never had birthday parties when I was younger we had family birthday parties – we had a few cousins come over and that was it – and it was much easier and it was much less harassment for my mother. I think it's a bit of 'keeping up with the Joneses'.

Although, in the past, Belinda keenly organised extravagant children's parties at home and expensive 'themed' activity-events in commercial venues, she describes more recent attempts to 'opt out' of an 'escalating party scene' by introducing a price-cap on her ten-year old son Jake's parties and suggesting simpler options – like football in the park with his best friends followed by burgers and chips at home.

While Julie and Belinda try to find ways to negotiate the sheer enormity of the commitment to children's parties with 'down-sizing' strategies, round the corner Camilla Knowles, mother of four young children, day-dreams about themes and novelties for her children's parties. In the summer her three-year-old daughter, Caitlin, had a 'gypsy' party and Camilla made a cake in the shape of a Romany caravan surrounded by fresh flowers (as described in the opening quotation). She made 'lucky-bags' (party gift bags) from hand-painted muslin filled with 'lucky charm' sweets and novelties that she had collected on numerous shopping trips for the fifteen child-guests to take away at the end of the party, along with a slice of birthday cake in monogrammed cake tins. Camilla is particularly proud of the unique party-bag gifts, small raffia donkeys and horses, which she bought whilst on holiday in a remote Italian village, as there is absolutely no equivalent in the local shops and they cost only 50 pence each. …

'Other mothers': Making a sociality of sameness

… In early infancy the child is almost entirely a construct of its mother but as this gives way to the increasing agency of the child, who demands everything from the style of their party outfit to the types of presents, the mother's ability to supervise and oversee the outcome of the social event becomes more limited. But also the woman's role as mother and her own identity and standing within these terms is less likely to need negotiation or reiteration as at the early stages of child-rearing. For some women the prospect of hosting birthday parties for their older children is filled with even more anxiety enjoyable only for those mothers with the least to risk, and the most to display, as expressed by Joanna:

> Well – I don't know. I sound as if I'm being a bit 'classist' here, but I wonder if it's [children's party culture] more of a middle class thing. That is to say, what I was used to when I was a younger – we were much more … I don't know whether it's access to money – having less money than we've got now but I can't remember being invited to birthday parties. So either I was a very unfriendly or unliked child or we just didn't do it. Some people seem to thrive on it as well – like my cousin's 'set', they seem to go to millions of parties and she looks on it, sort of all, very generously and thinks it's all great. And I just find throwing them traumatic. I'd do anything rather than give a party. I just don't like it.

The enormous pressure of children's parties, the increasing materialism and commercialisation identified by numerous informants, revealed an entirely contradictory relation between discourse and practice. On the one hand, like Joanna, mothers spoke nostalgically of the small scale, kin-based parties they experienced themselves as children and lamented the rise in commercial intervention. Yet on the other hand, the very same mothers regularly incorporated party services and mass-produced goods into their party provisioning.

A typical commercial enterprise aimed precisely at mothers like Joanna is *Party Pieces*, a catalogue and on-line service dedicated to the accessorisation of children's parties, offering goods such as fancy dress outfits, decorated paper cups, party games and prizes, banners and balloons. Mothers receiving the catalogue complete a form listing the dates of their children's birthdays and receive the catalogue in the post two months prior to the date of a specific child's birthday. As well as providing ideas for themed parties the catalogue appealed to mothers such as Philipa (despite awareness of paying over the odds for the merchandise) as an expedient way of shopping while creating innovative parties:

> I've bought things from the *Party Pieces* catalogue but you can try be a little bit less extravagant really – I probably wouldn't tend to depend completely on it – I don't think they are that pricey but the whole thing always adds up in the end – you end up buying more, rather than if you had just gone out and bought a few white plain paper plates – if you get the whole thing co-ordinated and masks and that sort of stuff.

The expansion of formal businesses into the previously 'home-made' arena of 'dressing-up' and 'fancy dress' costumes and accessories seems further testament to some mothers of the commercialisation of children's worlds. As well as catalogues featuring festive wares, more recently a local woman in the neighbourhood had been organising 'children's fancy dress direct-sales parties', showing a range of costumes from Dracula to Fairy Queens. Gathering together in the house of a volunteer hostess, mothers sip wine and handle a range of children's fancy and dressing-up wear and choose from a stand-up cardboard model showing prices, descriptions and costume types. In general, the costumes were considered overly simple in relation to the prices charged for them. A pirate costume, for example, consists of a black patch and a pair of shorts resembling pyjama bottoms; an ensemble several mothers considered insultingly easy to have put together themselves. ...

For some mothers the overt commodification of the catalogue undermines the entire project of the children's party and takes away the creativity of inventing games, costumes, decorations and prizes. Jane, for example, enjoys making homemade items, to create a co-ordinated theme. She used the closeness of Halloween to her daughter Rachel's birthday as a theme for her fifth birthday party, organised in conjunction with another mother, in the local church hall. As it was a fancy dress event, Jane had spent several evenings sewing a witch's outfit for her daughter from scraps of fabric from a local remnant store. She made jamboree bags filled with 'bits and bobs' from Woolworth's and had cut out paper decorations to string across the walls of the hall. Both mothers spent evenings carving out pumpkin lanterns and hand-made invitations with pop-up ghosts had been sent to around twenty children. A birthday cake in the shape of a 'scary monster' with the names of the two girls iced on top formed the centrepiece of the food. Working to a limited budget, Jane viewed the creative aspect of the party-making as a crucial element of its value and she encouraged Rachel and her small brother to make invitations and decorations at the kitchen table with her. ...

As well as the resources required for the organisation of children's birthday parties a number of strategies are employed to deal with the sheer volume of gifts required in the attendance of the yearly 'rounds' of parties. Jenny, for example, uses a two-tier approach to birthday gifts for her children's friends (as also described in Sirota's (199[8]) study of children's birthday gift-giving in Paris). For general school friends' parties she uses a collection of Woolworth's items, amassed throughout the year in the course of everyday household shopping trips. For closer friends' and best friends' birthday parties she uses the Early Learning Centre catalogue and specific shopping trips to make selections. She also keeps a bulk of children's birthday cards in a drawer of the living room cupboard and uses the corner shop 'in emergencies' if she runs out of appropriate cards. For members of her own family Jenny uses trips abroad, for example, to try to find items a little more special. Although family gifts can be postponed, delivered at a later date, gifts for the children of other mothers are a more pressing concern and onerous task:

> Most of the presents I buy are for the children to take to parties ... I owe my other cousin's little boy a present – he was four so I've got to get him something – I've got a huge family so it costs me a fortune in presents and also the kids have acres and acres of friends which is good, you want them to have friends, but sometimes the parties and the buying gifts can be a bit much.

Cultural economists (Levinson 2000; Zelizer 2002) have recently identified activities such as children's birthday parties, and their gift economies, as significant testament to children's economic activity. Unlike the gift relations between parent and off-spring (see Clarke forthcoming) the provisioning of birthday gifts does not involve overly complex mediations between child/adult. Rather choices of gifts (with the exception of 'best friends') relies on a heavily prescribed and general repertoire of material culture organised principally in accordance with gender/age appropriateness and cost allowing the easy circulation of goods and children in the production of social solidarity. Although, as asserted by more recent theoretical approaches to the research of childhood (James 1993; Christensen 2000), children are not merely objects of socialisation or 'adults-in-the-making', their agency here is internalised by the mothers and integrated as a vital part of the cultural and aesthetic repertoire of the general birthday party; child, gift and party attendance become one and the same.

Conclusion

… While birthday parties might be understood as a crude series of escalating potlatches (in terms of the colloquial concept of competitive gifting that followed the popularisation of the term after Mauss), in actual fact the parties are far removed from this sense of direct competitive giving. Rather, they involve subtle and skilful positioning through a series of normative stages, each of which has its associated strategies and potentials. While there is at once a desire to use goods and gifts to express relationships and their depth (honouring a particular mother or child, for example, with a more 'individually' chosen gift) the notion of the 'going rate' for the price of a children's party gift is crucial to the maintenance of 'sameness'. The expansion of the previously kin and home-based activity of the children's birthday party as a form of 'potlatch' (in which increasingly imaginative, commercialised or subtle variations of a theme are used to demonstrate the mother/child's worthiness and prestige) is testament to a contemporary British culture increasingly premised on the 'child' as a social object.

Despite the discourse regarding the unwanted intervention of the market into the 'authentic' relations of everyday domesticity, commercial services and goods are used by women to alleviate the pressures of potlatch party culture, and the potential for overly oppressive, idealised versions of competitive mothering. For venues such as Monkey Business soft-play venue, McDonalds fast food chain and the Party

Pieces catalogue offer a less risky, neutralised default to the individually organised event. While Martha Stewart (or Camilla Knowles) type renditions of creative, expressive mothering might be popularly aspired to, in this ethnographic context they are regarded with the highest suspicion as they pose the greatest threat to a culture of negotiated 'sameness'. The woman most likely to garner admiration is the mother who 'gets away' with pulling off the most affective party with the minimal effort and expense, all within the bounds of the accepted aesthetic of the group.

References

Christensen, P. and James, A. (eds) (2000) *Research with Children: Perspectives and Practices*, London, Falmer Press.

Clarke, A. J. (2004) 'Maternity and materiality: becoming a mother in consumer culture', in Taylor, J. S., Layne, L. and Wozniak, D. F. (eds) *Consuming Motherhood*, New Brunswick, NJ and London, Rutgers University Press.

Clarke, A. J. (forthcoming) 'Coming of age in suburbia: designing the normative child', in Gutman, M. and Connick-Smith, N. (eds) *Designing Modern Childhoods: History, Space and Material Culture of Children*, New Brunswick, NJ and London, Rutgers University Press.

DeVault, M. (1991) *Feeding the Family: The Social Organization of Caring as Gendered Work*, Chicago, IL, Chicago University Press.

James, A. (1993) *Childhood Identities, Self and Social Relationships: On the Experience of the Child*, Edinburgh, Edinburgh University Press.

Levinson, D. (2000) 'Children as economic agents', *Feminist Economics*, vol. 6, pp. 125–34.

Mauss, M. (1954) *The Gift. Forms and Functions of Exchange in Archaic Societies*, London, Cohen and West.

McKendrick, J. H., Bradford, M. G. and Fielder, A. V. (2000) 'Time for a party!: making sense of the commercialisation of leisure space for children', in Holloway, S. and Valentine, G. (eds) *Children's Geographies: Playing, Living, Learning*, London, Routledge.

Otnes, C., Nelson, M. and McGrath, M. (1995) 'The children's birthday party: a study of mothers as socialization agents', *Advances in Consumer Research*, vol. 22, pp. 622–7.

Sirota, R. (1998) 'Les copains d'abord. Les anniversaires de l'enfance, donner et recevoir', *Ethnologie Francaise*, vol. 4, pp. 457–72.

Zelizer, V. (2002) 'Kids and commerce', *Childhood*, vol. 9, no. 4, pp. 375–96.

Reading C
Buy a better baby

Christina Hardyment

Source: *Dream Babies: Childcare Advice from John Locke to Gina Ford*, 2007, London, Francis Lincoln, pp. 327–32.

In the last twenty years, parents have expended increasingly large parts of their disposable income on their children. The sight of estate cars and now 4 x 4s packed to the roof, to say nothing of the roof box, with equipment for the newborn baby became a matter of wonder to grannies who could not remember needing anything more than a bottle, a shawl and a pram. Thoroughly modern mothers are equally amazed that anyone ever managed without sterilizers, various styles of bottles, IQ-stimulating play-boards, clockwork mobiles that play classical music, orthopaedically approved bouncers and orthodontically approved dummies, slings, travel-cots, carrychairs, buggies, car seats, babygros galore, pallet-loads of disposable nappies, allergy-free mattresses, and a nursery kitted out from carpet to lampshade in a co-ordinated Mamas and Papas theme.

The under-fives became big business. Conferences began to be held to calculate the best way to market products to the 800,000 or so British women who give birth every year. In 1992, the Parent and Baby Care World Exhibition at Wembley offered 'the broadest spectrum of products and services for parents ever assembled under one roof' and promised to 'entertain, educate and inform' them. 'If this exhibition is about parenthood today,' commented *Independent* journalist Brigid McConville, 'then parenthood today is about consumerism.' She found the National Childbirth Trust stand deserted – 'Everyone was too busy shopping.' In 2007, Kensington Olympia hosts both the Baby Care Show and the Good Parent Exhibition, and there are similar opportunities to spend a fortune at Glasgow and Birmingham.

The manuals' lists of essentials for newborns lengthen annually. Views of what is a necessity and what is optional vary not only from writer to writer, but from edition to edition. In an increasingly mobile age, it was no surprise that Spock's 1992 list started with a 'dynamically [i.e. crash] tested' car seat. His second instruction was to have your water tested for bacteria and nitrates before the baby arrives. Cots' slats should have 'slats no more than 2 3/8 inch apart, a snug-fitting mattress, childproof side-locking mechanisms, no sharp edges or lead paint, and be at least

26 inches from the top of the rail to the mattress at its lowest level.' Among other new essentials were a rectal thermometer, an inclined plastic seat, and/or a cloth one (with a warning against using it too much), and an intercom between baby's room and that of its parents. Spock remained pro-playpen, though he conceded it was 'controversial', but became anti-baby-walker (describing it as 'useful' in 1975, it had become 'a major cause of injury' by 1992). Reins and harnesses were again 'controversial' (because of their restraint on infant spontaneity) but useful, 'especially in supermarkets'. Lightweight folding strollers have succeeded prams everywhere except in 'a few cities in the north-eastern parts of the United States'.

Green recommended rather less in fewer, wittier words. He recognized the dangers of babywalkers, but was more sanguine about their usefulness as 'sanity-savers for the parents of a certain type of child … give it a go if your child is bored being a baby, but not if he's a contented crawler'. Obviously not a yummy daddy, he too dismissed prams as cumbersome, British, and old-fashioned, and emphasized the advantage of pushchairs.

Juliet Solomon minimized the need for elaborate kit, recommending slings, baby-backpacks and, typically thoughtfully, pushchairs in which babies face backwards so that they 'can see mummy when they are out walking'. She was predictably caustic about the number of toys children were given. 'The sight of a small child, disgruntled because he is apparently unable to find anything to do in a room that looks like a toyshop will be familiar to many,' she writes. 'There is everything, and yet there is nothing. The adult equivalent is dissatisfied "grazing" with a TV zapper over several channels because there is "nothing on".' Most of the books agree with this, but in the real world their admonitions are as ineffectual as Canute's call for drier beaches. Toys 'R' Us and Children's World superstores flank the DIY warehouses; chain stores such as Hennes, Gap, and Next open kiddie-couture departments and yummy mummies trick out their cherubs in designer clothes.

Tracy Hogg called for a halt on the competitive stampede to acquire supposedly stimulating toys on the grounds that they could actually upset a baby. Hearing what one set of parents has done to cheer up their bawling three-week-old girl, she concluded that 'The poor little thing has been enduring an environment that – from her baby perspective – is like spending a day in Disneyland.' 'Put away anything that shakes, rattles, jiggles, wiggles, squeaks or vibrates,' she suggested.

'Try it for just three days and see if Baby calms down.' She might have added that baby's parents will get calmer too.

The nursery item on which parents spend most is the disposable nappy. In the 1970s, they were a last resort, stiff wads of absorbent wood-pulp, difficult to adjust and prone to leak. In the early 1980s elasticated edges arrived; a few years later adhesive tabs allowed nappies to be opened, checked, and resealed. The real breakthrough was in 1987 when an absorbent gelling agent was developed which could take up to twenty-eight times its own weight (rather than wood-pulp's mere four times) and which chemically bonded the moisture to itself. Added to wood pulp, this increased absorbency hugely reduced the bulk of the nappy, and kept the baby's skin feeling dry for much longer.

By 1992, 3 billion disposables a year were being sold and dumped after use in the UK alone. Waste disposal experts became concerned at the implications of the daily dumping of around 8 million sodden and dirty disposables. The working mothers' handbooks did not pander to environmentalism. 'Don't use terry nappies unless you really cannot afford the disposable kind,' advised Mary Beard, accepting philosophically that 'an average baby will use up most of his Child Benefit in nappies.' Spock however was quick to call disposables 'an ecological nightmare', a leading cause of a nationwide shortage of landfill space, not truly biodegradable (despite makers' claims), and a source of pollution. 'I think if I were a baby I would prefer to be snuggled up in a soft toweling nappy,' wrote Green in 1993. He cursed disposables with vivid eco-fervour: 'Each nappy costs a small branch and a cupful of crude oil to manufacture; they may be throwaway but the price certainly isn't.' Flush them down the lavatory, and the cost of the plumber will be 'almost as much as it costs for a good laundry service'. But he had recanted by 2001, emphasizing the improvements in disposables, omitting their eco-impact and ignoring the huge improvements in terry towelling nappies.

Today, with five million trees a year felled to keep UK babies in disposables, and each baby adding 2.5 tons to landfill from its nappies alone, almost all the manuals recommend the use of real nappies, now available in a myriad of cunningly crafted shapes and colours. Varieties listed in *Green Parent* peaked in 2006 at sixty; a year later the market had shaken down to thirty-seven options, including hemp, bamboo, organic cotton and wool versions. But today only around 20 per cent of UK parents are using washables. Many more intend to; the road to Pampers is paved with good intentions. Easy and inoffensive to the nose as the new washable nappy systems are, with their biodegradable liners that can be washed down the loo, most fastidious modern parents far prefer to 'bag it and bin it'. I bought some neatly shaped little washable nappies for my first grandchild; they were passed on all but unused to my second, where they lie in a bottom drawer, despite the fact that his mother is, in theory, a keen green. Yummy mummy Liz Fraser speaks for the majority of modern mothers when she admits that her urge to use real nappies

> lasted no longer than the first 24 hours, at which point I realised I was just kidding myself ... There is so much else to do, and you are so exhausted to start with that anything which makes your life easier is worth doing ... If you are a committed eco-warrior then all this will severely piss you off, and I do apologise and acknowledge that you are right. But for everyone else, don't beat yourself up about using disposables, try to do your bit for the environment in other ways.

Some of the blame must lie with the new system of chucking mothers out of hospital so fast (with a free pack of disposables, courtesy of their manufacturer). Nor was the cause of real nappies helped by a 2005 Environmental Agency survey claiming that because of the expenditure of energy washing and drying real nappies, there was little if any difference in the environmental impact to that done by disposables in destroying trees and creating slow-to-rot landfill. Real Nappy campaigners were quick to pick holes in the report (financed by disposable nappy companies), which assumed that forty-seven (rather than the usual twenty four) cloth nappies would be washed at 90° (much hotter than necessary) in an old-fashioned non-energy-efficient washing machine tumble-dried (rather than hung up to dry) and then ironed. It also ignored the fact that one set of nappies can be used for two or more babies. But the damage was done, and the report was quoted with elation on the Pampers website. Its distorting and imperfect research can now be defiantly cited by the 80 per cent of parents addicted to disposables, despite the fact that they have such efficient detergents and machines to deal with real ones. The green dream of the future is a national network of nappy-washing services to deliver clean nappies and take away dirty ones. Many local councils with waste targets to meet now offer these, even giving away sets of free washable nappies to new parents.

One unlooked-for side effect of the convenience and comfort of disposable nappies has been the postponement of potty-training. Disposables in larger and larger sizes are appearing on the shelves, exacerbating the global waste-disposal problem. 'They are so absorbent and do such a good job of keeping urine away that only grumpy babies seem to realise they are wet. When toddlers aren't toilet-trained by three, sometimes it's because paper diapers don't let them know they are wet,' warned Tracy Hogg. The manuals have grown increasingly vague as to the right age for toilet-training. They provide lists of signals of 'potty readiness', and warn parents to back off if any disinclination is shown. Freud still rules the bathroom.

Potty-training is another consumer opportunity. Potties need to amuse and enchant these days; manuals suggest you buy them in your toddler's preferred colour and shape; they can be had in every colour of the rainbow and play tunes as you tinkle. Sears suggests a gradual approach that spreads over some weeks (summertime is best) and involves first bare bottoms, then a succession of aids in the form of pants with inbuilt nappies (pull-ups), lightly padded training pants and finally real pants. Gina Ford prefers a week or weekend blitz, starting at between eighteen and twenty-four months, at a time when there are no distractions like a second baby or a change of house, and baby is dry after daytime naps. Necessary equipment includes two potties, a child's loo seat, ten pairs of pants, a selection of story books, cassette tapes and videos, a star chart, a booster step to reach the hand basin and a face cloth 'decorated with his favourite cartoon character' to use as a towel after washing hands. Yummy mummies don't seem to do potty-training at all; maybe they leave pre-prep school to do the business.

Easily the best reading on the subject is Christopher Green, firm but kind, and without many trimmings. Of three possible methods, he dismisses 'grunt and catch' (which requires an Olympic sprint) and 'broody hen' (in which being put on the pot comes AFTER action; 'the offering is placed in the sacred chamber, and the child made to sit above it like a hen incubating a new-laid egg') in favour of 'sit-and-wait', a regular postprandial session three times a day, made enjoyable by a story. 'Maybe at such a young age they don't appreciate the finer points of Goldilocks, but they sure understand the meaning of being the focus of all attention at centre stage.'

Often attached to advice on potty-training are a few impassive words on 'touching private parts'. Green explains that although this is now classed as a 'perfectly innocent habit' which should just be ignored, social convention still demands that it be discouraged when out and about or 'visiting maiden aunts'. 'Gently divert the offending hand or interest the child in something more sociable.'

References

Ford, G. (1999) *The Contented Little Baby Book*, London, Vermillion.

Green, C. (1992) *New Toddler Taming, A Parents' Guide to the First Four Years*, London, Vermillion.

Hogg, T. and Blau, M. (2005) *Secrets of the Baby Whisperer: How to Calm, Connect, and Communicate with Your Baby*, New York, Random House.

Sears, W. and Sears, M. (2005) *The Baby Book*, London, Harper Collins.

Spock, B. (1975, 1992) *Dr Spock's Baby and Childcare*, New York, Pocket Books.

Chapter 2

Childhood: a historical approach

Laurence Brockliss and Heather Montgomery

Contents

In this chapter, you will:

- consider the ways in which historians have approached the study of childhood
- develop an awareness of some of the problems with sources that historians face when studying children
- analyse the theories of Philippe Ariès on the 'invention' of childhood and the arguments of his critics
- critically examine some of the main themes in European constructions of childhood.

1 Introduction

Children's lives and daily experiences in the past have sometimes been dismissed by historians as unknowable because they leave so few traces in the historical record. Yet this is not to say that historians have been uninterested in children and they have long focused on particular aspects of children's lives, such as education or health and, importantly, on adults' views of childhood. This chapter traces the development of historical ways of looking at children, and examines the sources and methods that historians have used for doing so. It assesses how childhoods have changed and how different historians have understood and explained these changes. It will also show how certain ideas about childhood, while being products of particular times, places and contexts, continue to resonate in contemporary ideas of childhood.

2 How do historians study childhood?

History, as it has developed as an academic discipline over the past 200 years, has principally been the reconstruction of the past through the study of written documents preserved in institutional archives. Homo sapiens appears to have existed as a species for some 500,000 years, but it is only in the last four millennia that it has left any written record of its society and culture, and only in the last four or five centuries that keeping written records has gradually become a universal phenomenon. Historians therefore study humanity's most recent past as recorded in descriptions and reports of public events, criminal trials, witness statements, laws and government decrees which are catalogued and kept in archives. However, there are great swathes of time and place for which there is no written record and these remain the field of the pre-historian, archaeologist or anthropologist. In fact, as the specifically archival record of human activity in the UK and most other European countries is extremely fragmentary before AD 1200, conventional academic history about Europe tends to begin with the high Middle Ages (tenth to thirteenth centuries AD).

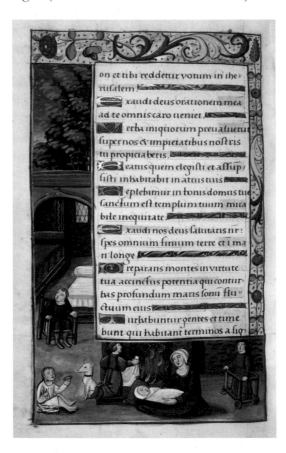

Figure 1 Sixteenth-century scene from an illuminated manuscript held in the Bodleian Library, Oxford University

It is customary to divide European historical time into four periods: the classical (ancient Greece and Rome), medieval (AD 400–1500), early-modern (AD 1500–1800) and modern (post-AD 1800). Writing archive-based histories of children and childhood which cover any period except the modern is very difficult. The material that survives in national, local and institutional archives for the pre-modern era mostly relates to matters of administration, justice and finance, and reveals little about children and childhood before 1800. These documents detail the world of the adult, not the world of the child. In the archival record before the nineteenth century, children and young people commonly only surface when they are living away from home as schoolboys, apprentices and students, when they suffer unexpected deaths outside the home, or when, in the absence of any family to look after them, they are institutionalised from an early age in city orphanages. Indeed, in the late Middle Ages and the early modern period, the day-to-day lives of the abandoned and orphaned can be charted much more fully than the lives of the majority of children who were raised within their families. The only comprehensive data that the pre-modern archives contain relating to children generally are demographic statistics. In early-modern England, for instance, thanks to the requirement from the early sixteenth century that all births, deaths and marriages should be recorded at the parish level, it is possible to know the numbers of children in the population as a whole, the level of child mortality and the proportion of children who survived to become adults (Wrigley and Schofield, 1981).

Figure 2   An entry from a coroner's record in 1569 which records the death of Jane Shaxspere, a two-and-a-half year old girl who drowned in a mill pond in Worcestershire

From the beginning of the nineteenth century the situation changed. With the dawning of the modern era, the state and local authorities began to take an ever closer interest in the upbringing of children. The era of Romanticism in the UK and Europe engendered a new view of the child as a precious and innocent vessel (see Section 4.3 for a fuller discussion of this). Children had to be kept away from the adult world – even from their own parents, if necessary – and there were particular concerns about parents allowing their children to perform hard physical labour. If many unsentimental members of the establishment only paid lip service to this novel viewpoint, and the demands of industrialisation led to large numbers of children working hard in harsh conditions, they accepted that children – in an age of fierce competition between nations – were an asset to the state and that their development could no longer be safely left entirely to parents, who were often judged too poor, too busy or too vicious to ensure their offspring were properly nurtured and educated. The consequent, if gradual, creation of the modern welfare state – beginning in the second half of the nineteenth century with the foundation of systems of mass education – resulted in a transformation of the archival record. The archives of the modern day are awash with details of children's lives across time. At one level, in the form of enquiries and audits by governmental agencies and private charities, they contain a record of elite concerns and aspirations. At another, through the plethora of surviving documentation about schools, health clinics, youth associations, and so on, they offer the possibility of uncovering the more mundane details about the daily lives of children across the social divide (Hendrick, 1994).

Figure 3   A young girl working in a coal mine pulling a tub of coal (1842)

Activity 1   Sources and informants

Allow about 45 minutes

Finding out about children in the past requires information from a wide variety of sources. Below are three different sources used by the historian Hugh Cunningham to examine child labour in the past.

Read through the two quotes and the table, and comment on the following questions:

- How useful do you find them in telling us about childhood in the nineteenth century?

- What problems are there in interpreting them?

1   Evidence given to the Factories Inquiry Commission 1833 (in British Parliamentary Papers 1968a, p. 587) by J. H. Green, Esq., FRS (a surgeon at St Thomas's Hospital in London):

> Children were not designed for labour, and although in the artificial state of society in which we live, and considering the imperative demands for sustenance which oblige the poor to employ their children, some labour must be permitted, yet both our conscience and our feelings equally demand that the labour of children should be under such restrictions as will ensure them against their being made the victims of avarice and disease, and as will render it compatible with their physical and moral welfare.
>
> *(Quoted in Cunningham, 2003, p. 86)*

2   Evidence to the Children's Employment Commission 1842 (in British Parliamentary Papers 1968b, pp. 252–3) by Sarah Gooder, aged 8 years:

> I'm a trapper [someone who controls the air vents] in the Gawber pit. It does not tire me, but I have to trap without a light and I'm scared. I go at four and sometimes half past three in the morning and come out at five and half past. I never go to sleep. Sometimes I sing when I've light, but not in the dark; I dare not sing then. I don't like being in the pit. I am very sleepy when I go sometimes in the morning ... I would like to be at school far better than in the pit.
>
> *(Quoted in Cunningham, 2003, p. 86)*

3   Employment of girls aged 10–14 in England and Wales from the 1851 census. This was the first nationwide census which recorded occupation and is therefore especially useful to historians studying child labour.

Table 1 Employment of girls aged 10–14 in England and Wales from the 1851 census

Occupation	No. employed	Per cent of 10–14 employed	Per cent of all 10–14
Domestic servants	50,065	26.5	5.3
Cotton	29,038	15.4	3.1
Worsted	10,586	5.6	1.1
Silk	10,533	5.6	1.1
Farm servants	10,085	5.3	1.1
Lace	8628	4.6	0.9
Wool	7333	3.9	0.8
Nurse	6938	3.7	0.7
Milliner	6048	3.2	0.6
Straw plait	5041	2.7	0.5
Other occupations	44,682	23.6	4.7
		100.0%	19.9%

(Adapted from Cunningham, 1990, p. 142)

Comment

These three pieces of evidence are all from official government publications and each provides a different insight into child labour in the nineteenth century. The first offers a campaigner's view against child employment, the second gives us a child's view, while the third provides statistical data on the extent of child labour among girls in 1851. Yet each of these sources needs further interpretation – how was this evidence created? By whom and under what circumstances? Might there be flaws in how it was collected and presented? All these questions are central to the historical interpretation of sources.

Child labour was a pressing social issue in the nineteenth century and many campaigned for its abolition. The first quote is from a surgeon who argues that child labour is both physically and morally damaging to children, although he still believes some children need to work. His concern focuses not only on the physical dangers to children, but also on their exposure to corruption and to moral degeneracy. The second is from a child herself, at first glance a rare case of a child's voice being captured in the historical record. However, we know a limited amount about her – did she write down her account or was she interviewed by someone from the commission? If so, who? The language she uses is sophisticated, and her speech articulate, and this must lead to questions about whether her account has been 'tidied up' or rewritten by others. Whether or not this really is the child's voice, therefore, is highly debatable. Finally, the census figures may be assumed to be an accurate reflection of the extent of child labour in England and Wales at the time, yet these must be treated with some caution as well. They were collected on house-to-house visits by data collectors who had to rely on what they were told. They suggest that the employment of children was much less widespread than is commonly supposed, with only 20 per cent of girls working, which may be due to the underreporting of domestic labour – especially when girls were working alongside their mothers at home. Therefore, while these figures are useful in describing the types of jobs children had, they may not be a reliable reflection of what children actually did or how hard they worked.

Each of these sources therefore gives only a partial picture about child labour in the nineteenth century, but taken together these pieces of evidence begin to build up a picture of the different views of childhood at the time, what children were thought capable of and how adults should best protect them.

Although archival material is of great importance to historians, it does not mean that a history of childhood cannot be written before the modern age. If archival history has traditionally been considered the most important, scholarly and prestigious form of historical writing, there has been a growing readiness since the 1970s to use other sources to supplement and sometimes subvert the archival record. Literary and visual sources were commonly seen by some academic historians as imaginative and unrepresentative records of life in the past with none of the supposed objectivity of archival documents. Now that it is understood that all records, however dry and mundane, are authorial creations with a point of view and cannot be seen as uncontested facts, historians have been free to find alternative means of recovering the experience and meaning of childhood in past societies. Although there remains an interest in using archival sources to discover the nature of children's lives in various periods, this has been tempered with a concern over the contexts in which they were produced and whether they need to be interpreted in the light of other material.

Figure 4   Pieter Bruegel (1525–1569), *Children's Games*, 1560

Literary sources have been particularly useful to historians of early-modern childhood. References to children in imaginative literature, law codes, childcare manuals and so-called 'ego-documents' (such as letters, diaries and autobiographies in which adults provide an account of their own childhood and that of their children) exist from the Graeco-Roman era. But they only became plentiful from about 1500 with the emergence of nation-states, the development of vernacular literatures, the division of Christendom into warring camps and a novel interest in individuality inspired by the Renaissance (Pollock, 1983; Fletcher, 2008). Visual sources, on the other hand, have been profitably pillaged by historians of all eras. By studying how children are presented in relation to adults, or on their own, on the funeral monuments of the Graeco-Roman era and in the religious sculpture of the high and late Middle Ages, the religious and historical paintings of the Renaissance, the family portraits of the eighteenth century and the photographs of the Victorian epoch, it has become possible to get a tangible idea of the changing concept of children and childhood across long swathes of time (Retford, 2006). Archaeology, too, although an independent discipline, has given the historian additional insights into the world of unrecorded childhood. Long before parish records began to provide the possibility of studying children as a demographic category, the excavation of settlement sites from the Neolithic Age to the late Middle Ages has uncovered information about child internment and children's diet, health and material culture.

Yet if the new respectability accorded non-archival sources makes it possible to write about childhood before the modern age, it also makes for controversy. Evaluating archival documents is difficult enough – even though they appear to be an official source of facts and figures they cannot be read literally, for reasons suggested previously – but non-archival sources also have to be approached with particular care and sensitivity, and an understanding of the context in which they were produced. They too can never provide a complete or uncontroversial picture. The very fact that the majority of the population was illiterate before the modern era means that diaries and autobiographics tend to be class and gender specific. They principally provide information about the childhood of well-to-do boys and frequently feature teenagers rather than young children. Histories written using these sources are accounts of an unrepresentative minority (Fletcher, 2008). It is only in the nineteenth century that the working-classes began to leave an account of their lives (Humphries, 2010). Visual sources equally provide elite rather than popular representations of children and childhood, but their evaluation is complicated further by the use of children as moral or spiritual emblems. One of the most famous Renaissance paintings of children is Pieter Bruegel's *Children's Games* painted in 1560. On the surface it shows children playing over 80 games in a town square. Should we believe, though, that these are games played by children, or are they rather adult games that Breugel, as a moralist, wished to present as childish and unworthy pastimes? Interpreting the evidence is particularly hard with the archaeological record. One of the peculiar features of the pre-Christian world is that children are frequently found buried apart from adults. Does that mean they were valued or under-valued? And what do we make of the absence of children's bones altogether in Bronze-Age Britain? Were they disposed of in some other way entirely? And how? These are all questions that historians cannot answer with any certainty.

The difficulties of writing histories of childhood before the modern era have only been compounded by our contemporary interest in children as agents. Before 1800 virtually all our sources are reflections on how adults perceived or remembered childhood, but not on how childhood was experienced by children. Even when the child 'speaks' in documents of any kind, the voice is filtered, as in the example of the child mine worker, Sarah Gooder, quoted in Activity 1. A further example of this is the testimony of a number of children who were caught up in the paranoia about witchcraft that engulfed Europe in the period 1550–1650 and appeared before the courts as either victims or witnesses (see Reading A). Their testimonies that were taken down by the clerk of the court introduce us to a world of children's games and customs that would otherwise remain hidden, but it must always be remembered that the children's answers were partly determined by the leading questions being put to them by adults. Even the odd collections of children's letters and the even rarer diaries that survive from the early modern period have to be treated with circumspection. The diary which the ten-year-old Dutch boy, Otto van Eck, began in 1791 and kept for six years is the most detailed so far discovered that was produced by a child before the modern era, and is a treasure trove of information about the activities, feelings and opinions of an adolescent in the age of the French Revolution. But Otto only kept a diary on his parents' behest and they read his daily entry each night; it was not a diary of his private, inner life but an account written for the benefit of adults (Baggerman and Dekker, 2009).

Figure 5 Children and adults found guilty of witchcraft could be put to death. This image shows the burning of three witches in Switzerland in 1585

Activity 2   Reading A

Allow about 35 minutes

Turn to Reading A, which focuses on a 12-year-old boy called Hans Merckler who lived in Germany in the seventeenth century. Lyndal Roper's work is based on trial transcripts written down at the time and held in the State Archive of Würzburg, Germany. In order to write this account, Roper would have gone to the town hall and state archives in Germany where the records of these trials are kept, spent many hours in their libraries going through boxes of papers and court records, some of which may never have been looked at before, and recreated the story of these children's lives. In the case of Hans Merckler, first the schoolmaster was informed, then witness statements were taken locally, then the case moved to Retzbach and from there to Karlstadt, the district administrative centre, and finally to the territory's capital. Records were kept at all these stages.

As you read through the text, comment on the following two issues:

* Where does Lyndal Roper get her information about Hans, and other children accused of witchcraft, from?

* How does she use her sources to gain an insight into children's worlds?

Comment

In researching this account Roper would have had to sift through a great deal of information which does not concern children directly. Part of the role of historians is to filter out much of the information they find, focus on a particular aspect of the data in front of them in a way that has not been done before and interpret what they have read. In this instance, there is nothing specific in these documents about child abuse, or about children's daily lives in their homes or in the orphanages in which they lived. There are, however, certain hints in the trial testimonies which enable historians to make inferences about these aspects of children's lives. Roper cannot say with absolute certainty that Regina Groninger from Augsburg was sexually abused, but her description, faithfully recorded in the court records, suggests a painful and unwanted sexual encounter. Similarly, the children's descriptions of witchcraft practices provide evidence of the prevalence and importance of witchcraft beliefs at the time but, in addition, they also suggest the importance of children's games, how children spent their time and their relationships with each other. However, this is only an interpretation, albeit a very plausible one, and could well be contested by another historian using the same material in a different way.

Despite the many difficulties of writing about children's lives, the history of childhood has undergone a veritable revival over the last 20 years. While there was a growing interest in children in the 1960s and early 1970s, this was often subsumed within two novel areas of historical enquiry: women and the family. It has only been since 1990 that children have once again become a subject of study in their own right. Today, it is a field that attracts a growing number of young as well as established historians, especially women, and has produced an extensive literature covering every period from the classical era to the present (Brockliss, 2012). For the most part, these studies reveal more about adult perceptions of childhood than the experiences of children, but some historians of twentieth-century childhood have at least attempted to write a new history of childhood which places the child at the centre of the narrative and uncovers their daily worlds, even their own ideas, as far as is humanly possible. A case in point is the recent study of German children in the Second World War by Nicholas Stargardt. Stargardt used a mix of archival records, diaries and contemporary letters in constructing his account. But he deliberately eschewed interviewing elderly Germans about their childhood in the 1940s. While oral testimony is a much favoured 'alternative' source used by some contemporary historians, it can be problematic when deployed to uncover the experience of childhood in earlier decades. For example, in the case of wartime Germany, Britain or any other part of the world, oral history is sometimes condemned by historians as peculiarly untrustworthy because individual memory has been inevitably affected and perverted by the internalisation of the myriad of images and accounts of the Second World War continually served up by television or Hollywood over the last 60 years. Stargardt therefore set out to identify sources that would reveal the world of the contemporary child, and his narrative is based on children's letters, diaries, classroom exercises and even their paintings (Stargardt, 2005). While Stargardt avoided oral history, however, it remains an important source of information for other historians and there are many histories that have been written (and will be written in the future) which draw on memories and witness testimonies (see Reading B).

Summary of Section 2

Historians must rely on a number of sources when looking at childhood in the past, including archaeological, demographic and visual ones.

> These must be interpreted within their historical context, but these interpretations are open to dispute.
>
> Histories of childhood are also strongly mediated by class, gender and race. Upper-class, literate boys are more likely to leave historical traces than poor children or girls.

3 Influential historians of childhood

3.1 Philippe Ariès

The first, and most influential, historian of childhood in the post-war period was Frenchman Philippe Ariès (1914–1984) who, in 1960, published *L'Enfant et la Vie Familiale sous l'Ancien Régime*. Originally written in French, it was translated into English as *Centuries of Childhood* in 1962. In this work Ariès argued that a concept of childhood had been largely lacking in the Middle Ages. Although medieval texts distinguished between infancy (0–7), childhood (7–14) and adolescence (14–21 or older), these divisions had little meaning in practice: once an infant could walk and talk, it immediately entered the world of adults. There was no room for sentimentality in parent–child relationships and children were regarded as economically useful, not as emotionally rewarding. Ariès wrote:

> In medieval society the idea of childhood did not exist; this is not to suggest that children were neglected, forsaken or despised. The idea of childhood is not to be confused with affection for children: it corresponds to an awareness of the particular nature of childhood, that particular nature which distinguishes the child from the adult, even the young adult. In medieval society this awareness was lacking. That is why, as soon as the child could live without the constant solicitude of his mother, his nanny or his cradle-rocker, he belonged to adult society.
>
> (Ariès, 1962, p. 128)

Ariès further claimed that due to the uncertainty of infants' survival in the Middle Ages, child-rearing was characterised by an indifference to babies. It was only after children's survival was assured (at around the age of seven) that people began to invest emotional energy in children, but as late as the eighteenth century, some were still claiming that small children 'did not count'. He argued that childhood as a distinct human condition started to emerge around the end of the fifteenth century when a modern understanding of childhood began to develop, as adults slowly started to value children for their own sake and sought to give them a separate identity. Then, beginning in the classroom (in an era where an increasing number of male children were being schooled), a new concept of childhood was born that would lay the foundations of our modern romanticised viewpoint. Ideas about the special nature of childhood gained ground during the seventeenth century, which saw the emergence of a specific costume for the under-sevens, specific children's games and toys, and the promotion of the belief that the young should be sheltered from adult concerns of sexuality and work. This culminated in what Ariès saw as the sentimentalisation of childhood and the birth of the 'child centred family' in the nineteenth and twentieth centuries.

Ariès maintained that the creation and diffusion of the modern idea of childhood went hand in hand with the development of two other significant social developments. The first was the invention of the modern family. There may have been affection in the medieval family, but the institution was not organised in a manner likely to encourage the close supervision of the young. Family life was community life: there was little distinction between public and private, and children – boys and girls – were commonly sent away from the family home at a young age (7–9) to live and work with relatives or neighbours. The sixteenth and seventeenth centuries, however, saw the emergence of a new idea of the affective family, where parents and children took a delight in each other's company and steadily cut themselves off from the outside world. In the modern age, the very public Twelfth Night festivities were finally replaced by the family Christmas. There was a shift in understanding about the responsibilities of parents who were now seen as 'responsible before God for the souls, and indeed the bodies too, of their children' (Ariès, 1962, p. 412). Ariès claimed that this led to new ideas about childhood which 'recognised that the child was not ready for life, and that he had to be subjected to a special treatment, a sort of quarantine, before he was allowed to join the adults' (1962, p. 412). The second development was the rise of the bourgeoisie. Ariès believed that the modern concepts of childhood and the family initially took root among the urban well-to-do. In the early-modern world the merchant and professional classes alone had the wealth and the kind of value system that was needed for these ideas to flourish. Therefore, the growing power of the bourgeoisie in the centuries before 1800, and its eventual dominance in the industrial era, guaranteed that the new concepts would become the norm.

Ariès' thesis relies heavily on an analysis of European art of the Middle Ages and early-modern period in which, he claimed, children were depicted as small adults. Although the infant Jesus was represented in many paintings, Ariès argued that he was pictured as a scaled-down adult, with the posture and muscles of an adult. Other children did not seem to appear and it was not until the sixteenth century that artists began to represent specific identifiable children in portraiture. Ariès used these observations to claim that before the sixteenth century the concept of childhood as a separate and different state did not exist, and children were therefore either not represented in art at all or were portrayed, like Jesus, as a miniature adult.

Activity 3   Representations of childhood

Allow about 20 minutes

The following pictures are similar to those that interested Ariès. Examine the pictures carefully and note the extent to which they support or challenge Ariès' thesis.

Figure 6   Duccio di Buoninsegna, *Madonna and Child* (also known as the *Stoclet Madonna* or *Stroganoff Madonna*), painted around 1300

Figure 7 Federico Barocci, *The Madonna of the Cat* (*La Madonna del Gatto*), probably painted about 1575

Figure 8 Cornelius Johnson, *Sir Thomas Lucy and His Family*, c.1630

Figure 9 William Powell Frith, *Many Happy Returns of the Day*, 1856

Comment

In these pictures there are very different representations of children. They are also representative of prevailing styles of their time. Ariès' thesis would hold that in the first one the child is not based on a real child, but is a stylised representation of Jesus. In it Christ's face is an adult face, the size of his head relative to his body shows adult, not child, proportions and the image clearly shows muscle tone that a young child would not have. In the second painting, although the theme is still religious, the children are represented much more naturalistically – they could have been modelled on actual children. By the third picture, the differences between children and adults are very clearly marked in dress, in the way they play with the dog and their position at the feet of the adults. The theme is secular and the family portrayed is aristocratic. The final picture shows a Victorian tea party, where the tone of the picture is much more sentimental. The children in this picture are playing, being brought gifts and are obviously separated from adult life. Looking at these pictures would support Ariès' theory that there was a change in the way that children were depicted in portraiture between the thirteenth and nineteenth centuries. His interpretation of that difference remains more controversial.

3.2 Criticisms of Ariès

Ariès was the first historian to look at how childhood changed throughout history and to emphasise the point that childhood is a social and historical construction which alters over time and place, and his pioneering book has deservedly become a classic. Nevertheless, it is also an object lesson in the pitfalls of using non-standard sources and the dangers of treating non-archival sources too cavalierly, and he has faced many criticisms over his sources and his interpretation of them. Other historians, especially medievalists, have continually shown over the past 20 years that his argument, however innovative, is based on a tendentious, literal and selective reading of literary and visual sources that can be easily undermined (Wilson, 1980; Orme, 2001).

Critics have claimed that Ariès' reliance on paintings is highly problematic. Works of art are not produced in a social and political vacuum but usually commissioned by a particular person or institution for a specific purpose (just as children's diaries mentioned earlier are also composed with a specific audience in mind). Paintings in the Middle Ages were almost exclusively connected with, and painted for, religious purposes. They illustrated religious themes and used symbolism to represent religious ideas and narratives. They were in no way concerned with the lives of ordinary, embodied children, but rather, with what the infant Jesus and child saints represented: innocence, purity and the soul. It was not until the fifteenth and sixteenth centuries that the growing wealth and confidence of the merchant classes resulted in them commissioning artists to paint portraits of themselves and their children in a secular rather than religious way. Even so, such paintings still relied heavily on symbolism and were used to convey certain ideas relating to the social and economic position of the child and its family. They were not therefore necessarily a 'realistic' or accurate representation of how individual children were perceived (Retford, 2006). What is clear, however, is that only certain, very special, children were represented. Poor children were rarely portrayed and boys were much more frequently represented than girls.

Ariès' reliance on paintings meant that he ignored other sources of information about children in the late-medieval period. For example, there were several scientific and medical books on children's illnesses which recognised childhood as a different stage from adulthood, with specific needs and attributes. The legal system of this period set out ages of criminal responsibility (the age at which children could be held responsible for their crimes), implying that children were seen as being different from adults, and not as morally aware. Finally, there were the teachings of the Church on the role and duties specific to children, which drew clear distinctions between childhood and adulthood (Orme, 2001).

Historians such as Linda Pollock (1983) have also challenged his central idea that children were treated with indifference in the Middle Ages and beyond, instead claiming that children were much loved, even from infancy. Child mortality meant parents were only too aware of the fragility of their children and placed a great emphasis on nurturing and protecting them. Although there are few first-hand accounts from parents in the Middle Ages, in the 1490s an Oxford schoolboy wrote, 'A great while after my brother died, my mother was wont to sit weeping every day. I trow that there is nobody which would not be sorry if he had seen her' (quoted in Orme, 1984, p. 4).

Ariès claims that attitudes of indifference survived as late as the end of the seventeenth century; up to this point, children under the age of seven simply 'did not count'. However, other sources dispute this, attesting to the deep feelings parents had about their children, and there is evidence of widespread parental grieving in the first half of the seventeenth century. William Brownlow (1594–1675) lost many children but was far from indifferent. He wrote upon the death of his first son: 'O Lord thou has dealt bitterlie with mee and broken me with breach upon breach, when wilt thou comfort mee.' On the death of his second, he wrote: 'I was at ease but Thou O God has broken mee a sunder and shaken mee to peeces.' The shopkeeper Nehemiah Wallington (1598–1658) wrote about his grief over his four-year-old daughter's death, 'The grief for this child was so great that I forgot myself so much that I did offend God in it; for I broke all my purposes, promises, and convenants with my God, for I was much distracted in my mind, and could not be comforted' (all quoted in Pollock, 1983, pp. 134–5).

The poet and playwright, Ben Jonson's seven-year-old son died of plague in 1603. He wrote a poem, *On My First Son*, expressing his pain.

Farewell, thou child of my right hand, and joy;
My sin was too much hope of thee, loved boy.
Seven years thou wert lent to me, and I thee pay,
Exacted by thy fate, on the just day.
Oh, could I lose all father now! For why
Will man lament the state he should envy?
To have so soon 'scaped the world's and flesh's rage,
And, if no other misery, yet age?
Rest in soft peace, and, asked, say here doth lie
Ben Jonson his best piece of poetry;

For whose sake, henceforth, all his vows be such,

As what he loves may never like too much.

(Jonson, 1985, p. 236)

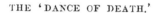

THE 'DANCE OF DEATH.'

THE CHILD.

Figure 10   Hans Holbein, *The Dance of Death – The Child*, 1538. The figure of Death steals the youngest child and causes much grief even in such a poor household

Other historians have accepted Ariès' contention that our present-day view of childhood is a relatively recent construction, but have taken issue with his timeline. Some argue that the crucial period of change was the eighteenth century under the influence of philosophers such as John Locke and Jean-Jacques Rousseau (this will be discussed in more detail in Section 4). Others have placed the changes much later. Hugh Cunningham, in his overview of the history of childhood in Europe, argues that it was the twentieth century which saw the most rapid change in how children were seen and conceptualised (Cunningham, 1995). This is not because parents in the last hundred years have showered affection on children as never before; levels of parental love, he believes, are impossible to measure in any epoch. It is rather that in the twentieth century the state became fully committed to an agenda based on the equality of children and adults, and children's right to grow up, enjoying a life of their own.

3.3   Lloyd deMause and 'the nightmare of childhood'

Ariès' narrative has stood the test of time better than another attempt to write a total history of childhood. In 1974, American psychoanalyst Lloyd deMause published a long introduction to a book of essays entitled *The History of Childhood* in which he plotted the child's experience of childhood from the Babylonians to the present. He began his book with the much quoted sentence:

> The history of childhood is a nightmare from which we have only recently begun to awaken. The further back in history one goes, the lower the level of child care, and the more likely children are to be killed, abandoned, beaten, terrorized, and sexually abused.
>
> (deMause, 1974, p. 1)

Essentially, until the recent past, he argued, childhood has been a story of universal pain and misery, the result of adult failure to empathise with children and see the world through a child's eyes. The history of childhood is the history of child abuse and deMause alleged that for most of recorded history, children were brutally treated by unkind and unloving parents, who were blinded by psychological ignorance, and their own unresolved psychological traumas and early childhood experiences. Drawing on theories from psychoanalysis, deMause argued that throughout history children were routinely beaten, killed and abused. The situation began to improve from the fourth century AD as the sexual abuse of children gradually declined, but it was only in the eighteenth century that children ceased to be considered sinful vessels which had to be literally whipped into an ideal shape (see Section 4.1). Even then, the emphasis continued to be on forming or socialising the child in a manner approved of by adults, albeit by training and guidance rather than force. It was the mid-twentieth century before parents really began to engage with children on their own terms, becoming facilitators rather than tyrants, and adopting what deMause called a 'helping' child-rearing mode.

Figure 11 William Hogarth, *First Stage of Cruelty*, 1750/1. This image suggests that abuse breeds abuse and that the boy has learned cruelty in his upbringing

---

Activity 4   Reading B

Allow about 35 minutes

Now turn to the second reading at the end of this chapter, by Hugh Cunningham. Read through Cunningham's account of childhood during the post-war years in the UK and then comment on the following:

- What changes does Cunningham identify in these years?

- What are Cunningham's sources for this account?

- To what extent does this extract support deMause's thesis that childhood has improved for children?

Comment

As previously noted, Hugh Cunningham argues that the twentieth century is the era in which adult–child relations changed most dramatically. In this extract he identifies three major changes concerning: (a) the distribution of food, (b) the distribution of income and (c) the greater openness between adults and children. There has been, he proposes, a shift in emphasis in the family so that while parents, and especially fathers, were once given the best food, this is now reserved for children and, in fact, parents are expected to sacrifice their own comfort for their children. In a similar way, money, which used to be given by children to their parents out of their wage packets, now flows in a different direction. Children do not work, they do not contribute financially to the family and instead are given pocket money by their parents rather than wages by an employer. Finally, Cunningham identifies another change in parent–child relationships – the greater openness and willingness to talk to children about matters such as menstruation which had previously been kept silent.

In the extract, Cunningham is relying partly on oral histories – people remembering their childhood and comparing them with those of their own children. Although some historians specifically reject adult memories as a reliable source, claiming that many people remember their childhoods as a golden time (which leads, in part, to the childhood in crisis thesis discussed in the previous chapter), others do use oral accounts and memories – alongside other sources – as a way of understanding the past. Here, by drawing on a variety of different accounts, Cunningham convincingly builds up a picture of social change after the Second World War.

Finally, on the surface, Cunningham's piece would seem to support deMause's theory that things are getting better for children and that the twentieth century represented a turning point when children started to be properly cared for. Cunningham, however, makes no such claims. He argues that both childhood and parent–child relations changed in the post-war period, but he does not insist that these are better – just different. Indeed, he notes that for some parents this change was unwelcome. Therefore, this extract does not support deMause's belief that the 'helping' mode of childcare was a welcome development or that children were treated better as a consequence.

In general deMause's argument has not been well received by historians. From the outset, it was dismissed as psycho-babble which had no regard for economic, social and cultural context, and deMause was accused of using evidence selectively, at worst of misreading it. Over the years his argument has been undermined empirically by historians, such as Pollock, who believe that parental love and concern were already alive and well in the late Middle Ages, and by other scholars who have shown that parent–child relations have continually changed and were influenced by war and peace, regime change and general levels of wealth, and also varied considerably within any population and across different countries. In consequence, in the light of the recent sensitive explorations of the plethora of archaeological and visual sources now available, it is hard to believe that the fate of children before 1400, let alone 1900, was as relentlessly dismal as deMause claimed.

Figure 12   Jan Steen, *The Village School*, from around 1665. This image depicts the ubiquity of corporal punishment in schools in Europe in the past

Yet deMause's argument should not be dismissed too quickly. If his overarching narrative is unconvincing, it did focus attention, from a modern perspective, on the significant and continual part played by violence, neglect and exploitation in adult–child relations. This is an uncomfortable topic that recent historians have tended to avoid and, if anything, abusive parenting practices in the European past have been downplayed. On the one hand, the worst kinds of child abuse, such as infanticide, are said to have occurred only rarely. On the other, currently unacceptable practices such as corporal punishment and child labour are admitted to have been common but deemed to be perfectly consistent with broader cultural values and not usually damaging. All this may be true, but deMause is surely right to believe that until the second half of the twentieth century most children in Europe would have been subject to levels of violence, neglect and exploitation which would seem shocking to many today. His critics are equally right to argue that most parents in the past would not have found corporal punishment offensive or demeaning and that they would have recognised clear boundaries between the acceptable and unacceptable: they, too, would have rated some forms of behaviour cruel and wrong. While deMause's argument may have been let down by his belief in the ubiquity of child abuse, his book continues to raise important questions about adult–child relationships in the past and the power differentials between adults and children.

Summary of Section 3

Ariès' thesis remains an important starting point for understanding ideas about childhood in European history.

Ariès claimed that the idea of childhood did not exist in medieval Europe and that during this period children under seven 'did not count'.

Critics have argued that his interpretation of pictures and his views about the lack of parental love for children were wrong, claiming that children have always been loved and valued.

deMause saw the history of childhood as a 'nightmare' and argued that only very recently had parents begun to treat children kindly.

Most historians reject the idea that childhood has been a 'nightmare' in the past or that recent years have been a story of upward progress. Nevertheless, deMause's work highlights features of the treatment of children in the past, such as widespread corporal punishment, that would be shocking to some people today.

---

4 Major themes in European constructions of childhood

While aspects of Ariès' thesis have been criticised, there is a general acceptance that ideas about childhood have changed over time. This section will give a short history of some major themes in European constructions of childhood and suggest how they continue to resonate today.

Activity 5   Attributes of childhood
Allow about 10 minutes

Write down, briefly, the chief attributes or fundamental characteristics of childhood as you see them. What qualities do children have that differentiate them from adults? Write down two lists: one including the good qualities that you think children possess and one including the bad qualities.

Comment

In our list of characteristics, we wrote down words like spontaneous, loveable, affectionate, happy, natural and trusting under the good characteristics. On the negative side, we wrote thoughtless, demanding and unwittingly cruel. How are two such contradictory views of childhood possible? Given that both children and adults can act badly, why do we think of the stereotypical image of a child pulling the legs off a spider and imagine this is a feature of childhood? Other people's lists would be very different, but what is important here is that everyone is drawing on different ideas and understandings of childhood, all of which have long histories.

4.1   Childhood as a time of evil and wildness

Ideas about the nature of children have been intensively debated in Christian theology over the centuries and it is impossible to talk generally about 'Christian thought'. Nevertheless, one strand of Christian thinking has promoted the idea that children are innately sinful. St Augustine (AD 354–430), one of the founding fathers of the Church and one of Christianity's most influential thinkers, suggested that even foetuses and newborns inherit humanity's original sin of disobedience to God (transmitted via their parents at the point of conception) and are thus morally unclean, even though they cannot commit actual sin.

Although tempered by other passages from the New Testament which suggest a more benevolent view of children and where the baby Jesus is venerated – Jesus is portrayed as the special protector of children, and children's qualities are presented as ideals to which adults should aspire – the idea of children as sinful has reverberated throughout the centuries. The sixteenth-century Reformation involved a revival of Augustinian doctrines and afterwards there are many references to the innate wilfulness or rebelliousness of children from which they needed to be saved, by beating if necessary. Susanna Wesley, mother of the founder of Methodism, John Wesley, was committed to child-rearing practices in which to 'spare the rod' was to 'spoil the child'. In a letter to her son in 1732, she wrote:

Break their will betimes: begin this great work before they can run alone, before they can speak plain, or perhaps speak at all … make him do as he is bid, if you whip him ten times running to effect it … Break his will now and his soul will live, and he will probably bless you to all eternity.

(Quoted in Jobling, 1978, p. 24)

Amongst Puritans (strict English and American Protestants of the sixteenth and seventeenth centuries), the idea of the sinful, wilful child was particularly strong. Puritans believed that God's authority in Heaven and the hierarchical structure of the holy trinity, with the all-powerful father at its apex, should be mirrored not only in the Church, but also in the family. Thus a father should control and rule over his wife, children and household. Just as 'Man' was fallen and had to submit to God to find redemption and enter Heaven, so children needed to submit to the will of their father. Sin and ill-discipline had to be beaten out of them and their will turned towards God. Puritan teaching, especially in New England, linked the harsh physical punishment of children to the concept of original sin. It was believed that as children were born in a state of sin, they had to be taught obedience and brought to God through physical punishment. As Cotton Mather (1663–1728), a famous Puritan minister and prolific author, put it, 'Better whipt, than Damned' (quoted in Heywood, 2001, p. 100).

A PURITAN FAMILY.
"*The whole Psalms in Four Parts.*" 1563.

Figure 13 *A Puritan Family*, from *The Whole Psalms in Four Parts* (1563). In this image, the father rules while the mother and children obey

4.2   Childhood as a blank slate

Although the Reformation placed particular emphasis on the Augustinian notion of original sin, it rejected the authority of the Roman Catholic Church and advocated a more personal relationship with God. In so doing it helped lay the way for the European intellectual movement of the late seventeenth and eighteenth centuries known as the Enlightenment or the Age of Reason. Nurtured by humanism and the revival of classical knowledge in the Renaissance, the Enlightenment emphasised the application of individual, human reason in matters of both religion and science. It also ultimately challenged the 'divine right' of monarchical rule in favour of secular and democratic alternatives. Ideas about childhood should be seen in this context: the figure of the child was a means to debate the new, more democratic forms that society might take.

The seventeenth-century empiricist and rationalist John Locke (1632–1704) rejected the idea of innate goodness or original sin and instead argued that at birth the mind was a blank slate (or *tabula rasa* in Latin) waiting to be imprinted. He believed that character and rationality emerged from experience, a perspective that emphasised the importance of education. In *Some Thoughts Concerning Education* (1693) Locke advanced the thesis that the child was an inadequate precursor to the real state of the human being, which was adulthood. Educators, by providing the proper guidance, examples, experiences and environment, could build on innate potential and shape the child's intellect and character to ensure it grew into a rational, self-controlled and responsible citizen. His emphasis on the importance of experience meant that he advocated systems of rewards and punishments so that the child learned to make positive associations with good behaviour and negative with bad. He thought it pointless to beat children when they were too young to understand what they were doing, but once they did know, he felt that the rod should put fear and awe into them (Gill, 2010).

Figure 14   John Locke (1632–1704)

Locke's view of childhood was relatively optimistic in that he saw children as capable of being educated, but in other ways it was problematic. By defining adulthood in terms of rationality, children were seen as inherently lacking in particular capabilities and were of much greater interest for what they would become rather than for what they were in the present. Furthermore, not only was the true goal of development adulthood, but this ideal was an implicitly gendered and racialised one. It was not only children who were deemed to fall below this standard, so too were the majority of women. Entire populations overseas were also categorised as child-like in demeaning ways that served as justification for the British Empire's project of expansion, colonisation and enslavement.

4.3   Childhood as a time of innocence

The eighteenth-century Romantic philosopher, Jean-Jacques Rousseau (1712–1778) was an influential exponent of a central conception of modern childhood – that children are special beings with a particular, cherished nature. Children, he argued, were born pure, but were corrupted by civilisation – which, in turn, had declined because of its progress away from nature. In the opening paragraph of *Emile, or On Education* (1762), he wrote: 'God makes all things good; man meddles with them and they become evil' (1966 [1762], p. 5) – a phrase that echoes his famous and politically radical declaration in *The Social Contract*, 'Man is born free; and everywhere he is in chains' (1923 [1761], p. 5).

In *Emile*, Rousseau sets out a method of education that is intended to turn children into uncorrupted adults. Under the care of a personal tutor, Rousseau argued that children (and unusually he discussed girls as well as boys) should be allowed to develop at their own rate in natural surroundings, where their goodness could be isolated and protected from the artificiality and misery of the adult world. The tutor's role was to filter out negative social influences on the child, to oversee the child's developmental processes and to offer appropriate knowledge and experiences at different stages. Rousseau was one of the first philosophers to construct childhood in terms of distinct developmental phases which education should respect: 'the education of the earliest years should be merely negative ... Leave childhood to ripen in your children' (1966 [1762], pp. 57–8). These phases began with the 'Age of Nature', lasting from when children learn to speak up to the age of 12; a period of idyllic innocence when they should be free and happy with 'nothing [to do except] to run and jump all day' (1966 [1762], p. 71) and when they learn their natural limitations. Only then, when children's rational faculties were beginning to develop, did Rousseau believe that they should be taught to read and introduced to the world of books. Even then they should learn to be self-sufficient before they were introduced to moral knowledge in their mid-teens (Gill, 2010). Although Rousseau's language might seem dated, his sentiments about childhood as a special time are not:

> Love childhood, indulge its sports, its pleasures, its delightful instincts. Who has not sometimes regretted that age when laughter was ever on our lips, and when the heart was ever at peace? Why rob these innocents of the joys which pass so quickly, of that precious gift which they cannot abuse?
>
> (Rousseau, 1966 [1762], p. 43)

The Romantic poets of the late eighteenth and early nineteenth centuries subsequently developed Rousseau's arguments about the particular sensibility or vital force of the child, which adults should worship for its redemptive power. They imagined childhood as a lost Eden, a magical realm from which adults were excluded and for which they could only yearn. In England the Romantic poets viewed the shift from nature to industrialisation with a particular horror and, for several poets of the era, children served as a symbol of humanity that it was feared would be destroyed by the oppressive effects of the Industrial Revolution.

Figure 15   Jean-Jacques Rousseau (1712–1778)

Activity 6   Contemporary ideas of childhood

Allow about 10 minutes

At the beginning of this section you were asked to think about the words you associated with childhood. Go back to your list and assign each of the words you noted down to one of the three different constructions of childhood discussed in this section.

Comment

Our 'positive' words were spontaneous, loveable, affectionate, happy, natural and trusting. All of these suggest a Romantic view of childhood while the others, 'thoughtless, demanding and cruel', suggest a much more negative view of childhood, closer to a Puritan one. More generally, however, we believe in the power (for both good and bad) of nurture and think that children can be shaped by the parenting and upbringing they receive – a position that puts us in closer agreement with John Locke. None of these positions is necessarily right or exclusive, but this activity shows the power of these ideas and the ways in which they continue to influence contemporary ideas about children. They also link to wider discussions outside our own personal beliefs. The previous chapter looked at how childhood is spoken of as being in crisis – this too draws on several of the constructions mentioned above: that childhood *should* be a time of happiness or innocence (a broadly Romantic perspective), but that there is a seed of unhappiness and destructiveness in children which, if left unattended to, will have terrible social consequences (a legacy of both Locke and a Puritan view).

Summary of Section 4

It is possible to identify three particular ways that children have been conceptualised by European constructions in the past, and to look at the impact these ideas have had on the way in which children were treated.

Some strands of Christian thought, particularly those associated with the sixteenth- and seventeenth-century Puritans, depicted the child as tainted by original sin, and used Biblical passages and the works of St Augustine to support this view.

John Locke saw children as blank slates; neither inherently good nor evil, but shaped by their upbringing and education.

Romantic ideas of childhood, initiated by Jean-Jacques Rousseau, saw children as inherently good until corrupted by adults.

5 Conclusion

Except for the children of the highest elites, the vast majority of children have left little evidence of their existence behind them. High mortality rates meant that many died before adulthood, and before the twentieth century those that survived rarely kept diaries. While their births and deaths may have been registered and recorded, finding out about their lives in-between remains problematic. Adult attitudes towards children have been easier to examine and it is possible to see how these have changed over the years, allowing speculation on the consequent impact on children. Historians have analysed how philosophers such as Locke or Rousseau conceptualised children and how they should be educated, and these ideas, first articulated in the seventeenth and eighteenth centuries, continue to inform contemporary attitudes about children. More recent historians of childhood, such as Ariès or deMause, have taken a broader historical sweep, examining the changing relationships between adults and children across many centuries, and their ideas, too, continue to be debated. Others have attempted to uncover the lives of children in the past by looking at coroners' records, demographic records and parish registers, as well as art and archaeological remains, and are beginning to find out more about children, how they lived, what their relationships with their parents and wider families were like, and how they spent their time. Despite the problems, shared by other disciplines in the social sciences and beyond, there is now a greater recognition among historians that childhood is an important and relevant area of the past that needs attention, and that leaving out childhood from a historical account of any society makes it incomplete.

References

Ariès, P. (1962) *Centuries of Childhood*, New York, Vintage Books.

Baggerman, A. and Dekker, R. (2009) *Child of the Enlightenment: Revolutionary Europe Reflected in a Boyhood Diary*, Leiden and Boston, Brill.

Brockliss, L. (2012) *Western Europe and Scandinavia*, Oxford Bibliographies Online: Childhood Studies, Oxford University Press.

Cunningham, H. (1990) 'The employment and unemployment of children in England *c*.1680–1851', *Past and Present*, vol. 126, no. 1, pp. 115–50.

Cunningham, H. (1995) *Children and Childhood in Western Society since 1500*, London, Longman.

Cunningham, H. (2003) 'Children's changing lives 1800–2000', in Maybin, J. and Woodhead, M. (eds) *Childhoods in Context*, Chichester, Wiley.

deMause, L. (ed) (1974) *The History of Childhood*, New York, Psychohistory Press.

Fletcher, A. (2008) *Growing Up in England: The Experience of Childhood 1600–1914*, London, Yale University Press.

Gill, N. (2010) *Educational Philosophy in the French Enlightenment: From Nature to Second Nature*, Farnham, Ashgate.

Hendrick, H. (1994) *Child Welfare: England 1872–1989*, London, Routledge.

Heywood, C. (2001) *A History of Childhood: Children and Childhood in the West from Medieval to Modern Times*, Cambridge, Polity Press.

Humphries, J. (2010) *Childhood and Child Labour in the British Industrial Revolution,* Cambridge, Cambridge University Press.

Jobling, M. (1978) 'Child abuse: the historical and social context', in Carver, V. (ed) *Child Abuse: A Study Text*, Milton Keynes, The Open University.

Jonson, B. (1985) *Ben Jonson – The Oxford Authors*, Oxford, Oxford University Press.

Orme, N. (1984) *From Childhood to Chivalry: The Education of the English Kings and Aristocracy 1066–1530*, London, Methuen.

Orme, N. (2001) *Medieval Children*, London, Yale University Press.

Pollock, L. A. (1983) *Forgotten Children: Parent–Child Relations from 1500 to 1900*, Cambridge, Cambridge University Press.

Retford, K. (2006) *The Art of Domestic life: Family Portraiture in Eighteenth-Century England*, New Haven, CT and London, Yale University Press.

Rousseau, J. J. (1923 [1761]) *The Social Contract and Discourses*, Toronto and London, J. M. Dent and Sons.

Rousseau, J. J. (1966 [1762]) *Emile, or On Education*, London, J. M. Dent and Sons.

Stargardt, N. (2005) *Witnesses of War: Children's Lives under the Nazis*, London, Jonathan Cape.

Wilson, A. (1980) 'The infancy of the history of childhood: an appraisal of Philippe Ariès', *History and Theory*, vol. 19, no. 2, pp. 132–53.

Wrigley, E. A. and Schofield, R. S. (1981) *The Population History of England 1541–1871: A Reconstruction*, London, Edward Arnold.

Reading A
Child witches in seventeenth-century Germany

Lyndal Roper

Source: 'Child witches in seventeenth-century Germany', 2010, in Brockliss, L. and Montgomery, H. (eds) *Childhood and Violence in the Western Tradition*, Oxford, Oxbow, pp. 292–9.

In 1628, Hans Merckler, an orphan aged twelve, was accused of witchcraft. He had forced two much younger boys, aged six and eight, to put a milk-bucket on a dung heap, place the Devil in the bucket, a board over the bucket and a chair on top. Then, perched on the chair, each was made to forswear God, Mary and the saints, while the other boy knelt. Merckler wanted, the witnesses said, to establish 'a witches' school'. In place of the prayers and catechisms children had to learn by heart, everyone was to learn the nonsense verse the Devil had taught him, starting 'Lyrum larum spoon game, old women eat a lot'.

This may look like a version of king-of-the-castle, nothing but a child's game. But this was not how the authorities saw it, and when the other boys' parents testified against him, Merckler soon found himself taken to the nearby town of Karlstadt where he was put through a criminal interrogation, and eventually, brought to the ... town of Würzburg, where one of the largest witch hunts ever seen in western Europe was reaching its climax. Things looked grim for young Merckler, who seemed to be in league with the Devil and could well have found himself executed for witchcraft. Yet he was lucky. By 1629 he was denying the whole story, and he wisely asked to be transferred to another school, that of the Jesuits. Six months later, he was returned to his guardian who was admonished to raise him well and take him to school and church.

Other children in the prince-bishopric of Würzburg at around the same period were not so fortunate. Valtin Winter claimed that his parents had seduced him into witchcraft: the resulting trial ended in the execution, first of his father, and then of himself. In the summer of 1628, fear erupted in the Juliusspital, a huge hospital established by the Counter-Reformation Bishop of Würzburg Julius Echter, which had a school attached to it; and a mass panic resulted in which scores of people met their deaths, many of them children. Probably over 1,200 people died during the witch-hunt in this large Catholic territory, and it was in its final stages that children and priests found themselves accused. In all we know that at least forty children died during the last two years of the panic in the city of Würzburg, about the same number as the total of clerics who also perished during this phase of the witch-hunting there. Not until 1629 was the panic, which had begun in 1590, and proceeded in waves, finally over.

It was unusual for groups of children to be suspected during witch hunts in this way, though it was certainly not unknown. The most notorious was that in Lutheran Mora, in Sweden in 1669–70; but there were others, including a small outbreak in 1683–4 in Calw (south Germany), and another in 1723 involving thirty children in Augsburg. Such episodes were deeply shocking to contemporaries. For Gottlieb Spitzel, who included the case in his *The Power of Darkness Broken* in 1687, such dreadful events were certain proof of the Devil's activity in the world and should be a warning to all parents. Yet for the witchcraft sceptic Balthasar Bekker, writing in 1691, the Mora debacle, with its involvement of children, was proof that witchcraft was nonsense. And it was axiomatic to Georg Hauber in his vast sceptical compendium on magic published in the late 1730s and early 1740s that the Swedish case had been a shocking miscarriage of justice: he included an illustration as well as a detailed account of the story …

Individual children were occasionally accused of witchcraft or became caught up in trials. Children's allegations were taken seriously in court because witchcraft was a *crimen exceptum*, a crime so serious that the normal rules of evidence could be suspended. Witches, it was believed, harmed young children and infants in particular; and this meant that children's stories often became part of witchcraft testimony. Children might become entangled in witch trials as suspects when their parents named them, under torture, as their accomplices; or they might, in the frenzied atmosphere of witch-hunting, give evidence against their parents, often under compulsion. Since only fellow witches could see the Devil in league with an accused individual, when children gave testimony about witchcraft itself (as opposed to statements about what harm had been caused by witches) they readily became suspected. It was believed that witchcraft travelled in the blood, and that witches offered their children to Satan, and so the children of convicted witches were likely to be witches too. On the whole, authorities did take account of the youth of offenders and their punishment was milder; but there were also occasions, like Valtin Winter's, where youth offered no protection.

Cases of witchcraft concerning children are amongst the most shocking documents of the European witch-hunt. They certainly betray a very different sensibility towards children, who, contemporaries believed, might be agents of the Devil. But they can also tell us something about children themselves. Difficult as such sources are, we can also use the records of the trials to offer a rare window onto the imaginative worlds of children, revealed in their games and in what they said about the Devil. Witchcraft cases always raised the question of imagination and fantasy, and even the author of the most infamous witch-hunting treatise, the *Malleus maleficarum* of 1486, dealt with the issue of the nature of illusion in its opening chapters. Authorities were only too well aware that children might confess to things that were not true and they themselves worried about reality and illusion in such cases – after all, the Devil was the master of illusion. Thus, for contemporaries as well, child witches raised the question of the limits of fantasy, which is also why they offer some of the few glimpses we have onto children's play.

Why did Merckler want to set up a witches' school? So far as I know, the idea of a school occurs nowhere in writing about the Devil and witches, and was Merckler's own invention. With it, Merckler took the idea of the Sabbath convention of witches and transposed it to the environment he knew, the school. This was a compensatory inversion of school life: it is no accident that his victims were younger children, who were to be trained not to become pious apprentices and servants, but to be the Devil's minions. What do we make of the perilous tower of bucket and plank on the dung-heap? His extravagant ritual of renouncing God and the Virgin was not unique: Anna Reuss, aged twelve, also stood on a dung heap and denied Jesus, and afterwards she rode on a cat to the Sabbath. She claimed her mother made her do it. Dung-heaps, then as now, were probably irresistible to children, and when Merckler staged his blasphemous renunciation of Christianity on the dung-heap, he desecrated the holy with excrement. The nonsense prayer the children were to be compelled to recite suggests what children may have felt about the stultifying rote learning that typified [contemporary] school education …

Above all, beatings figure repeatedly in what many children said about witches and the Devil, and suggest what a terrifying prospect they were in children's imaginations. Sometimes thrashings are mentioned in the context of explaining why someone had recourse to the Devil. Merckler saw the Devil standing by the house door one day while his mistress was beating him. One young student aged seventeen claimed the Devil had given him a special string and parchment charm which he could stuff down his trousers to prevent the pain of the rod. Here, witchcraft seems to be a kind of compensation fantasy, a way of coping with the routine violence of school discipline. Just as beating featured prominently in children's accounts of school routine, so also it was used, ironically enough, to force children to confess. Hans Philip Schuh, aged thirteen, was given 46 strokes and a further 77 strokes during interrogation in Würzburg: this brutal treatment eventually led him to confess to joining witchcraft at school; other children were beaten by their parents and masters during the eighteenth-century witch panic in Augsburg to make them confess, one child so severely that his finger was almost severed …

What is interesting about [Merckler's] case is that the stories emerged not from the adult world, because a parent had been suspected of witchcraft, but from the world of the children themselves …

Because children made the witch fantasy their own, they also tended to get it wrong. Witches generally saw the Devil as a man dressed in sombre black, occasionally green, but Merckler was adamant that he had been red, a striking colour that has nothing of the strict inversion of religious imagery implied by black. Merckler insisted that only he could see the Devil, and that he saw him in the presence of others – this too was unusual, because encounters with the Devil were usually secret, taking place when the individual was alone: here, the Devil has something of the character of an imaginary friend. Children made statements which were simply ridiculous, like the child who said the Devil came down the chimney on a donkey, or they got basic facts twisted: instead of whipping up fearsome storms, one child simply learnt to make rain. Merckler had sprinkled water on one boy's hand in an attempt to baptise him in the Devil's name – this was a standard demonology, except that Merckler managed only a hand, not the head. Valtin Winter was said to have gone about boasting he could make people 'lame and blind': normally, witches claimed only to harm or kill. The concrete nature of his boast suggests that he had mixed up fairy-tales with ideas about witches. Children's sense of play and fascination with dirt and insects is also reflected in what they confessed: Niclas Dornhauser of Alleshausen allegedly claimed he could conjure plagues of mice. Anna Krug aged eight-and-a-half said her mistress taught her how to make fleas: you poke a thorn into a cherry pip and out they crawl; while Valtin Winter said his parents and sisters knew how to make fleas out of black wax. The possibilities of magic to disrupt adult society were intensely fascinating to children.

But the issue over which their testimony was most likely to diverge from the standard adult confession was sex. Sex with the Devil was the key admission in most women's confessions to witchcraft, and the story of how the Devil had seduced her formed part of most stories women told. Men who confessed to witchcraft also confessed to diabolic sex, but in their case, the Devil usually took the shape of real women they knew: few men confessed to sodomitical intercourse with a male devil. Young and adolescent children's confessions to sex with the Devil are thus occasionally very revealing, because they lack adults' pre-formed words and narrative structures to talk about sex. ... Other children who confessed during the Juliusspital panic also admitted to kisses, and to 'committing shame' with each other and flying out to Sabbaths: they did not confess to sex with the Devil, or with other adults like carers or teachers, but only with each other. Like men accused of witchcraft, the boys named not the Devil but real girls as their sexual partners, and instead of claiming that the Devil came in the form of a girl, these children described sexual fondlings between real children. So Anna Marielein Fischer, a girl named by many of the other children, said that there was a bed on which they all lay with their lovers at the Sabbath ... Regina Groninger from Augsburg, aged twelve, in a confession which was highly idiosyncratic, claimed that the Devil came to her in the shape of a mysterious black man who 'lies on her whole body, and thus presses on her in such a way that her (if you will excuse the expression) shit goes out of her body'; he 'put something pointed like a spindle in the front part of her body..., from which she felt great pains, but she did not feel that anything was left behind in her body, and when he had to do with her thus, it lasted a quarter of an hour'. The precision of her description and her avoidance of any of the diabolic clichés that other children knew to use suggest this account comes from a real and deeply traumatic sexual experience. Again, sexual and excremental themes merge in stories about the Devil, a characteristic of children's witchcraft narratives.

Reading B
The kiddy and the pork chop: childhood 1950–1973

Hugh Cunningham

Source: *The Invention of Childhood*, 2006, London, BBC Books, pp. 213–19.

In Bethnal Green, in London's East End, Mrs Glass in the 1950s described the difference between her parents' generation and her own thus: 'Dad used to be very strict with us, we're different with our boy. We make more of a mate of him. When I was a kid Dad always had the best of everything. Now it's the children who get the best of it. If there's one pork chop left, the kiddy gets it.'

There are few things more important in family life than food. In working-class families in the nineteenth century and early twentieth, everyone agreed about the pecking order. Fathers came first, children next and mothers last. Now, in the 1950s, fathers seem to have given place to children; the child has become 'a mate'. Mothers in the 1950s and 1960s became acutely aware that the way they were bringing up their children differed from how they themselves had been brought up.

Mrs Glass was one of the participants in a famous study of the 1950s that compared Bethnal Green and the new model town of Dagenham on London's eastern outskirts. In a nutshell, they found a community in Bethnal Green and isolated families of parents and their children in Dagenham. And of course the future was Dagenham. In Bethnal Green grandmothers were involved in child care on a daily basis, and young mothers were in constant touch with one another. But for the families moved out to Dagenham, grandmother was still in the East End, and mother and the children tended to live behind net curtains. These new homes were becoming much more attractive places in which to spend time. Children began to get their own bedrooms. Radio had already helped bring entertainment into the home, but on nothing like the scale of television, which spread rapidly in the 1950s. At the outset there was a brief revival of community, the house with the television set becoming a magnet for the neighbours, but that soon passed. The nuclear family of father, mother and the children was driven in on itself.

The decades in the middle of the twentieth century witnessed one of the most important changes in the history of childhood. Until then, it had been assumed as a matter of course in the great majority of families that children would start earning as soon as they could and would contribute their wages to the family economy. They would tip up their earnings to their mother, who might give them something back for spends. As everyone knew, once the children started earning, the family as a whole enjoyed a better standard of living. In innumerable families across the country some kind of negotiation, spoken or unspoken, went on, the teenage worker torn between the sense of family needs and the wish to be able to spend on her or his own account.

In the post-war world the balance began to swing decisively in favour of the teenage worker. It was in the 1950s that sociologists started talking about 'the teenage consumer'. There is in fact much evidence of teenagers as consumers throughout the twentieth century, but undoubtedly they had more money at their disposal in the 1950s than they had had earlier. They were both earning more and contributing less to the family economy. What made this possible was a rise in living standards: the higher earnings of the male head of the household now began to make life less of a pinch. In addition, some wives were beginning to enter the labour market, normally part-time and in low-paid jobs, and what was often called their 'pin money' made its contribution to the family budget. The flow of cash that throughout history had gone from children to parents now began to change direction: parents spent on their children. The change was more than simply economic. Parents were beginning to think that their children might be able to have a better life than they had had and were willing to make sacrifices to help this to happen. An American historian, Viviana Zelizer, has described this process as a 'sacralization of childhood'. Family life began to be centred on the children, the parents investing in them emotionally as well as financially, their hopes inseparable from the happiness and success of their children.'

This consciousness of a change of generation can be seen in the history of pocket-money, which first began to be spoken about in the later nineteenth century. It only became an issue in the mid-twentieth century – and that because it was the poor who were most generous to their children. A wartime survey found that, 'school children in the poorer districts had far more pocket-money than those of the better class … These children spend their money largely on sweets, ice-cream and comics … [The] sweets [are] often of the most wretched quality [and the comics] generally poor to a degree.'

By the first half of the 1950s most parents were giving their children regular pocket-money by the time they started going to school. In the late 1960s it still seemed to be true, as in the 1940s, that poor parents spent more on pocket-money than the well-off. But the poorer you were, the greater the range of goods you were expected to buy with it. Parents varied in how they distributed money to their children, the one common factor being that they all did it. Mothers described what they did – or had done when their daughters were younger – in Swansea in the 1960s. At one end of the spectrum, there was a mother who said, 'I give them money when they ask for something and I never comes back from the shops without something for them – sweets and that. They moan sometimes that they don't get pocket-money like other children, but I tell them, "Look how much more in fact you get than the other kids."'

At the opposite end, the attitude was, 'I think it's very important in bringing up children to be strict on routine. I always gave them pocket-money every Friday – I wasn't allowed to forget it – they bought whatever they wanted with it.' But the most common attitude was expressed by another mother: 'Her father gave her [a few shillings] every week and if she wanted more, she came and asked me. Spoilt she was!' Children had come to occupy a new place in the working-class home.

By the 1960s, too, over half of all seven year olds were earning money from their parents for doing odd jobs, the child taking the initiative in negotiating this extra income. What in previous generations would have been an expected contribution to the family now became an opportunity to earn some money. Most children were exempt from any requirement to help. In the 1960s in Nottingham less than one-third of seven year olds were expected to do regular jobs and, particularly if you were a girl, the lower you were in the social scale, the less you were expected to do. Mothers took on the whole burden. 'I used to ask if she wanted me to help and she said, "Help me by keeping out of the way!"' One young woman who had had to help clearly felt she was picked on. She used to bath her brother and sister on Saturday nights until she was 17: 'And I used to stay in every Tuesday evening to do the ironing, and to do the washing up. My mother had a big womb op a few years ago – and she rather played up on it. She's *got* to do [the housework] now and so she *does* it. It was very inconvenient for my mother to let me get married – I did a lot of work.'

Alongside pocket-money and small earnings, children were becoming adept at extracting money from their parents: pester power, perhaps dating back to the eighteenth century, was now more vigorous, or, as one observer put it, there was a 'pressure towards the material indulgence of children'. A mother in Nottingham described how, 'I think myself you give in to your own where you couldn't have it – you think to yourself, well I didn't get this, and I'll see that he gets it. I think that's the whole attitude of a lot of people.'

If there were tensions between the generations, there was also a relationship between parents and children of a kind that could not have been imagined earlier. Children now found it much easier than in previous generations to talk to their parents … [I]n earlier centuries a prime virtue enjoined on girls was silence, and we all know the injunction that children should be seen and not heard. In many households the silence of the children remained the norm in the first half of the twentieth century. Mrs Peters in Lancashire recalled how you spoke when you were spoken to: 'I remember we had relatives in and they were talking about something and I spoke up. I'll never forget it. Dad turned right quickly on me, "Children should be seen and not heard." I can see him to this day pointing at me. I know I went crimson. I thought, I'll watch my step another time. They were kind and good, but firm. You'd to toe the line.'

One indication of this pre-Second World War lack of communication between mothers and daughters was that girls were left in complete ignorance about menstruation. Mrs Calvert, born in Preston in 1919, remembered: 'When I had been to the toilet I thought, oh, what have I done? I never thought anything and I were turned fifteen. I told her that I had all colour on m'pants. All she said was, "In my bottom drawer you will find some cloths. Put them up against you and keep warm and keep away from lads." That's all my mother ever told me about anything.' …

By the second half of the century, however, this had changed. Here is a shop manager's wife in Nottingham in the 1960s talking about her daughter Jennifer, aged 11:

> When I was Jennifer's age I didn't know – I was never told – and I don't think that's right. I think they *should* know as soon as they start to ask anything – I mean they *ought* to be told. Same as when your periods start – well, when mine started, oh, I was frightened to death, I didn't know *what was* the matter with me; and of course I didn't tell my mother until she found out. Well, Jennifer *knows*, and so of course she's not frightened … Well, as I say – she's just started, this week in fact, the first signs of it started; well, she

came straight away and told me. Well, I don't think there's anything if she wanted to know she wouldn't come and ask me; and if it came to it, I don't think she'd mind telling her Daddy, if I wasn't here. You see, they *can talk*.

But in this brave new world children's talk could be wearing on the parent. A lorry driver's wife said of her son 'He's got a terrible habit that he'll just talk and talk and talk and talk, until in the end you can hear his voice going through you, you know. I usually tell him to be quiet then. He'll say "All right" – and he just keeps right on! He doesn't take a bit of notice. He just keeps on, and on, and on, and on.'

Or as a railwayman's wife put it: 'It's her ordering me about. She'll want some water for her paint; I say "Wait a minute, will you, please?" "I want it *right away*, Mummy!" And she's on and on all the time until I go to get it her … I mean, when we was kiddies, we had to do as we was told, didn't we?'

Chapter 3

Childhood: a developmental approach

Martin Woodhead

Contents

In this chapter, you will:

- examine features of a developmental approach to childhood, explaining its historical roots and its global influence

- explore key concepts and methods used in the study of development, illustrated through examples of observational and experimental studies

- consider the way researchers test the adequacy of developmental theories by devising new experiments or carrying out new observations

- analyse debates about how far child development is a universal, stage-like process, and how far it is a social and cultural process

- evaluate the claim that developmental research and theories are a social construction of childhood.

1 Introduction

During the nineteenth and (especially) twentieth centuries, interest in the scientific study of childhood grew from strength to strength, including the establishment of child development as a field of academic research, as well as numerous applied fields concerned with educational, clinical, and health and social welfare policies and practices affecting children.

This chapter has two major aims. The first is to introduce developmental studies of childhood, with some examples of major research debates, including a discussion of the way Piaget's theories about children's competence at various stages of development have been challenged by more recent research. The second aim is to reflect on the significance of this way of studying children, in terms of what it tells us about the social construction of childhood. We will be asking about some of the ways that developmental psychology constructs the child, through the questions asked, theories formulated, research methods employed and practical implications proposed.

2 The emergence of child development

During the winter of 1799, people living in a rural community in Aveyron, France, noticed a dirty, naked boy in nearby woods. He was behaving strangely and apparently surviving alone on a diet of acorns and roots. During the harshest weather, the 'Wild Boy of Aveyron' (as he became known) stumbled into the village itself. Nobody knew where he came from, how long he had been living wild, or how he had managed to survive. He was reluctant to wear clothes, didn't speak and seemed retarded when compared with other village children of his age (about 12 years old). Many people thought he must have been abandoned during infancy and survived on his own ever since. The 'wild boy' was brought to Paris where he became the subject of widespread debate about how far his 'wildness' was due to the deprivations of his childhood. Some argued that capacities for mature rational thinking and cultured behaviour amongst adults is the product of society – transmitted to children through nurturance, teaching and training – of which the boy had clearly been deprived. Others argued that human civilisation is an expression of human nature – based on inborn human qualities that grow naturally through maturation – so the boy had probably been born 'mentally defective'. These competing beliefs about childhood will already be familiar to you from Chapter 2. Recall the writings of John Locke, especially the emphasis placed on the importance of children learning through experience and through good teaching. By contrast, Jean-Jacques Rousseau believed childhood is a natural state, and that children should be given freedom to grow and learn in natural surroundings, according to nature's plan.

A young doctor called Jean-Marc Itard heard about the case. He was more inclined to follow the principles of Locke than of Rousseau, believing that the child's strange and immature behaviour was the result of years of deprivation and social isolation. He felt many commentators were misguided in their expectations of the boy:

> The most brilliant and irrational expectations preceded the arrival of the Savage of Aveyron at Paris. A number of inquisitive people looked forward with delight to witnessing the boy's astonishment at the sights of the capital. On the other hand many people … believed that the education of this child would only be a question of some months, and that he would soon be able to give the most interesting information about his past life. In place of all this what

do we see? A disgustingly dirty child affected with spasmodic movements and often convulsions who swayed back and forth ceaselessly like certain animals in the menagerie, who bit and scratched those who opposed him, who showed no sort of affection for those who attended him; and who was in short, indifferent to everything and attentive to nothing.

(Itard, 1962 [1801], p. 4)

Itard was determined to put his own theories about the importance of social experience to the test, by demonstrating the possibility of reversing effects of social deprivation. He named the boy Victor, made a careful assessment of his capacities for speaking and thinking, and then set about to introduce basic skills. While some progress was made on each of these fronts, Itard was disappointed that the child never came close to his expectations for normal development. He eventually abandoned the project, but not before he had presented a detailed report on this pioneering experiment in child development to the French Minister of the Interior. A brief extract indicates the systematic way Itard approached the task. He began by training Victor to discriminate shapes and then sounds:

The aim of my first efforts was to make him distinguish the sound of a bell from that of a drum. Just as I had previously led him from the larger comparison of two pieces of cardboard, differently shaped and colored, to the distinction between letters and words, I had every reason to believe that the ear, following the same progression of attention as the sense of sight, would soon distinguish the most similar and the most different tones of the vocal organ. Consequently, I set myself to render the sounds progressively more alike, more complicated, and nearer together. Later I was not content with requiring him to merely distinguish the sound of the bell from that of a drum, but introduced the differences of sound produced by striking with a rod upon the skin, the hoop or body of a drum, or upon the bell of a clock, or a fire shovel, making a ringing noise.

(Itard, 1962 [1801], p. 56)

I start with the Wild Boy of Aveyron for two reasons. Firstly, because his case illustrates the power of competing cultural beliefs about childhood to inform the way children are understood and treated. Secondly, because the young doctor tried to resolve these debates through the application of systematic scientific principles. Itard's experiment was one of the earliest attempts to bring childhood within the domain of scientific enquiry – to adopt a positivist approach, based on the idea that observation and measurement lie at the heart of scientific endeavour. Henceforth, issues surrounding children's development, care and education weren't just debated by parents, priests and pedagogues. Increasingly, they were subject to scientific scrutiny – applying principles of observation, measurement and experimentation originating from the natural sciences.

2.1   Science or social construction?

The focus of this chapter is on scientific knowledge about children. One of the goals of scientific research has been to evaluate competing theories, beliefs and claims about childhood, in order to find out what children are really like – the basic principle of a positivist approach. This is certainly what Itard hoped to do when he embarked on research with young Victor and his faith in the power of science is echoed in textbooks to this day. For example:

> Developmental psychology today is a truly objective science ... Today a developmentalist determines the adequacy of a theory by deriving hypotheses and conducting research to see whether the theory can predict and explain the new observations that he or she has made. There is no room for subjective bias in evaluating ideas: theories of human development are only as good as their ability to account for the important aspects of children's growth and development.

> (Shaffer, 1993, p. 38)

Science can and does offer a great deal in shedding light on many important issues. Academic libraries are filled with volumes of journals and books reporting what children know and are capable of at different ages, how their growth and adjustment is shaped by their circumstances, what the most effective approaches to teaching and learning are, and so on. But I will argue that developmental research isn't a straightforward enterprise of establishing the truth about the way children really are in a once-and-for-all way. The storehouse of knowledge may be much greater than in Itard's day, but many of the underlying debates live on; especially where scientific understanding about how children develop merges with beliefs about how they should develop, how they should be treated, and the importance of care, play, learning, discipline, and so on.

"George! What are you doing with the baby?"

Figure 1   Thc child as subject of study

Recognising 'child development' as a particular way of thinking about (or constructing) childhood is also important for the reason that it has been so influential. Besides informing the treatment of children at home, in hospitals, childcare centres, schools, etc., developmental concepts have become part of everyday language. Questions about milestones in a baby's life, about what's normal for this or that age, about which kinds of experience might harm and which promote development, about whether adolescent rebellion is a natural stage of growing up, and so on, all draw heavily on research and theories about these themes.

One of the questions adults in the UK often ask when they meet a child for the first time is 'How old are you?' – or if the child is too young to answer for themselves, they ask the parent about the baby's age. Knowing a young person's age is an important way to position them, linking their appearance and behaviour to knowledge and expectations about competencies and social experiences. It opens the way to such questions as whether they've started talking yet, whether they go to playgroup, what class they are in at school, whether they have learned to read, how well they are getting on compared with others their age, etc. In other words, knowing a child's age is a clue to knowing how to place them within the childhood life-phase. The very familiarity of developmental ways of thinking and organising children's lives means it is easy to overlook how powerful age/stage thinking has become in contemporary constructions of childhood, as well as respects in which these expectations of childhood may be culture specific.

In Bangladesh, for example, birthdays have not traditionally been recorded or celebrated. And expectations of children have not been so strongly linked to their age. One anthropologist with extensive knowledge of Bangladesh observed:

> When children are asked about their age, they are likely to reply, 'How do I know? Ask my mother,' as if this information did not concern their individual self. ... As for mothers, when pressed to give the age of their children, they commonly reply by giving a range. For example, my son is 8 to 9, my daughter is 11 to 12 years old.
>
> (Blanchet, 1996, p. 41)

Blanchet goes on to explain that expectations of children are linked to their life circumstances as much as with their age. Expectations hinge around when children are seen as having achieved understanding or competence appropriate to their situation:

> A child who is orphaned, for example, is expected to develop rapidly a state of 'understanding'. A poor child placed as a domestic servant, a pre-pubertal girl given in marriage are under

similar pressures. They are excused for behaving as small irresponsible children, but not for long. Middle class children on the other hand are expected to show an early maturity about school work, but in other aspects of their development, for example sexuality, they are expected to remain innocent and act as though they did not understand.

(Blanchet, 1996, p. 48)

Another example comes from a study of beliefs about development amongst the Navajo people of North America. Chisholm (1996) explains that Navajo view maturity in terms of how much responsibility an individual takes. When he asked: 'What is the goal of development?', he was told:

Being a leader is the highest goal. Being a leader of the people is the highest form of development, like its goal. The whole thing is responsibility—taking care of things. First you just learn to take care of yourself. Then some things, then some animals, then your family. Then you help all your people and the whole world. Talking real well is when you're ready to help the people, talking real well in front of big crowds of people, then you're ready to start helping.

(Quoted in Chisholm, 1996, p. 171)

Another feature of Navajo thinking is that development isn't seen as applying only to children, but continues well into adulthood (see below).

An outline of the Navajo model of development

Stage 1 'One becomes aware' (2–4 years)
A child's awareness is said to begin when he or she no longer has to be restrained from touching a hot stove or from wandering away and getting lost. These are seen as the first indicators of self-discipline.

Stage 2 'One becomes self-aware' (4–6 years)
Children are said to become aware of their own thought, perceptions and intentions to do things. Children of this age are

thought to be able to begin learning the importance of kinship relations and to show 'respect' for others.

Stage 3 'One begins to think' (6–9 years)
Now that the child has begun to learn the importance of kinship relations, he or she must begin at least to imitate, if not always fully carry out, action that embodies this 'respect'. For example, children at this stage are expected to offer morning prayers (respect for the Holy People) and to begin to care for lambs and kids (respect for the means of making a living).

Stage 4 'One's thought begins to exist' (10–15 years)
This is the transitional stage to adulthood, in which children are expected to carry out all activities without help or supervision. During this stage, a girl's puberty ceremony is also performed. The key at this stage is knowing not only what one's responsibilities are, but 'how they came to be'. This includes knowledge of the complete versions of certain legends and, thus, full understanding of the hierarchy of Navajo clans, one's place within this scheme, and the basis in kinship for one's responsibilities to all others.

Stage 5 'One begins to think for oneself' (15–18 years)
At this stage parents say to young people, 'You are on your own now; I cannot think for you.' Except for marriage, they are considered fully adult, and expected to manage all their affairs on their own – except that they are still responsible for helping with the duties of their parents' household.

Stage 6 'One begins thinking for all things' (17–22 years)
The young person has now mastered every aspect of the responsibilities of the adult life, including raising and trading in livestock. The training of the past culminates in marriage.

Stage 7 'One begins to think ahead for oneself' (22–30 years)
In this stage, the successes of one's life are manifested in one's own children. 'Success' here means not only jewellery, nice clothes and a good appearance, but increasing herds, a good marriage and evidence of 'good thought' in one's children.

Stage 8 'One begins to think ahead for all things' (30+ years)
The qualities of the previous stage are further developed, and one begins to acquire recognition as 'one who has the knowledge and ability to speak and plan ahead for both his children and neighbors' (Begishi et al., n.d., p. 23).

(Adapted from Chisholm, 1996, pp. 172–3)

While all societies recognise that children are growing, learning and acquiring culturally valued competencies, there is considerable variation in how far expectations are strongly linked to their age, and how far other factors come into play, notably gender and social class or caste. Despite these cultural variations in the way children's development is understood, minority-world beliefs and expectations play an increasingly important role, through processes of globalisation, especially with the spread of schooling systems, as well as through the influence of expert knowledge, and the interventions of UNICEF and other non-governmental organisations concerned with children. The Geneva Declaration of the Rights of the Child (1924) and the UN Declaration of the Rights of the Child (1959) were both framed in terms of promoting children's 'normal development'. The UN Convention on the Rights of the Child (UNCRC) (1989) also draws heavily on child development concepts, especially Article 6:

> 2. States Parties shall ensure to the maximum extent possible the survival and development of the child.
>
> (UNCRC, Article 6)

2.2   Defining development

The global influence of developmental approaches to understanding childhood and promoting children's rights can be seen as a positive indicator of the value attached to scientifically based theories of children's development. But dissemination of good scientific knowledge is not straightforward (Boyden, 1997; Woodhead, 1999). 'Development' is neither a precise concept, nor a neutral one. With some notable exceptions, most research in children's development has been based on the lives, experiences and expectations of children growing up in minority-world societies, according to the theories and methodologies adopted by researchers living within those societies, especially in Europe and North America. But they have been applied much more widely, to the lives of children growing up in very different circumstances, and with very different prospects for development.

This chapter will introduce you to some examples of developmental research and theory, including some major debates about how best to understand the child. But I also want to convey a sense of the distinctiveness of these ways of thinking, debating and researching childhood, and the sense that developmental research (and indeed all scientific research) is a product of time and place, reflecting, to a greater or lesser extent, the concerns of the period.

Activity 1   What is development?

Allow about 25 minutes

Let us establish what researchers mean when they talk about studying children's development.

Read the explanation below, taken from a widely used introductory child development textbook. What do you see as the main features of a developmental approach?

> The term 'development' refers to the process by which an organism (human or animal) grows and changes through its life-span. In humans, the most dramatic developmental changes occur in prenatal development, infancy and childhood, as the newborn develops into a young adult capable of becoming a parent himself or herself …
>
> Generally, developmental processes have been related to age. A typical 3-year-old has, for example, a particular mastery of spoken language … and a 4-year-old has typically progressed further. A developmental psychologist may then wish to find out, and theorize about, the processes involved in this progression. What experiences, rewards, interactions, feedback, have helped the child develop in this way?
>
> (Smith et al., 2011, p. 6)

Comment

I have grouped together some of the key ideas in this quote.

Human, animal, organism:

Development doesn't just apply to children. Reference to animals and other organisms draws attention to the evolutionary significance of human development, as will become clear in Section 2.

Foetus, prenatal, newborn, infancy, childhood, young adult, lifespan:

Development isn't just about the childhood life-phase. Legal definitions and cultural practices may formally define when childhood begins and ends, but in developmental terms, the foundations of the child's nervous system are established during the foetal stage, and processes of learning and development continue throughout adult life.

Age, growth, change, progression, mastery:

The emphasis on charting growth and change, most often linked to chronological age, is one of the most distinctive features of a developmental approach to childhood. But the emphasis on progression and mastery signals that development is about change in a particular direction, towards more mature 'adult' ways of functioning, about becoming more competent, more autonomous, etc.

Typical:

Another distinctive feature is the emphasis on normal, universal processes of growth and change. Differences are recognised, for example related to gender or social class, but overall the emphasis is on what's shared in common within a group rather than on what is unique to an individual.

Experiences, rewards, interactions, feedback:

Describing children's development is only one goal of developmental research. Explaining development is another goal. For example, developmental researchers want to find out what factors promote development, as well as how deprivations can be overcome. This was Itard's motive for trying to help Victor and it continues to inspire much research, especially applied studies in education and childcare.

One other feature of developmental approaches is the imbalance in research attention paid to particular age groups. Major theories do cover the full age range from infancy to maturity. But as a general rule, younger children have received disproportionate attention compared to older children – perhaps because growth and change appear so rapid on so many fronts. As confirmation of the point, one of the introductory textbooks on my bookshelf devotes more than 350 pages to infancy and early childhood (up to about six years old), but less than 200 pages to the rest of childhood and adolescence (Sroufe et al., 1996). Studies of adolescent change are an exception to this general rule, again because this appears to be a major period for personal change in minority-world societies (see Barnes, 1995; Morrow, 2003).

You will find a similar emphasis on research and theory related to early childhood in this chapter. It's also important to point out that within one chapter it isn't possible to convey the diversity of approaches to studying childhood within the field of developmental research. This chapter concentrates mainly on development of children's intellectual and social understanding, and introduces examples of both observational and experimental research. Inevitably, in the space of one chapter, other major traditions of child research cannot be covered. For example, psychoanalytic approaches originating from the work of Sigmund Freud are only briefly referred to (in Section 3), and no attention is given to behavioural approaches, for example linked to the work of B. F. Skinner (see Das Gupta, 1994).

Summary of Section 2

The story of the Wild Boy of Aveyron illustrates the origins of scientific studies of childhood as well as the link with wider cultural ideas about childhood.

Developmental research has been the dominant academic framework for studying childhood. It has been very influential on the treatment of children, as well as on everyday ways of talking about young people.

Developmental research is founded on scientific principles, but it also constructs particular images of the growing child.

---

3 A new science of child study

In this section I continue to trace the early history of developmental research, and consider the impact of the new science on social issues during the twentieth century.

I began Section 2 with Itard's account of the 'Wild Boy of Aveyron'. Another landmark piece of child research was written by a young parent living in London during the 1840s. He kept a detailed diary of his son William (affectionately nicknamed Doddy). This account was especially influential because the parent was Charles Darwin – who went on to write *The Origin of Species* (1859). Towards the end of his life, Darwin returned to the diary and wrote it up in an article for the journal *Mind* (published in 1877).

3.1   The impact of Darwin

Figure 2   Darwin's research included observation of his son

Activity 2   Reading A

Allow about 30 minutes

Now turn to Reading A and read the short extracts from Darwin's 'A biographical sketch of an infant'. Note the way he approaches the task of recording his son's 'biography' – he talks about his son in an impersonal way (e.g. as 'this infant'), emphasising the goal of objectivity, achieved through precise observation and description. Also note how he makes these observations within a time framework – linked to the baby's age – and the simple experiments employed to try to find out what his son feels and understands. As you will see, Darwin wasn't content to describe what he saw each day. He was searching for patterns of growth – evidence of progress from immaturity to competence. Consider the questions that seem to be guiding Darwin's enquiry, especially about how far observed behaviours are the expression of 'instinct' or shaped by experience and learning, about how his son's development compares with his daughter's, and how this human child's development compares with other species.

Comment

When I first read this account, I was struck by the way Darwin set about recording his son's 'biography' as well as by the topics he focused on, many of which connect with research traditions continuing to this day. Darwin was one of the first, and certainly one of the most influential, to offer an evidence-based account of early development, in keeping with traditions of the physical and biological sciences. Darwin's approach is cool and unsentimental. At the same time he isn't judgemental about his young son's immaturity, but concentrates on trying to understand what makes him behave the way he does. He frames his observations in terms of a series of categories – reflex actions, vision, movement, anger, fear, reason, moral sense – and charts each category in relation to age. As well as making precise observations, Darwin carried out experiments to test hypotheses about his son's capacities. For example, he tested Doddy's reflex reactions when touched on the sole of his foot, his fearfulness of 'strange and loud noises', his reactions to being approached by his father in a strange way (backwards), and his empathy towards his nurse when she pretended to cry. Several of these experiments anticipate major research traditions. For example, children's reactions to seeing their mirror image have been studied as an indicator of self-recognition (Lewis and Brooks-Gunn, 1979).

Darwin's observation that Doddy first showed clear preferences for his nurse's affection at five months hints at the emergence of 'emotional attachment' (which will be discussed in Section 3.3). The boy's sympathy towards his nurse's distress, his sensitivity to ridicule and his attempts to deceive his father resonate with recent debates about young children's capacities for social understanding (which is elaborated in Section 5, Reading B).

Another important feature of Darwin's scientific approach is that he acknowledges the gaps in his understanding, such as how to explain Doddy's early recognition of his mother's breast. At the same time, Darwin doesn't always hesitate in making judgements, which perhaps reflect his cultural values as much as his observations. For example, Darwin compares Doddy's development as a boy, compared with that of his daughter at the same age, judging that his daughter was 'not nearly so acute' when faced with an image in a mirror, and asserting that 'a tendency to throw objects is inherited by boys'! (Gender issues are followed up in Chapter 5.)

Most significantly, Darwin makes comparisons between human children and other species (e.g. locating his son's reactions to seeing himself in a mirror alongside the reactions of 'higher apes' to the same procedure). Darwin's approach to studying children made a big impact on the research community and on society at large. From now on children came to be viewed as scientifically interesting, especially because their development was seen as related to that of other species, which reinforced the interest in studying children as part of 'nature' that had been kindled by Rousseau's writings.

Following Darwin, the study of human childhoods became firmly established as a respected subject of scientific scrutiny, detailed description, theorisation and experimentation. Pioneers of the science of childhood included James Sully (who established child psychology at London University during the 1880s), Wilhelm Preyer (a biologist who carried out influential early studies in Germany) and G. Stanley Hall (who became an advocate for basing child-rearing on scientific principles in the United States and offered some of the earliest accounts of adolescence as a distinctive life stage). Another advocate of the new, scientific approach was Arnold Gesell (see below).

Figure 3   Arnold Gesell's observation dome

Arnold Gesell

Dr Arnold Gesell was a pioneer in the systematic study of child development. He began by studying abnormal development, but became frustrated by the lack of detailed information about normal development. In 1911 he founded the Yale Clinic of Child Development in the USA. Gesell's approach emulated the science laboratory. It was based on observing children's natural behaviour unobtrusively, devising simple tests and recording their behaviour in minute detail, following a standard procedure. The photograph in Figure 3 shows white-coated Gesell working with a child in a large glass observation dome he had specially constructed. He took advantage of the new technologies of the day (photography and film cameras) to assemble a massive databank of young children's behaviour at various ages. For example, in his major work on the first five years of life, he organised his observations under a list of categories broadly grouped into Motor, Language, Adaptive Behaviour, and Personal and Social Behaviour. He distilled this research into what he called 'normative summaries', charts representing the milestones of normal development for each age group.

An example at four months old is given below.

Motor Characteristics

Prefers to lie on back

Tries to raise self, lifting head and shoulders

Can roll from side to side (or back to side)

Holds head erect when carried

Lifts head when prone

Pushes with feet against floor when held

Language

Coos

Smiles

Laughs aloud

Makes several vocalizations

Adaptive Behavior

Notices large objects

May notice spoon on table

Hands react to table

Personal-social Behavior

Shows selective interest in animated face

Makes anticipatory postural adjustment on being lifted

Not much affected by strange persons, new scenes or solicitude

Turns head to voice

Plays with hands

(Gesell, 1925, quoted in Beekman, 1977, pp. 156–7)

3.2   Developmental science and social issues

Valerie Walkerdine (1984) summed up the new enthusiasm for studying children during the early years of the twentieth century:

> Children's bodies were weighed and measured. The effects of fatigue were studied, as were children's interests, imaginings, religious ideas, fetishes, attitudes to weather, to adults, drawings, dolls, lies, ideas and, most importantly for us, their stages of growth. (All this is a full twenty years before Piaget began to study children.) What is important is that children as a category were being singled out for scientific study for the first time …

(Walkerdine, 1984, p. 171)

In the UK, seeds of knowledge from systematic studies of children's development fell on fertile ground. The social climate was sympathetic to the application of scientific method to social issues, especially where generalisations could be made about large numbers of children. The new knowledge seemed particularly relevant to social issues associated with industrialisation, urbanisation and mass schooling, especially with the increased attention being paid to children as a group, and the growth in provision of health, education and welfare services for all children – not just for elite groups (Hendrick, 1997).

Interest in scientific studies can be detected even during the early decades of the nineteenth century. Employment of young children en masse in the textile factories of northern England had already prompted politicians and social reformers to start asking questions about whether labouring long hours from an early age would harm children's young growing bodies and their morals. Child study offered the research tools to monitor how far early deprivations might be stunting their growth. By the early twentieth century, monitoring children's health and growth was becoming normal practice, coinciding with the development of child health services.

Figure 4 The development of child health services

Thinking about children in terms of ages and stages, normality and abnormality wasn't restricted to professionals. Parents shared the new knowledge, as an increasingly literate society was receptive to the earliest child-rearing manuals (Hardyment, 1984).

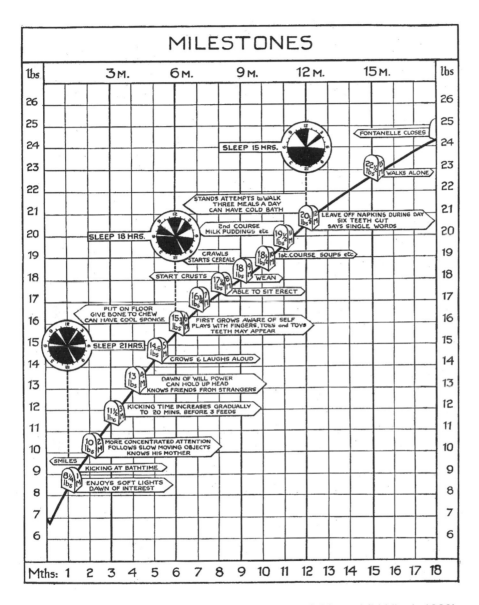

Figure 5   A chart for parents from *The Mothercraft Manual* (Liddiard, 1923). Strict schedules of feeding and sleeping were advocated, following the principles of childcare expert Truby King

Defining the stages in children's 'normal' development became even more salient with the establishment of mass education, culminating in the Education Acts of 1870 and 1880, which laid the framework for a compulsory system. Confronted with a group of children all aged around six, eight or 11, teachers needed to know – what is it reasonable to expect of a child this age? What standard should be set in relation to the range of abilities in a class of 30 or 40 children?

Figure 6   Child development included intellectual, moral and physical development

Evidence of what is 'normal' or 'typical' became a standard to judge which children were 'subnormal' or 'retarded', not just in physical and motor development, but also in intellectual development. The first intelligence tests were developed by Binet and Simon in Paris, as a direct response to a French Ministry of Public Instruction Commission into the problems of low-ability children within the public school system. In due course a new profession would emerge, able to apply these new techniques to sort and classify children according to their aptitudes and abilities – the educational psychologist.

Writing in the 1970s, Newson and Newson reflected back on the growth of interest in the psychological development of children:

> Seen in historical and anthropological perspective, perhaps the most interesting aspect of the contemporary preoccupation with childrearing is that today we are self-consciously concerned with the possible *psychological* consequences of the methods which we use in bringing up our children. This attention to the total psychological development of the child is indeed a new phenomenon, in that earlier generations of parents have been chiefly preoccupied by the related themes of physical survival and moral growth, rather than with concepts of mental health or social

and emotional adjustment. So massive a change of emphasis must be of fundamental significance, not only to the anthropologist and the social historian, but to the child psychologists, psychiatrists and psychotherapists whose very existence as a group depends upon the climate of opinion which regards their professional skills as valuable and necessary, and which places them on an equal footing in social esteem with the more anciently respected callings of the paediatrician and the pedagogue.

(Newson and Newson, 1974, pp. 53–4)

Newson and Newson draw attention to the growing interest in children's mental health, and social and emotional adjustment. The rest of the section focuses on this topic, because it very clearly illustrates the way scientific theories connect with wider discourses about children's needs, especially when research is closely tied to applied issues.

3.3   Natural needs?

Babies and young children often get upset if they are separated from their parents, or from the people who most often care for them. What's less well known is that babies' tendency to get upset follows a developmental pattern. Separation protest (as psychologists call this kind of crying) happens much more often when babies are around seven to eight months of age. Younger babies are less sensitive to being separated – or at least they don't protest so loudly. Separation protest typically reaches a peak around 12 months and then gradually becomes less common as most babies become better able to cope with brief separation. Cross-cultural research has also found the same developmental patterns in very varying cultural contexts. These are generalisations, of course, and there can be marked individual, as well as cultural, differences in the ways separations are managed. Also, a change of care arrangements (e.g. starting nursery) can cause renewed upset in much older children.

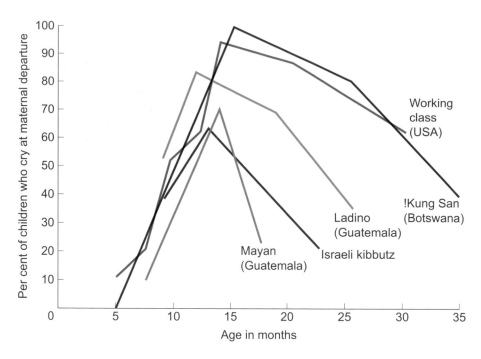

Figure 7 A graph comparing separation protest from different societies

You may recall that Darwin included the development of affection in the study of his son Doddy, noting that Doddy was several months old before he seemed to show a clear preference for his nurse's affections. The onset of separation protest during the second half of the first year is now recognised as an indicator that the young child has formed close emotional attachments to their parent or other caregiver. This line of research into children's early emotional attachments can be traced back to the originator of psychoanalysis, Sigmund Freud, and to his daughter, Anna Freud, who studied children in residential care during the Second World War. But research on attachment is most closely associated with the work of John Bowlby. Bowlby began his research by exploring the effects on children of being deprived of maternal care. Bowlby wanted to explain why children brought up in institutions so often have relationship difficulties and behavioural problems later on. He was also concerned about the emotional distress experienced by young children in hospital who were deprived of contact with their parents (common practice in England at the time). Notice the parallels between Bowlby's interest in the effects of social deprivation, and Itard's interest in the deprivations suffered by the 'Wild Boy of Aveyron'.

Figure 8   Children in institutional care

Bowlby's background was in medicine and he was trained in psychoanalysis. He was also very interested in evolution, especially the lessons from research into animal behaviour that built on Darwin's theory and appeared to suggest some of the mechanisms that might be at work in human babies. Ethological studies of baby geese seemed to show that young goslings imprint on their mother (or indeed the first moving thing with which they come into contact) (Lorenz, 1981). Bowlby saw a strong parallel in the way young babies become attached (or bonded) to their mothers (or other principal carers). He argued that when a baby becomes distressed and resists separation this is due to a biologically adaptive mechanism which evolved to protect the young of the human species by ensuring they maintain a close relationship to their mothers.

One of the most controversial features of Bowlby's early theories is that he took the bold step of trying to prescribe children's needs for care. He argued that some ways of caring for babies are natural and adaptive; others are unnatural and harmful. Bowlby's often-quoted conclusion at this time was:

what is believed to be essential for mental health is that the infant and young child should experience a warm, intimate, and continuous relationship with his mother (or permanent mother-substitute) in which both find satisfaction and enjoyment.

(Bowlby, 1967 [1951], p. 11)

Bowlby's work had a major impact on reforming practices in childcare, especially in residential and hospital care. At the same time his theories were criticised on two counts concerning the claim that children's emotional needs are an expression of their human nature.

The first set of criticisms drew attention to the dangers of over-generalising from behaviours of other species. Human infants don't 'bond' to their caregivers in a mechanical or instinctual way equivalent to imprinting. A baby's first relationships are also built on communication and the beginnings of shared understanding.

The second set of criticisms centred on claims made for 'natural' care. Critics argued that these so-called natural patterns of care were a reflection of minority-world cultural values, projected on to children as being about their needs. They were seen as a social construction, reinforcing dominant attitudes to family life in the post-war UK, by emphasising women's responsibilities for meeting the needs of their infants through offering full-time mothering (Tizard, 1991; Singer, 1992; Woodhead, 1997). For example, Bowlby's original work argued that children's needs for love and security are focused on one person (the mother or mother substitute). This principle (known as monotropism) was widely criticised as telling as much about mid-twentieth century English attitudes to family, nursery care and gender divisions as about the fundamental needs of children. It flew in the face of a wide range of evidence in cultural contexts where shared care is the norm, for example the widespread practice of older siblings (usually older sisters) sharing care of young children (Weisner and Gallimore, 1977).

In short, a first lesson was that human children certainly have needs for care and nurturance, but their attachments aren't necessarily focused on one person and they may be distributed amongst several consistent caregivers. A second lesson was that developmental theories may be informed by careful empirical research, but the interpretation of that research is shaped by available discourses about children's needs for care and nurturance.

These cultural dimensions of early emotional development are highlighted below.

Cultural dimensions of early emotional development

Robert LeVine and colleagues were interested in the way universal developmental processes may be expressed in different ways in different societies, according to the contexts of care, the demands on parents and other caregivers, and the values for children's adjustment. They compared child-rearing practices in an urban community in Boston, USA, with those amongst a rural Gusii community in Kenya. Note that the study was carried out during the 1970s and describes practices at that time.

Amongst the Gusii community, there was a high birth rate, but also a high mortality rate, so careful nurturance was a high priority. Mothers kept their babies in close physical contact, breastfeeding on demand and sleeping alongside them. But this nurturant style did not incorporate high levels of stimulation or play between mother and infant. Instead, mothers concentrated on keeping their babies quiet and comfortable, without encouraging lively interactions, so there was little emphasis on playing and talking to babies. These mothers were responsible both for managing their large family and for cultivating the fields. They relied on the help of older children, especially older daughters who would carry the baby on their back, play with it and bring it to the mother for feeding. By the age of three, toddlers were already being trained to carry out small domestic chores, in the context of a subsistence economy where even the youngest members were expected to play their part. The emphasis was on deference to elders and obedience to the mother's instructions; praise was offered sparingly, but there were opportunities for play and mischief as part of children's wider ranging familial and peer relationships. LeVine et al. argued that this picture of Gusii childhoods contrasts sharply with the affluent, technically and medically sophisticated US for the very reason that the conditions, priorities and goals for childhood are so different. For infants growing up in Boston, survival was virtually assured. There were strong expectations on mothers and other carers to establish a close emotional and playful relationship with their infant; a relationship in which there was reciprocity and mutual responsiveness, where the subdued infant was stimulated, and the curious infant encouraged to explore. Children were provided with plenty of psychological space, treated as individuals and encouraged to express their feelings and wishes. Clashes of will were not only expected, but to some extent encouraged, within a framework that emphasised autonomy, assertiveness and independence.

(Adapted from LeVine et al., 1994)

Finally, note that extensive research has been carried out since Bowlby originally formulated his theories, especially into the formation of emotional attachments, and the effects of separation or other disturbed relationships (see Schaffer, 1996, for a review).

Summary of Section 3

Darwin's observations illustrate the establishment of child study as a research tradition, as well as the links to evolutionary biology.

One of the goals of early research was to identify norms of development, as a standard for measuring children's developmental progress.

The new scientific approach to childhood was established against a background of social changes, in which the new knowledge and techniques could be applied to practical social issues.

Theories about emotional development and the effects of deprivation illustrate the links between scientific research and theory, and cultural discourses about children's needs for specific kinds of care. Cross-cultural studies provide a broader perspective of these issues.

---

4 Stages of development

For the rest of the chapter we will be concentrating on children's intellectual development, including their understanding of their social world. Probably the most influential developmental theory in this area was constructed by Jean Piaget (1896–1980).

Figure 9   Piaget observing a child

Piaget first became interested in children's thinking abilities when he was working with Binet in Paris, constructing the earliest intelligence tests. He wanted to explain why young children of a certain age tended to make the same kinds of error on simple reasoning tasks, and what led them to make correct judgements a year or so later. He began to study these questions at the Institut Jean-Jacques Rousseau in Paris, but spent most of his long career at the university in Geneva. The connection with Rousseau is no coincidence. Piaget's theory of universal stages in children's development is the most powerful elaboration of Rousseau's basic idea that children's distinctive ways of thinking and behaving reflect their progression through natural phases of development.

Activity 3   Piaget's account of development

Allow about 25 minutes

Jean Piaget was an influential developmental theorist. For one of his early experiments he watched groups of boys playing marbles. He noticed that at different ages they approached the game in different ways. The youngest child did not seem to follow any rules at all. But older boys started playing according to the rules of the game and had arguments when rules were disputed or not followed. Some boys devised new rules and new games. From observations like this, Piaget built up a theory of how children's thinking capacities develop. He claimed that children's cognitive development passed through a sequence of stages that can be summarised as:

Sensori-motor: 0–2 years

Pre-operational: 2–6 years

Concrete operational: 6–12 years

Formal operational: 12 years and older

Think about these stages in relation to children you have contact with and your own memories of development. Then answer the following questions:

- How do you respond to these stages as a model for development?
- How have Piaget's theories had an impact upon the way children are organised and treated?

Comment

You may be in general agreement with the stages drawn up by Piaget. They correspond to a generally held view that younger children understand less than older children, and that children become more competent as they get older.

Piaget's stages have a certain familiarity as they have passed into mainstream thinking in minority-world societies through social policies and practices such as paediatric care, education and health visiting. His ideas have had an enduring impact on the way children are schooled, as many pedagogic practices are based on ideas of the child as developing cognitively with age.

Generations of undergraduate students replicated many of Piaget's 'classic' experiments, and generations of children have as a result been classified as either 'pre-operational' or 'concrete operational' thinkers. During the 1960s and 1970s these experiments also circumnavigated the globe, as cross-cultural psychologists enquired as to whether all the world's children pass through the same stages. Dasen (1974) constructed a graph comparing children in 26 communities in terms of the percentage of children who had attained the stage called 'concrete operational reasoning'. While he found some evidence for universal stages, children in communities exposed to modern 'European style' schooling tended to reach these stages earlier than other children.

4.1   Piaget's influence

Piaget's image of children as active learners engaging with the world
through play and exploration, and progressing through a series of stages
towards mature adult understanding, has been enormously influential,
especially because it connected with powerful discourses in minority-
world societies about what childhood is about and how children should
be treated (Walkerdine, 1984). Piaget's stage theory could be used as a
basis for judging children's capacities for understanding and taking
respsonsibilities for their actions. For example:

> The child, the boy, the man, indeed, should know no other
> endeavour but to be at every stage of development wholly what
> this stage calls for. Then will each successive stage spring like a
> new shoot from a healthy bud; and, at each successive stage, he
> will with the same endeavour again accomplish the requirements of
> this stage: for only the adequate development of man at each
> preceding stage can effect and bring about adequate development
> at each succeeding later stage.
>
> (Froebel, 1887, quoted in Bruce et al., 1995, p. 16)

This was written by the German originator of the kindergarten
movement, Friedrich Froebel, in 1887. So, the image of the child as an
active learner progressing through stages didn't originate with Piaget.
What Piaget's theory did was to offer scientific endorsement for
progressive, child-centred education. The following extract is taken from
an influential official report on British primary education published
during the 1960s (known as the 'Plowden Report'), which drew
explicitly on child development research, including Piaget's theory:

> At the heart of the educational process lies the child. No advances
> in policy, no acquisitions of new equipment have their desired
> effect unless they are in harmony with the nature of the child,
> unless they are fundamentally acceptable to him. We know a little
> about what happened to the child who is deprived of the stimuli
> of pictures, books and spoken words; we know much less about
> what happens to a child who is exposed to stimuli which are
> perceptually, intellectually or emotionally inappropriate to his age,
> his state of development, or the sort of individual he is. We are
> still far from knowing how best to identify in an individual child

the first flicker of a new intellectual or emotional awareness, the first readiness to embrace new sets of concepts or to enter into new relations.

(Central Advisory Council for Education, 1967, paragraph 9)

Note the way the authors draw on ideas about children's nature, and stages of development in terms of children's readiness for learning. Note, too, that the emphasis is on the individual child's development and learning, with no explicit mention of the role of teaching. This example is from the late 1960s, but the impact of stage theory remains powerful to this day, and is widely taken up as a scientific basis for prescribing children's needs. For example, the major US professional organisation for early childhood education (the National Association for the Education of Young Children, or NAEYC) prepared an important curriculum document on what they called 'Developmentally Appropriate Practice', based explicitly on child development research. It was, in part, a response to the political pressure on early years teachers to introduce more formal teaching of academic skills (Bredekamp, 1987).

Piaget's stage theory is by no means the 'last word' on how children learn to think and how they should be educated. I will conclude this section by showing how some enterprising variations on Piaget's classic experiments led some developmental researchers to challenge some aspects of stage theory and then, in Section 5, I will introduce a rather different theoretical framework for studying the child in development, within which social and cultural processes, including teaching, have a more significant role.

4.2   Critical experiments

The following activity encourages you to think about the limitations of Piaget's theories. While they have been enormously influential in understanding how children develop, subsequent studies have questioned the ideas of children passing through stages that define their cognitive abilitiy. Further studies have questioned the universalism of Piaget's approach.

Activity 4   Two experiments

Allow about 30 minutes

Now study the two experiments described below. They were first carried out with children in the UK during the 1970s, and were amongst the first to raise questions about Piaget's theory.

Experiment 1 is a variation on the classic 'conservation of liquids' experiment – which was one of the indicators of whether children had reached the operational stage of thinking. This new version of the experiment altered the way the task was presented and the results were rather different. Children were more likely to make the 'correct' judgement from a younger age, suggesting they were capable of operational thinking much earlier than predicted by Piaget.

Experiment 2 is a variation on the 'three mountains task'. Once again, the problem introduced to the child is similar to Piaget's experiment, but it is presented in a different way. And, once again, researchers found that much younger children showed capacities for perspective taking than in Piaget's experiments.

For both experiments, think about what might account for the difference in children's ability to make the correct judgements. Pay particular attention to the materials used, and how the problem is posed by the experimenter. If the same children are capable of reasoning correctly in some situations but not in others, what is the implication for the idea of stages of development?

Making sense of experimental tasks

Experiment 1: 'The chipped beaker'

Two children were shown two beakers (A and B) filled to the same level (as in Piaget's experiment). In this version pasta shells were used rather than water. The children were asked whether the beakers had the same amount as a preliminary to a game they were going to play with the shells, where it was important for each child to start with the same amount (i.e. so that the game was fair).

When the children judged the quantities to be the same, the experimenter handed them each a beaker in turn, but suddenly 'noticed' one of the beakers was chipped to a sharp edge, then 'found' another container (C) into which they poured the contents of the chipped beaker. ...

The experimenter then asked the standard question: is there more in the new beaker than in the other beaker, or less, or the same amount?

(Light, 1986)

Figure 10 The task

Experiment 2: Hiding from policemen

Two intersecting 'walls' were constructed on a board, to form a cross, as in Figure [11]. Dolls representing a 'policeman' and a 'little boy' were used as props. With the policeman at the position shown in the Figure [11], the 'little boy' was placed in section A and the child asked: 'Can the policeman see the little boy?' The question was then repeated with the little boy placed in position B, C and D. Next, the policeman was placed in a new position, and the child was asked to place the little boy where the policeman couldn't see him. Finally, the task was made more complex, with two policemen positioned at different points, and the child asked to hide the little boy from both policemen. This final task required the child to coordinate two different points of view.

(Hughes, cited in Donaldson, 1978, pp. 20–2)

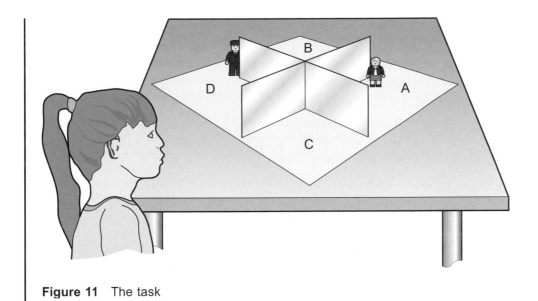

Figure 11   The task

Comment

These different results drew attention to questions about how children make sense of the tasks set by adults, especially through the way they are presented and the language that is used. Children seem to understand the task in a different way when it is presented as about chipped beakers or about little boys and policemen, because it makes greater 'human sense' to them in relation to everyday experiences, familiar story themes and games (Donaldson, 1978). So, in the context of making a game fair, replacing a chipped beaker in Experiment 1 doesn't alter children's view on whether quantities are the same. In Experiment 2, while most children don't have direct experience of being chased by policeman, this kind of situation is one they recognise, and draw into in their play.

These examples illustrate the way results of well-designed experiments can lead researchers to abandon (or at least modify) a well-established theory. They offered a challenge to any attempt to link ages to stages in a rigid way, since children's reasoning abilities apparently varied according to the way the task was presented and the way it was understood. More broadly, these studies illustrated the dangers of representing child development as a generalised progression through stages, as if 'the developing child' is an isolable unit that can be studied in a vacuum.

Summary of Section 4

Piaget's influential account of stages in intellectual development links to progressive traditions of theory and practice in education.

A comparison between Piaget's classic investigations into children's thinking and more recent experiments highlights how 'human sense' alters children's apparent competence.

These experimental studies illustrate scientific methods of hypothesis testing, and show how empirical research can challenge dominant theories.

5 Development in context

Think about the following question: If we want to study child development, what should we study? This may seem an odd question at first. The answer seems obvious – we should study a child, or children in general. So, in order to understand physical development, measurements can be taken of children's growth at various ages. For motor development, milestones can be recorded from sitting, to crawling, to walking. For mental development we study children's abilities to solve problems at various ages, like Piaget did to arrive at his account of the stages of development. The problem is that measuring developmental milestones stripped of context constructs an image of development as happening within a child. We turn now to a very different view, in which development is seen as something that happens between a child and others, in specific social and cultural settings. This view is especially linked to Lev Vygotsky, a Russian psychologist and contemporary of Jean Piaget (they were both born in 1896). Vygotsky challenged the idea that development is a universal, natural process. He described child studies of this kind as a search for the 'eternal child'. He proposed that child psychologists should instead study the 'historical child', arguing that any particular child's development – their social relationships, sense of self, ways of thinking, etc. – is embedded in the social and cultural contexts of their lives at a particular point in history.

One implication of Vygotsky's view is that features of child development (including the modern, minority-world childhoods that are often taken as a standard for all) are understood as a product of specific economic, social and cultural contexts. For example, the idea that children do not work is specific to minority-world experience, yet work is a major influence in the lives of most of the world's children. An ideal of childhood is constructed as a time of dependency, play and learning, carried out mainly at home and school. By contrast, a cultural approach emphasises the ways in which children's development is constructed within particular settings and communities, and is more cautious about assuming that commonly found patterns of development are necessarily universal. On this view, there is nothing fundamentally 'natural' about children's care and learning, either at home or within a school setting. The environments children inhabit, and the ways in which they are treated, are shaped by generations of human activity and creativity, mediated by complex belief systems, including about the 'proper' way for children to develop and learn. The cross-cultural contrasts highlighted in LeVine et al. (1994) illustrate the point (see case study at the end of Section 3), as does the way advice on child-rearing practices has changed over the past century, even within minority-world societies (Hardyment, 1984).

5.1   Naturally social

Some researchers take the argument a step further, claiming that one of the few universal features of human development is children's orientation to engage in social relationships, cultural activity, communication and meaning making, in all its diversity. According to this view, the most significant features of any child's environment are the humans with whom they establish close relationships, learn to communicate, seek guidance, and from whom they receive instruction and training. The baby becomes connected psychologically, not least through the processes of attachment discussed in Section 3.3. Babies also become more – not less – psychologically interconnected as they grow and learn in the context of social relationships. They learn with others and they learn through others – parents, brothers and sisters, friends, grandparents, teachers, and so on. Through these close relationships children's experiences are structured and given meaning. By learning to communicate, especially through language, children gain access to shared knowledge and cultural understanding. In this way, mental development is closely tied to social and emotional development. It is not primarily an individualised process (as charts showing stages of development tend to emphasise); it is a social and a cultural process. Vygotsky placed great emphasis on the idea that psychological development is not something that happens *within* the child. Development of human skills, knowledge and beliefs during childhood takes place through relationships between the child and others able to guide, communicate and scaffold their learning.

Studies of early infancy suggest that human babies may be 'pre-adapted' to engage in these early communicative relationships:

> Watching and listening to infants and toddlers, I have come to the view that being part of culture is a need human beings are born with – culture, whatever its contents, is a natural function. The essential motivation is one that strives to comprehend the world by sharing experiences and purposes with other minds …

> (Trevarthen, 1998a, p. 87)

Figure 12 Face-to-face conversation between parent and baby

Very soon after a baby is born, it is common for parents to feel that their newborn already recognises them and that they are able to communicate with each other, many months before the first words are uttered. Related to this, many carers discuss the thoughts and emotions of their baby when interacting with them, a feature sometimes called 'mind-mindedness' (Meins et al., 2011). Research with very small babies provides some clues as to why parents may start to feel this way. A newborn baby's vision is still immature in lots of ways, but in one respect babies are quite discriminating – they prefer looking at other human faces. For example, experimental studies have demonstrated that newborns try to track a picture of a human face when it is moved, but they are much less interested in other equally complex patterns (Johnson and Morton, 1991; Pascalis and Kelly, 2009). Very soon, they begin to discriminate between faces, showing preferences for their mother or other main caregiver. The fact that babies show a special interest in the human face from birth isn't just the starting point for establishing relationships. Reading faces becomes one of the basic tools through which babies learn about other aspects of their social world, especially as their attention gradually begins to incorporate the world of objects as well as people:

> What happens when you show a baby something new, something a little strange, maybe wonderful, maybe dangerous—say a walking toy robot? The baby looks over at Mom quizzically and checks her out. What does she think? Is there a reassuring smile or an expression of shocked horror? One-year-olds will modify their own reactions accordingly. If there's a smile, they'll crawl forward to investigate; if there's horror, they'll stop dead in their tracks.
>
> (Gopnik et al., 2001, p. 33)

While this US baby was learning how to react to toy robots, other babies in other settings might have used similar techniques to learn about what is fun and what is dangerous in their environment. At the same time as babies are monitoring facial expressions, they also listen for cues in the sounds they hear, about how to react to people and events in their lives. For example, the tone of voice adopted by a parent is sufficient signal as to whether the four-legged furry creature coming towards them is friendly or frightening. Just as for vision, babies seem especially oriented to listen to the sound of the human voice from birth. Even when they are only a few days old, they already show preferences for their mother's voice compared with a female stranger's voice (DeCasper and Fifer, 1980; Belin and Grosbras, 2010).

These are just a few examples of ways that babies are actively oriented to making sense of their social environment and learn from watching others. From studies like these, Trevarthen goes a step further, arguing that human babies are born with a capacity for 'inter-subjectivity' which is the foundation for many distinctively human qualities: social sensitivity, empathy, imaginative play, communication, conversation, teaching and learning (Trevarthen, 1998b). Or, as Gopnik et al. put it:

> For human beings, nurture *is* our nature. The capacity for culture is part of our biology, and the drive to learn is our most important and central instinct ... our unique evolutionary trick, our central adaptation, our greatest weapon in the struggle for survival, is precisely our dazzling ability to learn when we are babies and to teach when we are grown-ups.
>
> (Gopnik et al., 2001, p. 8)

5.2 Understanding children

As further evidence for young children's skills in relating to others, I turn finally to a well-known study by Judy Dunn. Reading B is an edited version of a chapter in which Dunn summarises a series of studies carried out on the development of social understanding in very young children, aged two to three years old.

This study belongs to the continuing tradition of detailed child observation illustrated by Reading A, written more than a century earlier. Towards the end of Reading A, Darwin comments on the early development of 'moral sense'. As evidence, he refers to several incidents between two-year-old Doddy, his sister and his father: Doddy pretends to be angry; Doddy praises his own generosity, echoing the words a parent might use; Doddy is sensitive to what he believes is ridicule; and Doddy tries to deceive his father over the sugar. Indicators of very young children's capacities for social and moral understanding were also the starting point for Dunn's study. She also uses careful narrative records as evidence for children's capacities at various ages, and towards the end of the article she explores some of the processes that drive their developing understanding.

Observation is a strong tradition of developmental research, but so is experimentation using specially designed tasks like those used by Piaget and his successors (e.g. as in the experiments examined in Activity 4). From her observational work, Dunn became aware of a discrepancy with the findings of experimental studies on the same topics. Piaget's work has been extended in important new directions by subsequent researchers, using what is termed the 'false-belief' paradigm. Dolls and toys are used as props in telling stories like the following (based on Wimmer and Perner, 1983).

Sally and Anne are playing together. Sally puts a marble in her basket and then leaves the room. While Sally is outside, Anne takes the marble out of the basket and hides it in a box. Sally comes back into the room and looks for her marble. Where will she look for it?

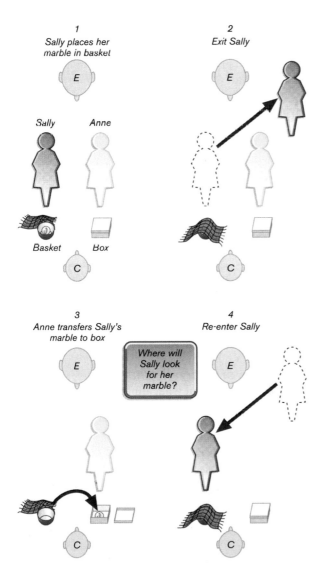

Figure 13   Experimental studies have extended Piaget's work (E = Experimenter, C = Child)

Wimmer and Perner (1983) found three year olds consistently expected that Sally would look for the marble in the box – where the children themselves knew it had been put. From the age of four, children began to be able to make a judgement based on Sally's perspective – her (false) belief that she would find the marble in the basket. These experiments seemed to confirm the children's stage-like progression from naivety about everyday social situations towards reasoned understanding and sound judgement. However, there are disputes about these conclusions. The findings from experimental studies of false-belief have been challenged, much as Piaget's experiments were challenged, because they fail to take account of personal meaning and context, with it being proposed that even young infants have some form of understanding of others minds (e.g. Reddy, 2007).

Activity 5   Reading B

Allow about 35–45 minutes

Now study Reading B by Judy Dunn, 'Young children's understanding of other people'. Dunn begins by reviewing the evidence of babies' sensitivity to other people, extending the discussion above. She summarises four aspects of two and three year olds' day-to-day encounters, and then draws some conclusions about the influences on their development.

As you read, make notes on Dunn's evidence for the following:

- Very young children have a practical understanding of other people's feelings and intentions, indicated by knowing what teases their sibling, by selectively appealing to mother for help according to who had initiated the dispute; and by distinguishing an intentional from an accidental act.

- During their third year, children became skilled contributors to shared play with their siblings, adapting their play to their partner's intentions, and adopting a repertoire of 'pretend' roles.

- They display growing curiosity about other people's feelings and social rules, as expressed through their use of questions.

- They are already learning to make jokes, including differentiating between siblings and parents in terms of which kinds of joke they will react to.

- Children seemed to become most sophistaed in using reason in support of their self-interest and rights.

- Children's understanding about other people's feelings and intentions appears to be enhanced where their families engage in discussion about these themes.

Comment

Like previous generations of developmental psychologists, Dunn uses observation as a key method for studying children. However, she shifts the focus of the research gaze from testing in laboratory conditions to observing daily life. She finds that young children have capacities that extend beyond what is normally expected of them by developmental models. Very young children interact with other family members in ways that reveal high levels of understanding, reason and empathy.

In short, by observing children in familiar settings – in everyday interactions with siblings and parents – Dunn sees much stronger evidence of their practical understanding of other people's point of view, than is suggested by tests that require children to make a judgement about a hypothetical, story situation. Her research emphasises children's active engagement in making sense of their social world. They are active participants in the cultural practices that structure and shape their childhood:

> By 36 months of age, the children 'managed' their family lives very effectively: they anticipated and manipulated the reactions of others, 'read' their emotions, used others to reach their own ends, and influenced the feeling states of others intentionally and practically by teasing, comforting, and joking. They questioned and disputed the application of social rules to themselves and others and they successfully redirected blame onto others.
>
> (Dunn, 1988, p. 114)

Dunn's study is based on close observation of children's engagement with everyday cultural life in specific domestic settings within the UK and the USA. As Dunn herself acknowledges, children's experience of early social interaction – play, talk, jokes, disputes and teasing – may be quite different within other settings or cultural contexts. The assumption of much developmental research is that children are seen as individuals, dependent during infancy, but gradually growing towards autonomy. In this respect researchers may share the same cultural assumptions about children's development as the families they research. Anthropologists have long pointed out that this is a dangerous assumption to make:

> The Western conception of the person as a bounded, unique, more or less integrated motivational and cognitive universe, a dynamic center of awareness, emotion, judgment, and action organized into a distinctive whole and set contrastively both against other such wholes and against a social and natural background is, however incorrigible it may seem to us, a rather peculiar idea within the context of the world's cultures.
>
> (Geertz, 1975, p. 48)

For example, the rich field data in Dunn's study have been collected in settings where it is accepted that very young children have strong feelings. Their vocal assertion of their wishes is tolerated, or even encouraged, in a cultural context which recognises these outbursts as an important feature of becoming a separated identity. In many English-speaking countries, children who are beginning to assert their sense of self are described as the 'terrible-twos'. But cross-cultural studies suggests it may be wrong to assume these experiences of child development are natural, normal and universal:

> the classic account of the toddler's drive for autonomy and separateness … appears incorrect as a thematic description of toddler development in many non-Western cultural communities … For example, in Zinacantan, Mexico … the transition from infancy to early childhood is not typified by resistant toddlers demanding and asserting control over toileting and other self-help skills (the familiar 'No! *I* can do it!'), but instead by watchful, imitative children who acquire toilet training and other elements of self-care with a minimum of fuss.
>
> (Edwards, 1995, p. 47)

Finally, the image of the developing child conveyed by Dunn's account is rather different from the image conveyed by conventional theories about stages in normal development. First, there is the evident precocity of children's understanding of many aspects of their social world, especially within the intimate environment of their homes. These children seem to have quite a strong practical 'moral sense' even by the age of three, when they would still be very immature in terms of more formal tests on these themes. Secondly, the children in Dunn's study appear very 'worldly' by the age of three. They are close observers of the day-to-day events around them, and keen to understand what is going on. They are already learning how to tease and upset their siblings, engage in 'word play on forbidden topics' and negotiate their self-interest. These social skills also coincide with children's developing sense of empathy. Young children can be highly sensitive to expressions of pleasure and pain in others and they are capable of quite touching expressions of sympathy towards a parent who feels unwell or upset.

This line of research raises intriguing questions about how young children are thought about and understood. Are they best seen as dependent innocents in need of protection, or as assertive individuals, interested and engaged in their social world?

Summary of Section 5

Lev Vygotsky represents a different tradition of developmental research, drawing attention to the ways in which childhood is a social and cultural process.

Research into early infancy suggests human babies are pre-adapted to social interaction and cultural learning.

In Judy Dunn's research, very young children appear highly socially competent in everyday situations at home, raising questions concerning cultural beliefs about young children's innocence.

---

6 Conclusion

We've come a long way from the story of the 'Wild Boy of Aveyron', which captured the imagination of the French public in the winter of 1799. During the intervening two centuries the idea that childhood is a period of development that can be studied systematically has become increasingly significant, both as an end in itself (in research and teaching about child development) as well as feeding into the design of systems of childcare and education. This concluding section draws together some of the main themes of earlier sections, by asking how the study of child development constructs its subject – the child.

In the opening sections of the chapter, I explained that early scientific studies of childhood concentrated on identifying normal patterns of children's physical, emotional and cognitive development, as well as variations from the norm. I have drawn attention to the risks that attach to these normative accounts of developmental processes, especially in so far as they construct an image of a universal child, even though it is mainly based on minority-world cultural contexts and expectations for childhood. At the core of much developmental theorising is the idea that childhood is an extended period, during which all children progress through a series of stages from immaturity to maturity, which tends to overlook respects in which routes to maturity, as well as maturity itself, are culturally defined. Positioning children on a developmental trajectory related to their age is seen as a distinctive feature of modern societies. From a social constructionist perspective, developmentalism is a discourse within which children are constructed as 'not yet adults', as in a 'process of becoming', rather than persons in their own right (Burman, 1994; James et al., 1998). They are a set of potentials, a project in the making (Verhellen, 1997).

So developmental theories can be seen as a powerful discourse (or discourses) on childhood. But developmental research also claims status as a field of scientific enquiry. I have tried to show what this means in practice, by illustrating a range of research traditions, including examples where a new experiment or set of careful observations can serve to challenge a powerful theory or paradigm. In the final section especially, I contrasted Piagetian approaches that convey an image of the individual child progressively constructing mature capacities for reasoning and thinking, with Vygotskian theory which emphasises child development as a social, interactive and cultural process. For me, the lesson of social constructionism is not to abandon empirical research and theory building, but to be aware of the various ways theories, research methods and findings construct the child in development (as also argued in Chapter 1).

This leads to the final point about the status of the child in research and theory. I have tried to convey a sense of the challenges of studying child development within a scientific framework, especially how the child is understood as a growing human organism, as a social actor and as a subject for research.

The cartoon in Figure 14 illustrates one of the most basic dilemmas. Compare it with the cartoon at the beginning of the chapter (Figure 1). These cartoons sum up some features of two very different ways to approach developmental research. The first represents a strictly positivist approach: the parent/scientist studies the child's learning much as a chemist might record what happens to chemicals in a test tube, or a zoologist might observe animal behaviour. It may remind you of the objective methods of observation and experimentation, symbolised by Gesell's observation dome (Figure 3). In the second, the scientist is also making a systematic study of the child. What he may not have observed is that the child is equally intent on making his own study of the scientist – and will probably react to the situation according to his understanding of what is going on. The second cartoon is a reminder that the child is not a passive object of research. Researching children's development is not like carrying out a chemistry experiment, because a human relationship is involved: researcher and child are both accessing cultural knowledge to make sense of what is going on. They are also relying on cultural communicative practices, notably language, to share their understanding. Each, in their own way, is a participant in the process of human meaning making (Woodhead and Faulkner, 2000). Asking about the status of children as participants in research is part of a much broader question about their status in society – how far they are viewed as immature and dependent or as citizens with rights. These questions are the subject of the next chapter.

Figure 14   The researcher and the researched

References

Barnes, P. (1995) 'Growth and change in adolescence', in Barnes, P. (ed) *Personal, Social and Emotional Development of Children*, Oxford, Blackwell.

Beekman, D. (1977) *The Mechanical Baby: A Popular History of the Theory and Practice of Child Raising*, New York, New American Library.

Belin, P. and Grosbras, M. H. (2010) 'The developmental origins of voice processing in the human brain', *Neuron*, vol. 65, no. 6, pp. 852–8.

Blanchet, T. (1996) *Lost Innocence, Stolen Childhoods*, Dhaka, University Press.

Bowlby, J. (1967 [1951]) *Maternal Care and Mental Health*, New York, Schoken.

Boyden, J. (1997) 'Childhood and the policy makers: a comparative perspective on the globalization of childhood', in James, A. and Prout, A. (eds) *Constructing and Reconstructing Childhood*, 2nd edn, London, Falmer Press.

Bredekamp, S. (ed) (1987) *Developmentally Appropriate Practice in Early Childhood Programs Serving Children from Birth through Age 8*, Washington, DC, National Association for the Education of Young Children.

Bruce, T., Findlay, A., Read, J. and Scarborough, M. (1995) *Recurring Themes in Education*, London, Paul Chapman.

Burman, E. (1994) *Deconstructing Developmental Psychology*, London, Routledge.

Central Advisory Council for Education (1967) *Children and Their Primary Schools* (Volume 1), London, HMSO.

Chisholm, J. S. (1996) 'Learning "respect for everything": Navajo images of development', in Hwang, C. P., Lamb, M. E. and Sigel, I. E. (eds) *Images of Childhood*, Mahwah, NJ, Lawrence Erlbaum.

Darwin, C. (1859) *On the Origin of Species by Means of Natural Selection*, London, John Murray.

Dasen, P. (1974) in Berry, J. W. and Dasen, P. R. (eds) *Culture and Cognition*, London, Methuen.

Das Gupta, P. (1994) 'Images of childhood and theories of development', in Oates, J. (ed) *The Foundations of Child Development*, Oxford, Blackwell.

DeCasper, A. J. and Fifer, W. P. (1980) 'Of human bonding: newborns prefer their mother's voices', *Science*, vol. 208, no. 4448, pp. 1174–6.

Donaldson, M. (1978) *Children's Minds*, London, Fontana.

Dunn, J. (1988) *The Beginnings of Social Understanding*, Oxford, Blackwell.

Edwards, C. P. (1995) 'Parenting toddlers', in Bornstein, M. H. (ed) *Handbook of Parenting*, Mahwah, NJ, Lawrence Erlbaum.

Geertz, C. (1975) 'From the native's point of view: on the nature of anthropological understanding', *American Scientist*, vol. 63, pp. 47–53.

Gesell, A. (1925) *The Mental Growth of the Preschool Child: A Psychological Outline of Normal Development from Birth to the Sixth Year, Including a System of Developmental Diagnosis*, New York, Macmillan.

Gopnik, A., Meltzoff, A. and Kuhl, P. (2001) *How Babies Think*, London, Phoenix.

Hardyment, C. (1984) *Dream Babies: Child Care from Locke to Spock*, Oxford, Oxford University Press.

Hendrick, H. (1997) *Children, Childhood and English Society, 1880–1990*, Cambridge, Cambridge University Press.

Itard, J. M. (1962 [1801]) *The Wild Boy of Aveyron (L'enfant Sauvage)*, Englewood Cliffs, NJ, Prentice-Hall.

James, A., Jenks, C. and Prout, A. (1998) *Theorizing Childhood*, Cambridge, Polity Press.

Johnson, M. H. and Morton, J. (1991) *Biology and Cognitive Development: The Case of Face Recognition*, Oxford, Blackwell.

LeVine, R. A., LeVine, S., Liedermann, P. H., Brazelton, T. B., Dixon, S., Richman, A. and Keffer, C. H. (1994) *Child Care and Culture: Lessons from Africa*, Cambridge, Cambridge University Press.

Lewis, M. and Brooks-Gunn, J. (1979) *Social Cognition and the Acquisition of Self*, New York, Plenum.

Liddiard, M. (1923) *The Mothercraft Manual*, London, Churchill.

Light, P. (1986) 'Context, conservation and conversation', in Richards, M. and Light, P. (eds) *Children of Social Worlds*, Cambridge, Polity Press.

Lorenz, K. Z. (1981) *The Foundations of Ethology*, New York, Springer-Verlag.

Meins, E., Ferneyhough, C., Arnott, B., Turner, M. and Leeckam, S. (2011) 'Mother- versus infant-centered correlates of maternal mind-mindedness in the first year of life', *Infancy*, vol. 16, no. 2, pp. 137–65.

Morrow, V. (2003) 'Moving out of childhood', in Maybin, J. and Woodhead, M. (eds) *Childhood in Context*, Chichester, John Wiley/Milton Keynes, The Open University.

Newson, J. and Newson, E. (1974) 'Cultural aspects of childrearing in the English-speaking world', in Richards, M. P. M. (ed) *The Integration of a Child into a Social World*, Cambridge, Cambridge University Press.

Pascalis, O. and Kelly, D. (2009) 'The origins of face processing in humans: phylogeny and ontogeny', *Perspectives on Psychological Science*, vol. 4, no. 2, pp. 200–9.

Reddy, V. (2007) 'Getting back to the rough ground: deception and "social living"', *Philosophical Transactions of the Royal Society of London B*, vol. 362, pp. 621–37.

Schaffer, H. R. (1996) *Social Development*, Oxford, Blackwell.

Shaffer, D. R. (1993) *Developmental Psychology*, 3rd edn, Pacific Grove, CA, Brooks/Cole.

Singer, E. (1992) *Childcare and the Psychology of Development*, London, Routledge.

Smith, P. K., Cowie, H. and Blades, M. (2011) *Understanding Children's Development*, 5th edn, Chichester, Wiley.

Sroufe, A. L., Cooper, R. G., DeHart, G. B. and Marshall, M. E. (1996) *Child Development: Its Nature and Course*, New York, McGraw-Hill.

Tizard, B. (1991) 'Working mothers and the care of young children', in Phoenix, A. and Woollett, A. (eds) *Social Construction of Motherhood*, London, Sage.

Trevarthen, C. (1998a) 'The child's need to learn a culture', in Woodhead, M., Faulkner, D. and Littleton, K. (eds) *Cultural Worlds of Early Childhood*, London, Routledge.

Trevarthen, C. (1998b) 'The concept and foundations of infant intersubjectivity', in Bråten, S. (ed) *Intersubjective Communication and Emotion in Early Ontogeny*, Cambridge, Cambridge University Press.

Verhellen, E. (1997) *Convention on the Rights of the Child*, Leuven, Garant Publishers.

Walkerdine, V. (1984) 'Developmental psychology and the child-centred pedagogy: the insertion of Piaget into primary school practice', in Henriques, J., Holloway, W., Urwin, C., Venn, C. and Walkerdine, V. (eds) *Changing the Subject*, London, Methuen.

Weisner, T. and Gallimore, R. (1977) 'My brother's keeper: child and sibling caretaking', *Current Anthropology*, vol. 18, no. 2, pp. 169–90.

Wimmer, H. and Perner, J. (1983) 'Beliefs about beliefs: representation and constraining function of wrong beliefs in young children's understanding of deception', *Cognition*, vol. 13, pp. 103–28.

Woodhead, M. (1997) 'Psychology and the cultural construction of children's needs', in James, A. and Prout, A. (eds) *Constructing and Reconstructing Childhood*, 2nd edn, London, Falmer.

Woodhead, M. (1999) 'Reconstructing developmental psychology: some first steps', *Children and Society*, vol. 13, no. 1, pp. 3–19.

Woodhead, M. and Faulkner, D. (2000) 'Subjects, objects or participants? Dilemmas of psychological research with children', in Christensen, P. and James, A. (eds) *Research with Children: Perspectives and Practices*, London, Falmer.

Reading A
A biographical sketch of an infant

Charles Darwin

Source: 'A biographical sketch of an infant', 1877, *Mind*, 2, pp. 286–94.

During the first seven days various reflex actions, namely sneezing, [hiccupping], yawning, stretching and of course sucking and screaming, were well performed by my infant. On the seventh day, I touched the naked sole of his foot with a bit of paper, and he jerked it away, curling at the same time his toes, like a much older child when tickled. The perfection of these reflex movements shows that the extreme imperfection of the voluntary ones is not due to the state of the muscles or of the co-ordinating centres, but to that of the seat of the will. At this time, though so early, it seemed clear to me that a warm soft hand applied to his face excited a wish to suck. This must be considered as a reflex or an instinctive action, for it is impossible to believe that experience and association with the touch of his mother's breast could so soon have come into play. ...

With respect to vision,—his eyes were fixed on a candle as early as the 9th day, and up to the 45th day nothing else seemed thus to fix them; but on the 49th day his attention was attracted by a bright-coloured tassel, as was shown by his eyes becoming fixed and the movements of his arms ceasing. It was surprising how slowly he acquired the power of following with his eyes an object if swinging at all rapidly; for he could not do this well when seven and a half months old. At the age of 32 days he perceived his mother's bosom when three or four inches from it, as was shown by the protrusion of his lips and his eyes becoming fixed; but I much doubted whether this had any connection with vision; he certainly had not touched the bosom. Whether he was guided through smell or the sensation of warmth or through association with the position in which he was held, I do not at all know.

The movements of his limbs and body were for a long time vague and purposeless, and usually performed in a jerking manner; but there was one exception to this rule, namely that from a very early period, certainly long before he was 40 days old, he could move his hands to his own mouth. ...

When between 80 and 90 days old, he drew all sorts of objects into his mouth, and in two or three weeks' time could do this with some skill; but he often first touched his nose with the object and then dragged it down into his mouth. After grasping my finger and drawing it to his mouth, his own hand prevented him from sucking it; but on the 114th day, after acting in this manner, he slipped his own hand down so that he could get the end of my finger into his mouth. This action was repeated several times, and evidently was not a chance but a rational one. ...

Anger. It was difficult to decide at how early an age anger was felt; on his eighth day he frowned and wrinkled the skin round his eyes before a crying fit, but this may have been due to pain or distress, and not to anger. When about ten weeks old, he was given some rather cold milk and he kept a slight frown on his forehead all the time that he was sucking, so that he looked like a grown-up person made cross from being compelled to do something which he did not like. When nearly four months old, and perhaps much earlier, there could be no doubt, from the manner in which the blood gushed into his whole face and scalp, that he easily got into a violent passion. A small cause sufficed; thus, when a little over seven months old, he screamed with rage because a lemon slipped away and he could not seize it with his hands. When eleven months old, if a wrong plaything was given him, he would push it away and beat it; I presume that the beating was an instinctive sign of anger, like the snapping of the jaws by a young crocodile just out of the egg, and not that he imagined he could hurt the plaything. When two years and three months old, he became a great adept at throwing books or sticks &c., at anyone who offended him; and so it was with some of my other sons. On the other hand, I could never see a trace of such aptitude in my infant daughters; and this makes me think that a tendency to throw objects is inherited by boys.

Fear. This feeling probably is one of the earliest which is experienced by infants, as shown by their starting at any sudden sound when only a few weeks old followed by crying. Before the present one was 4½ months old I had been accustomed to make close to him many strange and loud noises, which were all taken as excellent jokes, but at this period I one day made a loud snoring noise which I had never done before; he instantly looked grave and then burst out crying. Two or three days afterwards, I made through forgetfulness the same noise with the same result. About the same time (viz. on the 137th day) I approached with my back towards him and then stood motionless. He looked very grave and much surprised, and would soon have cried, had I not turned round; his face instantly relaxed into a smile. ...

Affection. This probably arose very early in life, if we may judge by his smiling at those who had charge of him when under two months old; though I had no distinct evidence of his distinguishing and recognising anyone, until he was nearly four months old. When nearly five months old, he plainly showed his wish to go to his nurse. But he did not spontaneously exhibit affection by overt acts until a little above a year old, namely, by kissing several times his nurse who had been absent for a short time. With respect to the allied feeling of sympathy, this was clearly shown at six months and 11 days by his melancholy face, with the corners of his mouth well depressed, when his nurse pretended to cry. Jealousy was plainly exhibited when I fondled a large doll, and when I weighed his infant sister, he being then 15½ months old. Seeing how strong a feeling jealousy is in dogs, it would probably be exhibited by infants at an earlier age than that just specified, if they were tried in a fitting manner.

Association of Ideas, Reason, &c. The first action which exhibited, as far as I observed, a kind of practical reasoning, has already been noticed, namely, the slipping his hand down my finger so as to get the end of it into his mouth; and this happened on the 114th day. When four and a half months old, he repeatedly smiled at my image and his own in a mirror, and no doubt mistook them for real objects; but he showed sense in being evidently surprised at my voice coming from behind him. Like all infants he much enjoyed thus looking at himself, and in less than two months perfectly understood that it was an image; for if I made quite silently any odd grimace, he would suddenly turn round to look at me. He was, however, puzzled at the age of seven months, when being out of doors he saw me on the inside of a large plate-glass window, and seemed in doubt whether or not it was an image. Another of my infants, a little girl, when exactly a year old, was not nearly so acute, and seemed quite perplexed at the image of a person in a mirror approaching her from behind. The higher apes which I tried with a small looking-glass behaved differently; they placed their hands behind the glass, and in doing so showed their sense, but far from taking pleasure in looking at themselves they got angry and would look no more. ...

Moral Sense. The first sign of moral sense was noticed at the age of nearly 13 months: I said 'Doddy (his nickname) won't give poor papa a kiss,—naughty Doddy.' These words, without doubt, made him feel slightly uncomfortable; and at last when I had returned to my chair, he protruded his lips as a sign that he was ready to kiss me; and he then shook his hand in an angry manner until I came and received his kiss. Nearly the same little scene recurred in a few days, and the reconciliation seemed to give him so much satisfaction, that several times afterwards he pretended to be angry and slapped me, and then insisted on giving me a kiss. So that here we have a touch of the dramatic art, which is so strongly pronounced in most young children. About this time it became easy to work on his feelings and make him do whatever was wanted. When 2 years and 3 months old, he gave his last bit of gingerbread to his little sister, and then cried out with high self-approbation 'Oh kind Doddy, kind Doddy.' Two months later, he became extremely sensitive to ridicule, and was so suspicious that he often thought people who were laughing and talking together were laughing at him. A little later (2 years and 7½ months old) I met him coming out of the dining room with his eyes unnaturally bright, and an odd unnatural or affected manner, so that I went into the room to see who was there, and found that he had been taking pounded sugar, which he had been told not to do. As he had never been in any way punished, his odd manner certainly was not due to fear, and I suppose it was pleasurable excitement struggling with conscience. A fortnight afterwards, I met him coming out of the same room, and he was eyeing his pinafore which he had carefully rolled up: and again his manner was so odd that I determined to see what was within his pinafore, notwithstanding that he said there was nothing and repeatedly commanded me to 'go away,' and I found it stained with pickle-juice; so that here was carefully planned deceit. As this child was educated solely by working on his good feelings, he soon became as truthful, open, and tender, as anyone could desire.

Reading B
Young children's understanding of other people

Judy Dunn

Source: 'Young children's understanding of other people: evidence from observations within the family', 1998, in Woodhead, M., Faulkner, D. and Littleton, K. (eds) *Cultural Worlds of Early Childhood*, London, Routledge, pp. 101–15.

In infancy, babies are apparently both interested in and responsive to the emotions and behavior of other people. They are born predisposed to attend to stimuli with the characteristics of the human face and voice, and they develop quickly 'remarkable abilities to perceive the actions and expressions of other people' (Spelke and Cortelyou, 1981). They learn rapidly about stimuli that change in a manner that is contingent upon their own behavior – as does the behavior of other people interacting with them. By 2 months of age, they respond differently to a person who intends to speak to them than to one who speaks to someone else (Trevarthen, 1977). By the second half of the first year, they have begun to share a common communicative framework with other family members, and, as we have learned from the elegant experimental studies of *social referencing* (Klinnert, Campos, Sorce, Emde, and Svejda, 1983), in situations of uncertainty, they monitor the emotional expressions of their mothers and change their behavior appropriately in response to those expressions. As the work of those studying early language has shown particularly clearly, their comprehension of social procedures is surprisingly subtle. Bruner, for example, has persuasively argued that children have mastered the culturally appropriate use of requests, invitations, and reference well before they are correctly using the conventional linguistic forms (Bruner, 1983). ...

The findings that I discuss (described fully in Dunn, 1988) are drawn from three longitudinal studies of secondborn children in their second and third years: six children followed at 2-month intervals through the second year, six followed similarly through their third year, and 43 families studied when the secondborn children were aged 18, 24, and 36 months. The families were middle- and working-class families living in and around Cambridge in England, and all the observations, which were unstructured, were made while the children were at home, playing, fighting, and talking with their mothers and siblings. Examples are also cited from an ongoing study of children in Pennsylvania. ...

Disputes

Within each domain that we studied – disputes, jokes, empathetic and prosocial behavior, cooperation, pretend play, and conversations about other people – we found evidence for children's growing grasp of the feelings of others, of their intended actions, and of how social rules applied to other people and to themselves. In disputes, for example, the children showed a growing sophistication in teasing – actions that demonstrated a practical grasp of what would upset or annoy a particular person. Early in the second year, acts that we categorized as teasing were pretty simple; for example, children in disputes with their older siblings often seized or removed their siblings' transitional object or most special toys, or attempted to destroy something that had special significance for the siblings. In the course of the second year, such teasing acts became more frequent and more elaborate. One 24-month-old, for instance, whose older sister had three imaginary friends called Lily, Allelujah, and Peepee, would, in the course of disputes with this sister, announce that *she* was Allelujah. It was an act that was reliably followed by anger or distress on her sister's part, and it was also an act of notable sophistication for a 24-month-old, because it involved both some grasp of what would upset her sister and a transformation of her own identity.

Our analysis of disputes between the siblings showed, too, that early in the second year the children's attempts to enlist the aid of their mothers on their own behalf differed sharply according to whether the siblings had acted in an aggressive or hostile fashion first or whether they themselves had done so. The probability that the children would appeal to their mothers was high (66%) if the sibling had been first to act in an aggressive or teasing manner. In contrast, they rarely appealed to their mother for help in incidents when they *themselves* had acted in such way: in only 4% of such incidents did they do so. Such a distinction in the children's behavior, and indeed the evasive actions that second-year children take to avoid future punishment (see Dunn, 1988), indicate some anticipation of the mothers' actions, although, of course, they imply no elaborate understanding of the mothers' *minds*. This grasp of how other people can be expected to behave in relation to social rules becomes strikingly evident during the third year, when children's language abilities increase. Our analysis of disputes showed, for example, that *blaming* the sibling for incidents in which the child might be in trouble, and drawing the attention of the mother to the sibling rather than the self, are both common by 36 months – demonstrating a ready anticipation of how the mother will respond to another's transgression. The children's justifications showed, then, that notions of responsibility and of blame are well in place by 36 months, and that these were used frequently by the children, revealing an effective grasp of how their mothers would react to cultural breach.

Particularly illuminating were the excuses that the children used in their attempts to avoid disapprobation. The nature of the excuses that the children used in disputes showed an increasingly elaborate grasp of how social rules applied to different people in different contexts and of how these rules could be questioned. For our present purposes, it is excuses of intent that are of special interest. In our culture, we see as crucial the distinction between acts that are intended to harm others or transgress rules of conduct and acts that have similar consequences but are accidental (Darley and Zanna, 1982). The question of when children begin to make this distinction is, however, a matter of some dispute. Piaget (1965) considered that there was 'some reason to doubt whether a child of 6–7 could really distinguish an involuntary error from an intentional lie … the distinction is, at the best, in the process of formation' (p. 145). In contrast to this view, Shultz (1980) reported observations that children as young as 3 may make such a distinction. The children in our studies made the excuse that they 'didn't mean to' rather infrequently during the observations. However, among the incidents when they did refer to intentions were some that involved children as young as 26 months:

Example 1: Child aged 26 months (Study 3)

Child climbs on Mother to investigate light switch:

M: You're hurting me!
C: Sorry. Sorry. I don't mean to.

This example could be interpreted as a 'rote-learned' strategy for getting out of trouble, rather than evidence that the child really understood the significance of his intentions for his mother. For several of the earliest examples of the references to intentions, such explanations in terms of the child having learned to repeat phrases without understanding their meaning can be offered (cf. Astington, 1991). However, the wide variety of situations and the appropriateness with which these phrases are used should be borne in mind: it should be noted that there is not one example of such a phrase being used inappropriately. The children in both the Cambridge and Pennsylvania studies very clearly understood the significance of the phrase that an act (either against them or by them) had been done *on purpose*, and they used this in their attempts to obtain comfort or help, to good effect. The following example comes from an observation of a 33-month-old girl in the Pennsylvania study, who came crying to her mother after her brother had deliberately bitten her on the forehead:

Example 2: Child aged 33 months (Pennsylvania study)

C:	Look what Philip did!
	He bited me!
	(crying)
M:	He bit you on the head?
C:	Yes.
M to Sib:	Philip is that true?
S:	No.
C to M:	Yes!
	On purpose!
M to C:	He did it on purpose?
C:	Yes!
M to Sib:	Come on over, Philip.
Sib to M:	I didn't do it on purpose Mom.
C to M:	Yes he did.

The possible significance of family discourse

The second theme that should be highlighted in any consideration of the processes that are important in the developments in understanding of others is the contribution of family discourse about others. The evidence from studies in both the United States and Britain shows that young children in our cultures grow up in a world in which there is much conversation within families about the feelings and behavior of others and about their motives, intentions and the permissibility of their actions. Messages – implicit and increasingly explicit – about such matters are conveyed to them each day in a wide variety of ways (see also Shweder, Mahapatra, and Miller, 1987). Children are participants in conversations about such matters from a very early age: they monitor, comment on, and join in such discussions between others, and they question, joke about, and argue as to the causes and consequences of the feelings and behavior of others. It appears very likely that children's differentiated understanding of other minds is influenced by such discourse. Here, the analysis of individual differences supports such a contention. Differences between families in the frequency and extent of discussion of others' feelings, motives, and behavior are striking; in our studies in Cambridge, correlations were found between such differences in the first three years of children's lives and in a variety of 'outcome' measures, such as the child's own participation in conversation about inner states (Dunn, Bretherton, and Munn, 1987), their friendly behavior towards their younger siblings (Dunn and Kendrick, 1982), and, most strikingly, their performance three to four years later on affective perspective-taking tasks (Dunn, Brown, and Beardsall, 1990).

References

Astington, J. W. (1991) 'Intention in the child's theory of mind', in Frye, D. and Moore, C. (eds) *Children's Theories of Mind: Mental States and Social Understanding*, Hillsdale, NJ, Lawrence Erlbaum Associates.

Bruner, J. (1983) *Child's Talk*, New York, Norton.

Darley, J. M. and Zanna, M. P. (1982) 'Making moral judgements', *American Scientist*, vol. 70, pp. 515–21.

Dunn, J. (1988) *The Beginnings of Social Understanding*, Cambridge, MA, Harvard University Press.

Dunn, J. and Kendrick, C. (1982) *Siblings: Love, Envy and Understanding*, Cambridge, MA, Harvard University Press.

Dunn, J., Bretherton, I. and Munn, P. (1987) 'Conversations about feeling states between mothers and their young children', *Developmental Psychology*, vol. 23, pp. 132–9.

Dunn, J., Brown, J. and Beardsall, L. (1990) 'Family talk about feeling states, and children's later understanding of others' emotions', *Developmental Psychology*, vol. 26.

Klinnert, M. D., Campos, J. J., Sorce, J. F., Emde, R. N. and Svejda, M. (1983) 'Emotions as behavior regulators: social referencing in infancy', in Plutchik, R. and Kellerman, H. (eds) *Emotion: Theory, Research and Experience* (Vol. 2), New York, Academic Press.

Piaget, J. (1965) *The Moral Judgement of the Child*, New York, Free Press.

Shultz, T. R. (1980) 'The development of the concept of intention', in Collins, A. (ed) *Minnesota Symposium on Child Psychology* (Vol. 13), Hillsdale, NJ, Lawrence Erlbaum Associates.

Shweder, R. A., Mahapatra, M. and Miller, J. G. (1987) 'Culture and moral development', in Kagan, J. and Lamb, S. (eds) *The Emergence of Moral Concepts in Young Children*, Chicago, IL, University of Chicago Press.

Spelke, E. S. and Cortelyou, A. (1981) 'Perceptual aspects of social knowing: looking and listening in infancy', in Lamb, M. E. and Sherrod, L. R. (eds) *Infant Social Cognition*, Hillsdale, NJ, Lawrence Erlbaum Associates.

Trevarthen, C. (1977) 'Descriptive analyses of infant communicative behaviour', in Schaffer, H. R. (ed) *Studies in Mother–Infant Interaction*, London, Academic Press.

Chapter 4

Childhood: an anthropological approach

Heather Montgomery

Contents

In this chapter, you will:

- learn about the various ways that anthropologists have studied children

- develop a knowledge and understanding of the contribution of some of the key theorists in the field

- consider the distinctive features of an anthropological approach, including ethnography, participant observation, cultural relativism and social constructionism

- critically evaluate the features of child-centred anthropology

- examine the links between anthropology and the other social sciences.

1 Introduction

Put very simply, social anthropology is the study of culture, especially, in the early days of the discipline, of 'other' cultures; that is, those outside the minority world. Although this description is no longer accurate because many anthropologists now work all over the world, including at 'home', it remains the case that anthropologists are interested in the social relationships of human beings. They are interested in culture: in family structures, religion, political and economic life, and in how societies 'work'. The term 'culture' is a much contested and defined one, but this chapter uses the definition given by literary critic Terry Eagleton:

> Culture can be loosely summarized as the complex of values, customs, beliefs and practices which constitute the way of life of a specific group.
>
> (Eagleton, 2000, p. 34)

The important point here is that the word does not simply refer to 'high culture', such as fine art or literature, but to a complete way of life. Although the popular image of an anthropologist is of a white man in a pith helmet discovering previously unknown tribes, anthropologists today are just as likely to be women and found working in schools, hospitals or studying social relationships on the internet. Today they are also likely to be funded from a wide variety of sources. Whereas once anthropologists would have been funded by European or North American universities, now money often comes from business, marketing and even the military, all of whom realise that understanding human culture is important not just in the interests of pure research, but also as a potential precursor for changing behaviour. Children are very much part of this story, and this chapter will look at how anthropologists have studied children in the past and how they study them now.

2 The emergence of anthropology: from the armchair to the field

The first lectures in social anthropology in England were given to undergraduates at Oxford University's Pitt Rivers Museum in 1884. In the earliest days of the subject there was a large overlap between archaeology, anthropology and geography, and the focus was on studying 'primitives' and their relationship to 'civilised' people, as well as on how humans interacted with the landscape around them. Anthropologists were heavily influenced by ideas of evolution and saw societies in terms of evolutionary stages, developing from simple, hunter-gatherer ones, through to settled agricultural communities and on to complex industrialised cities. Many early pioneers of anthropology relied on secondary sources, drawing on tales from travellers, missionaries, ancient texts and other second-hand sources. Few actually met or studied first-hand the people they were supposedly interested in – they remained 'armchair anthropologists.'

By the end of the nineteenth century, however, anthropologists began to mount expeditions to what were then remote parts of the world and to work directly with the people being studied. In 1898 an expedition set off from Cambridge to the Torres Strait in Papua New Guinea to study the natural world and the landscape of these islands, as well as the psychological and social life of the people who lived there. In charge of the expedition was W. H. Rivers, a psychologist and anthropologist who later became famous for his work with soldiers suffering from shell shock during the Great War. He was particularly interested in the colour vision of people in these islands and found that while colour blindness and myopia were rarer than in Europe, the islanders had no word for the colour blue and would use the same word to refer to the colour of everything from the sky to the deepest black.

Figure 1 Badu Islanders pose with members of the 1898 Cambridge University anthropological expedition to the Torres Strait

In the USA anthropologists were also going out to the field to collect data. Franz Boas, one of the founding fathers of American anthropology, went to Baffin Island in the Canadian Arctic in 1883 to look at the impact of the physical environment on the ways that Inuit populations migrated. Later he conducted systematic work on the children of immigrants to the USA, examining how and why their physiology changed after they had settled in the USA.

Although working on very different peoples, and having very different perspectives and interests, Boas and Rivers were both pioneers of fieldwork. Fieldwork lies at the heart of the anthropological method and one of the most prominent proponents to leave behind a theory of fieldwork was Bronisław Malinowski. Malinowski was a Polish-born scholar who came to London to study at the London School of Economics in 1910. In 1914 he set off for the Trobriand Islands (located off Papua New Guinea) to study first-hand the lives of the people there. Stranded by the Great War, Malinowski remained with the Trobriand Islanders for four years, learning their language, joining in with their religious and social rituals and becoming, as far as he was able, part of their lives. He published his account of their lives and how he found out about them in *Argonauts of the Western Pacific* (1922).

Figure 2 A photo of an Inuit girl (about age 4) in traditional clothing, taken by Franz Boas around 1920

2.1 Participant observation

Malinowski called his method of doing research participant observation. This involved intensive fieldwork and studying people in their natural environment. It meant learning the local language, watching how people went about their daily lives, participating in their rituals and asking questions about the meaning and significance of certain actions. Data was collected from observation and also from informants. People themselves were considered the experts on their own lives (even though they did not always see wider cultural patterns) and by asking questions of informants, anthropologists like Malinowski could fill in the gaps in their own knowledge. These observations and answers to questions were then written up daily in field notes, another important part of the anthropological method. The aim of participant observation was to create an intimate portrait of people in every arena of their lives, from domestic routine to public ceremony.

Malinowski placed equal weight on observation and participation. It was not enough simply to watch people or to ask questions; in order to understand the full picture, the anthropologist had to be part of the community, participating in everyday life. If the people being studied were hunters, then the anthropologist went hunting with them, if they were farmers, the anthropologist farmed alongside them. Although this was not always practical and Malinowski admitted in his field notes that he was not always able to participate fully in the Trobriand Islanders' lives, he believed it was only by total immersion that a holistic picture of the lives of other people could be built up. This model has remained central to anthropology until this day, although many have criticised it as over-romantic, as well as practically impossible. Indeed, even Malinowski himself struggled with it and in 1967 the publication of his personal diary from fieldwork, *A Diary in the Strict Sense of the Term*, caused an academic scandal. Despite its lyricism and observations on methods, it also detailed his frustration with the Trobriand Islanders, his dislike of them at times and his sexual fantasies about them. It showed a fieldworker struggling with the method that he had promoted so assiduously and it revealed the difficulties of remaining a detached, scientific observer while participating in the lives of other people.

Figure 3   Bronisław Malinowski in the Trobriand Islands, 1918

2.2 Ethnography

The word 'ethnography' comes from two Greek words – *ethos* (people or folk) and *graphia* (writing) – and represents the anthropologist's attempt to explain and interpret facts of social and cultural life. The term can be defined as both a research method (anthropologists conduct ethnography) and the outcome of this process (the book, film or journal article in which anthropologists attempt to explain and interpret facts of social and cultural life). One important feature of ethnographic writing is that it goes beyond simple description or a list of facts. It attempts not only to describe but also to explain life and culture; crucially, it attempts to do so from an insider's perspective. Malinowski summed up this approach:

> [Ethnography has a] goal, of which an Ethnographer should never lose sight. This goal is, briefly, to grasp the native's point of view, his relation to life, to realise *his* vision of *his* world. We have to study man, and we must study what concerns him most intimately, that is, the hold which life has on him. In each culture, the values are slightly different; people aspire after different aims, follow different impulses, yearn after a different form of happiness. In each culture, we find different institutions in which man pursues his life-interest, different customs by which he satisfies his aspirations, different codes of law and morality which reward his virtues or punish his defections. To study the institutions, customs, and codes or to study the behaviour and mentality without the subjective desire of feeling by what these people live, of realising the substance of their happiness—is, in my opinion, to miss the greatest reward which we can hope to obtain from the study of man.
>
> (Malinowski, 1922, p. 25)

Again, this represents an ideal on Malinowski's part and it is one which anthropologists have often struggled to put into practice. Such a statement is also a product of its time and this particular version of ethnography is shot through with racial and sexual assumptions that need careful handling. However, it expresses the idea that ethnography, at its heart, aims to take account of how people view themselves and their societies.

Ethnographic methods first developed by anthropologists, such as long-term and intensive fieldwork, the use of local informants and the attempt to gain an insider's perspective, are now used by many scholars outside anthropology, including researchers in disciplines such as education, cultural studies, geography and sociology. Many of these may never have heard of Malinowski and would not call themselves anthropologists but would still see themselves as ethnographers. Ethnographic research therefore is now an important element of much social science, but it has not been adopted uncritically and there has been much debate on the extent to which any outsider can straightforwardly document another culture from one of its members' points of view. So many concepts do not translate easily and the ethnographer is forced to use his or her own language in a way that can unintentionally distort and reflect the concerns of the researcher rather than those of the people being studied. The problems with the ethnographic method will be discussed in greater length in the final chapter of this book.

Activity 1   Ethnography and thick description

Allow about 20 minutes

Ethnography, as American anthropologist Clifford Geertz argued, is what practitioners of anthropology do and 'it is in understanding what ethnography is, or more exactly what doing ethnography is, that a start can be made toward grasping what anthropological analysis amounts to as a form of knowledge' (1973, pp. 5–6). In order to demonstrate this point he described a particular gesture and the many ways of interpreting it. The gesture he discussed was the rapid contraction of the eyelids – an ambiguous gesture which could be described either as a wink or a twitch.

Imagine you are watching a silent film of a person rapidly shutting and opening her eyes. Make notes on the multiple ways that this gesture could be interpreted, what further information you would need to know to interpret this properly and how you could differentiate between the meanings of these different gestures.

Comment

A twitch and a wink both involve identical movements of the eyes. Yet they are very different, as this one gesture has multiple meanings. A twitch might mean someone had something in their eye or the light was too strong. It might simply be an involuntary movement, meaning nothing. However, if we called it a wink rather than a twitch, then we are implying that the person making the gesture meant something specific by it. A wink is a form of communication. It might be friendly or even flirtatious; it might also be malicious or conspiratorial. In order to make sense of it though, the person watching would need to know the context, the relationship between the people and the circumstances in which this communication took place.

Geertz used this example to show the difference between thin and thick description in ethnography. A researcher using thin description would simply say that a person had contracted their eyelids. An ethnographer using thick description would supply the entire context; who these people were, what their relationship was, what the circumstances and context of this gesture were and, most importantly of all, what it meant. Although in everyday life most people can provide thick descriptions when they describe an event or a gesture, it is much harder to do so as an outsider in an unfamiliar situation. Geertz's identification and definition of the thick description, and his example of the wink, reminds anthropologists writing up their field notes to be aware of the need to take context into account at all times, and to recognise that many gestures have multiple meanings and histories, and cannot always be understood simply by asking questions or watching what is going on. Geertz's descriptions of thin and thick description, although originating in anthropology, have been extremely influential outside the discipline as well. Many ethnographers, whatever their disciplinary background, argue that they provide thick description and quote Geertz as a source.

2.3 Cultural relativism

Nineteenth-century anthropologists have been heavily criticised for their European ethnocentrism – the idea that the culture, social life, morals and manners of Europeans or Americans were necessarily better than those of others – and for arguing that those who held different beliefs (by worshipping several gods rather than one, for example) were in some way primitive or strange. As a way of countering this, Franz Boas and his followers emphasised the importance of cultural relativism or the idea that all cultural beliefs and practices are of equal value and need to be studied neutrally. Cultural relativists argue that the moral frameworks of different cultures differ very radically from each other and therefore need to be judged in their own terms.

Such a stance is problematic. Although in principle neutrally describing the practices of others might seem straightforward, it can quickly become contentious. Male circumcision performed on newborns is one such controversial example. For the majority of Jewish people, circumcision (*bris* or *brit milah*) is a central part of their social, cultural and religious identity, divinely sanctioned and binding them together as a people, legitimised through the Torah. The UK's Chief Rabbi describes circumcision thus: 'Since the days of Abraham, this has been the sign, for males, of the covenant between God and the people' (Office of the Chief Rabbi, 2009). Circumcision therefore is a long-standing religious and cultural tradition, and also an identifier of belonging and religious heritage. Yet others condemn the practice, describing it as child abuse which involves removing a healthy body part from a child who is too young to consent. In the USA, in particular, debates over the legitimacy and morality of circumcising boys have recently become very heated, with increasingly entrenched arguments between children's rights activists and those for whom circumcision is a vital part of religious and cultural identity. In June 2011, a judge in San Francisco refused to allow a ban on the circumcision of boys to be voted on as part of a ballot, citing religious freedom.

Figure 4   An activist van campaigning against infant circumcision in the USA

As this example suggests, the issue of cultural relativism is an important one when it comes to understanding children. Childhood can be a very emotive issue and, as the various debates over contemporary parenting practices in the UK and elsewhere have shown, ideas about the best ways to raise children can cause deep controversy. Whether children should be put to bed with a routine or kept up with their parents until they fall asleep when they are ready, if they should be fed on demand, or whether or not they should sleep with their parents are all issues which cause much anxiety, as Chapter 1 suggested. When looking at other cultures such debates can be even more explosive as certain cultural practices which appear wrong and even abusive to some people are acceptable elsewhere. While people in the minority world might baulk at weaning a child by putting hot chilli on the mother's breasts until the child learns not to want his or her mother's milk any more (a common practice in central and lowland South America), some minority-world child-rearing practices can seem equally damaging to outsiders. Putting children in separate rooms from their parents, not feeding them when they cry, not carrying them the whole time and, indeed, not circumcising them are viewed so negatively in some parts of the world that people believe that Europeans and Americans do not know how to look after children (Korbin, 1981). Reading A describes an instance where an anthropologist found the idea of cultural relativism very difficult when she witnessed the harsh disciplining of children. Even as she understood it and placed it in context, the severity of the punishments sometimes made her feel as if she was witnessing abuse rather than discipline.

Activity 2   Reading A
Allow about 35 minutes

Go to the readings at the end of the chapter and look at Reading A 'Dealing with the dark side in the ethnography of childhood: child punishment in Tonga', by Helen Kavapalu.

Helen Kavapalu has carried out extensive fieldwork on child-rearing in Tonga and has focused particularly on discipline. Her work examines why children are beaten with such frequency, what the effects of this are and how it relates to indigenous ideas about power, status and correct social behaviour. In this reading she describes the harsh disciplining of children in Tonga while trying to understand it within its context. Nevertheless, she struggled very hard with ideas of cultural relativism, and the severity of the punishments made her feel uneasy.

As you read this extract, make notes on:

- your own feelings about what you are reading and whether you think these practices are acceptable

- whether or not you believe that anthropologists should seek to describe these practices in a neutral way.

Comment

You may have reacted in a number of ways to this reading and there is no right answer. Kavapalu herself seems to have conflicting views. On the one hand, she understood that the beatings she saw were not random violence or cruelty but linked to wider ideas about the nature of childhood and the necessity of shaping children in particular ways. On the other, she was obviously concerned that children were beaten, sometimes severely, from a young age and felt that this could inflict serious physical and emotional damage. You may have felt differently – believing that beating children is always wrong, in whatever situation, and that cultural difference does not take precedence over children's safety.

How you react to this extract will determine how you feel about the second bullet point above. Anthropologists always try to understand what they see in relation to the context in which it occurs – without making value judgements – but here, and in many other cases, there is no simple conclusion to be drawn. Anthropological descriptions raise important questions about how far studies of childhood can be truly culturally relativistic (without making value judgements) or, indeed, whether they should be. Anthropologists struggle with such issues throughout their work.

Figure 5   School children from Tonga in uniform on parade

It is very difficult to read about parenting practices and accounts of how children are treated without judging them, or making assumptions about what would be a correct or better way of raising children, but anthropologists and other social scientists try to suspend judgement in order to understand the nature and causes of the practices concerned. Anthropological studies of childhood cannot answer questions about the correct ways to raise children, and rarely try. Instead, they raise questions about the limits of understanding and the extent to which anthropologists should simply describe without judging. Like all research with human subjects, this ideal does not always match up to the reality. It is extremely difficult to describe a situation, let alone another cultural system, without interpreting and commenting on it in some ways. Judgements can be both implicit and explicit, and cultural relativism is sometimes a difficult position to maintain.

Summary of Section 2

The central method of anthropological research is participant observation, carried out during fieldwork and written up as ethnography.

Anthropological fieldwork can be carried out in any institution or area of the world.

Anthropologists try to understand how the people they are studying see the world.

Ideally, cultural relativism allows for an acknowledgement of the differences between cultures without the imposition of value judgements. However, in many cases, this is not possible.

---

3 Margaret Mead and childhood

At the same time that British and European anthropologists were making the transition from the armchair to the field, participant observation was also being actively promoted in the USA by anthropologists such as Frank Boas, who worked on the native people of Canada (now known as the Inuit). He was also interested in child development, particularly the impact that environment had on children, and how this could change and shape their physical bodies. Boas was writing at a time when psychology was developing as a discipline, based on very different premises to anthropology. One important strand of psychological thinking was that personality and behaviour were biologically determined, so that people acted in certain ways because of in-built biological impulses which could be recognised and studied. As all human beings had the same biology, it was possible to identify universal patterns of behaviour. One of the most famous proponents of this view was G. Stanley Hall who, in his influential 1904 book, *Adolescence: Its Psychology, and Its Relations to Physiology, Anthropology, Sociology, Sex, Crime, Religion and Education*, claimed that adolescence was a universal, transitional process in the life cycle between childhood and adulthood, characterised by particular traits and behaviours brought on by the biological changes at puberty. Most famously, Hall described adolescence as a time of storm and stress, when young people were in the grip of powerful biological changes they could not control. He wrote:

> every step of the upward way is strewn with wreckage of body, mind, and morals. There is not only arrest, but perversion, at every stage, and hoodlumism, juvenile crime, and secret vice …

> (Hall, 1904, p. xiv)

For Hall, adolescence was universal and would be characterised by the same behaviours regardless of setting. He believed an adolescent in Africa would display the same recklessness and delinquency as one in the USA. However, Boas rejected this, arguing that culture and environment were as important as biology.

With Boas's encouragement, his student, Margaret Mead, began her studies of Samoa and the South Pacific. Like Boas, she viewed the differences between various peoples as cultural rather than biological and set out to Samoa with the explicit aim of disproving Hall's universal, biological determinism. In *Coming of Age in Samoa* (1971 [1928]) she analysed the daily lives of Samoan girls from infancy, through early childhood, until adolescence. Based on close observation and discussions with young women and girls in Samoa, Mead found none of the tensions inherent in the lives of American adolescents, concluding that adolescence was not necessarily stressful and disruptive for either the child or the society, and that any disorderly behaviour in adolescence was caused by cultural conditioning rather than biological changes. Mead identified several cultural reasons why growing up in Samoa was less stressful to both the individual and society than it was in the USA.

Firstly, North American adolescents were bombarded with choices and options which made their lives more difficult as they had to decide what they wanted. In contrast, young people in Samoa had very limited choices that revolved around staying in their villages with their families, marrying and having children in due course, and remaining within their communities until they died. Their society was homogeneous, believing in one religion and attending one church. There were no alternative belief systems or models that children could follow and rebellion was not an option. Children and young people, thus, had fewer choices and could not be made miserable by them. Mead also argued that the clear ritual markings of transition from one stage of development to another gave the girls a structured path through the life cycle, which enabled them to negotiate the processes of growing up more easily.

Figure 6 Margaret Mead sitting between two Samoan girls around 1926

Secondly, attitudes to sexuality were very different in the two societies. Girls in Samoa were much freer to take lovers and experiment with sex. Sexuality was identified as a source of pleasure rather than tension and the flexibility of adolescent girls' sexual behaviour gave them freedom from many of the problems suffered by their counterparts in the USA. According to Mead, the girls whose lives she studied started to take a series of lovers just after puberty. Usually a girl's lover would be much older than herself and before her marriage she was expected to have many lovers or casual sexual partners. As long as these lovers were within certain social groups (i.e. not family members), these sexual affairs were accepted. Mead concluded that, in Samoa, stress and strain were not an inevitable part of adolescence and that:

> adolescence represented no period of crisis or stress, but was instead an orderly developing of a set of slowly maturing interests and activities. The girls' minds were perplexed by no conflicts, troubled by no philosophical queries, beset by no remote ambitions. To live as a girl with many lovers as long as possible and then to marry in one's own village, near one's own relatives, and to have many children, these were uniform and satisfying ambitions.
>
> (Mead, 1971 [1928], p. 129)

Despite the certainties of such statements, others have disagreed profoundly with Mead's views and Derek Freeman (1999) has argued that her work was fundamentally flawed. He claims that she overlooked many of the sources of tension in Samoa and played down the strict control that elders had over girls' sexuality. He argues that Mead's informants hoaxed her, telling her what she wanted to hear rather than giving her accounts of their actual behaviour and beliefs, which were in fact very different. Based on his own fieldwork and interviews with surviving informants, Freeman maintained that the young women of Samoa had lied to Mead, claiming that they indulged in casual and premarital sex, when, in fact, virginity was a highly prized cultural ideal. It has proved hard to either confirm or refute these accusations. By the time they were interviewed by Freeman, Mead's informants were elderly women, many of whom had converted to Christianity after years of missionary activity and who may well have played down their experiences as girls and were now expressing changed cultural ideas of chastity. They may also have been more comfortable talking about their sexual experiences with another woman of a similar age than they would be with a much younger man many decades later. Whatever the criticisms of Mead, however, her most important contribution to the study of childhood was that she was the first anthropologist to take children, as children, seriously. She was interested in their lives and how they perceived their world.

Summary of Section 3

Margaret Mead was one of the pioneers of anthropological studies of childhood.

Through her work she challenged the idea of universal psychological traits based solely on biology and unaffected by environment.

She showed that children from different cultural backgrounds could experience adolescence in very different ways.

4 Anthropology within 'the new social studies of childhood'

Margaret Mead was not alone in her interest in childhood. Over the years many other anthropologists have studied particular aspects of children's lives, such as education, socialisation, language learning, child-rearing practices and techniques, or initiation ceremonies at birth or adolescence (Lancy, 2008; Montgomery, 2009). Particularly in the USA, anthropologists have conducted longitudinal studies of infant care and the long-term effects of different types of care (LeVine and New, 2008), and of different understandings of child development (see, for example, the Navajo model of development discussed in Chapter 3), and they have also worked on large-scale cross-cultural comparisons of child-rearing in parts of Africa and the USA (LeVine et al., 1994).

In the 1970s, however, there was a shift away from these sorts of studies, especially among British and Scandinavian anthropologists who argued that discussions of child-rearing said little about children themselves and much more about the adults caring for them. Jean La Fontaine argued:

> Anthropology has only just begun to question Western cultural assumptions about children. To begin with: a view of culture as inculcated rather than innate required a concept of children as the raw material of social reproduction, the 'empty vessel to be filled' in another telling phrase (James & Prout 1990). Arguing against those who would claim a genetic basis for the different behaviour and 'customs' of peoples other than their own, or would interpret

them as indicating a lower rung on the evolutionary ladder, anthropologists insisted that social behaviour was learned. If it was learned, then there must be some stage at which human beings had not yet begun to learn. The physical process of maturation must therefore be accompanied by another process, of enculturation as the American anthropologists called it, or socialisation, the preferred term of British social anthropology. The description of this process of learning and its cultural variations may have been seen as a study of children but in fact children were merely the objects under transformation. What was studied was the process of social reproduction, the transmission of culture to the next generation and the maintenance of society through the process of inducting new members of it. To describe and understand social reproduction and explain continuities of culture is still a valid intellectual concern, but it has the disadvantage of perpetuating a view of children as human material to be moulded by adults into replicas of themselves.

(La Fontaine, 1998, pp. 14–15)

Figure 7   In the USA in particular, anthropologists have looked in detail at child-rearing practices such as how babies are carried, where they sleep and how often they are fed

Inspired by wider political and social movements, anthropologists began to study groups such as women, children or the ethnically and socially marginal, who had not always been studied in the past. Just as women's studies began to explore women's sometimes hidden place in history, art or literature, so studies of childhood began – throughout the social sciences – to stress the importance of understanding children's lives, and also the implications of the previous neglect for studies of culture and social organisation.

Figure 8 Sociologist William Corsaro with children from Head Start, a programme which promotes the school readiness of children from low-income families

One of the first people to use children as informants was Charlotte Hardman, who published a ground-breaking article in 1973 in which she claimed that children's lives were as worthy of study as any other section of society and, furthermore, that a focus on children could reveal aspects of social life not found in most conventional ethnographies. She posed the question as to whether there could be a meaningful anthropology of childhood and concluded that there could, basing her argument on two sources. Firstly, she was inspired by a quote from Peter and Iona Opie, the folklorists who had collected children's rhymes and games throughout Great Britain. They wrote:

> And the folklorist and anthropologist can, without travelling a mile from his door, examine a thriving unselfconscious culture (the word 'culture' is used here deliberately) which is as unnoticed by the sophisticated world, and quite as little affected by it, as is the culture of some dwindling aboriginal tribe living out its helpless existence in the hinterland of a native reserve ... 'The world-wide fraternity of children is the greatest of savage tribes, and the only one which shows no sign of dying out.'
>
> (Opie and Opie, 2001 [1959], pp. 1–2)

Despite the problems with the language of this quote (and the unfortunate drawing of parallels between children and 'savages'),

Hardman proposed that children, as the Opies had suggested, did indeed exist within a separate subculture; they had their own ways of thinking, their own world views and their own cultural understandings in the form of games and rhymes.

Secondly, she drew heavily on the newly emerging anthropology of women and its examination of the ways in which women had been overlooked by both male and female anthropologists in the past who were more interested in observing and participating in the public life of men, so that religious rituals were given more attention and prominence than cooking or childbirth. This had the impact of effectively marginalising women and overlooking their experiences – Hardman suggested that this was accompanied by a parallel neglect and sidelining of children.

Along with colleagues in sociology, cultural studies and geography, anthropologists contributed to what has become known as the 'new social studies of childhood'. This way of analysing children's lives is often described as 'child-centred' or 'child-focused' and in anthropology demands the use of children as primary informants, focusing on their agency and experiences of childhood. There is sometimes still a resistance to this on the basis that children are not useful or proper subjects for research and are unreliable informants: they do not communicate in proper sentences, they tell tales and lie, their perspectives are very partial and limited, and as researchers are not generally children either, they cannot properly access children's views of the world (for a fuller discussion of these differing views see Montgomery, 2009). Such arguments can be countered by arguing that they do not refer only to children. Adults too are unreliable, do not always tell the truth, and there are often miscommunications between anthropologists and their adult informants. Doing research with children means taking all these issues into account, realising that children are very likely to be bored by an adult stranger asking endless questions, while trying to focus on children's own experiences and understandings. There are no easy solutions to this, but those anthropologists who specialise in childhood try to work with children, recognising their own expertise about their lives, rather than on children as passive subjects.

Activity 3   Reading B

Allow about 30 minutes

Now study Reading B, 'Children's views of death' by Myra Bluebond-Langner, one of the earliest advocates for child-centred anthropology, and Amy DeCicco. Bluebond-Langner worked with terminally ill children, comparing their knowledge of, and reactions to, their illnesses with those of their parents and doctors. This extract is taken from her work with DeCicco, where she discusses and summarises children's views of death, and how children negotiate knowledge about their illnesses with their parents and those who look after them. As you read it, note down:

- how children become aware of their condition
- how using child-centred research methods helps to draw out different perspectives.

Comment

As Bluebond-Langner and DeCicco argue, most studies of children and death are either medical or psychological. Few people actually ask children for their thoughts or look at how they react to diagnoses of their illness. By focusing on the children themselves, Bluebond-Langner shows that her child informants understood very clearly that they were dying, even though their parents and doctors had specifically kept the information from them. By talking to children she shows the ways in which children understand and interpret their parents' attitudes towards their own illness, and she demonstrates the desire on both sides to protect shared ideas of innocence and ignorance. She also shows that knowledge is a negotiation between parents and children, and that children are not just the passive recipients of the information that their carers want them to have.

By the 1990s children's lived experiences, as described by children themselves, had become the focus of several anthropologists who studied issues such as the nature of children's friendships in British schools, children's daily lives at home in Norway, the struggles of street children in Brazil, the role of child soldiers in armed conflict in the Democratic Republic of Congo or the experiences of child prostitutes in Thailand (for a fuller discussion of these ethnographies see Montgomery, 2009). Children's lives in schools were also a significant part of this work and many important ethnographic studies with children took place in schools in the UK during this time (see Hammersley, 1990). All of these studies took children's participation in research, and their role as informants, as vital. Taking children themselves as a starting point meant that they could no longer be seen as a homogeneous group with views and priorities that depended only on their physical advancement. Child-centred research reflected a recognition that children possessed agency and that they could, and did, influence their own lives, the lives of their peers and that of the wider community around them.

Figure 9 A pencil drawing by a 13-year-old boy in New Guinea, collected in the 1920s by Margaret Mead and which she then used to describe children's understanding of space and place

4.1   Childhood as a social construction

Margaret Mead emphasised that adolescence and childhood were always 'social constructions' rather than biological facts and this idea was enthusiastically endorsed by the new social studies of childhood. Seeing childhood as a social construction does not mean that childhood doesn't exist, or that children are the same as adults, rather it acknowledges that childhood 'is always a matter of social definition rather than physical maturity' (La Fontaine, 1986, p. 19). Furthermore, seeing childhood as a social construction emphasises how differences in the ways that children are perceived have important implications for understanding how children experience childhood and how they are treated by adults. This insight is not unique to anthropology, but with their tradition of cross-cultural study, anthropologists are well placed to examine different childhoods in different parts of the world – as well as within cultures –

and to show that the differences between children are not only biological but also cultural.

Activity 4   Childhood as a social construction

Allow about 20 minutes

Read through the following short passages about Balinese and Taiwanese views on infants. An American anthropologist writes the first extract as if they are an ingenious healer writing childcare advice for local mothers. The second is also by an American anthropologist who conducted fieldwork in the 1970s. Make notes on the different constructions of childhood in each case and the implications they have for how the child is treated.

Your infant as a God

> At birth, your child will be divine, closer to the world of the gods than to the human world. Having just arrived from heaven, your infant should be treated as a celestial being. Provide the attention that a god deserves, and address your child with the high language suitable to a person of higher rank. You should hold your newborn high, for gods and members of a higher rank should always be elevated relative to their inferiors. For the first 210 days (or 105 days, depending on region and status), never put your baby down on the ground or floor, which is too profane for a god. Until then, your baby should be carried at all times.
>
> *(Diener, 2000, p. 105)*

Childhood in rural Taiwan

> For the first six weeks of life, a Taiwanese infant spends most of her time on the family bed or in a wheeled bamboo crib that can be rolled about the house. It is considered dangerous for an infant to be carried too much before she is at least six weeks old. After that she is tied on her mother's back with a long strip of cloth that crisscrosses both of their bodies and in effect swaddles the child. Unfortunately, it provides no support for the infants' rubbery neck. I find the sight of these delicate little heads bobbing loosely very distressing, but Taiwanese mothers assured me it did not matter a bit ...

We asked forty-one mothers, 'Do you think crying hurts a baby or do you think that it doesn't matter?' Twenty-three of the mothers felt that crying not only did not matter but in some ways was even beneficial. Five of the 'pro-crying' mothers felt that crying was a form of infant exercise; five others quoted a proverb to the effect that a child must cry to grow; one mother quoted her grandmother, who had claimed that crying made a child's intestines large ...

(Wolf, 1972, pp. 57–8)

Comment

In the first piece, infants are thought of and treated as divine until they are about nine months old. They are considered better than adults; purer and much closer to the gods. This means they are treated as very important, celestial beings for whom everything must be done and to whom respect must be paid. In contrast, the majority of Taiwanese mothers saw their infants as robust and resilient and did not necessarily take great efforts to stop them crying. In contrast to both these models, the general European and American view of babies is that they are helplessly dependent, very vulnerable and must be in close contact with their mother at all times. Not everyone believes they should be soothed as soon as they cry, but few people think crying is 'good' for them or a form of exercise. What we see in these two vignettes are the very different ways in which babies and young children are socially constructed and the impact this has on how they are treated. These views may differ across and between societies, and individual parents may believe and act very differently towards their children. Parents may be acting according to the way they think is best or most natural for their children, but they are also acting according to cultural beliefs about the nature of the infant and their needs.

Activity 5   Reading C

Allow about 30 minutes

Now turn to Reading C, 'The spiritual lives of Beng infants' by Alma Gottlieb. This extract is about a people called the Beng who live in the Côte d'Ivoire, West Africa. Among the Beng, childhood is constructed very differently from the USA (where Alma Gottlieb is from) and she explicitly contrasts Beng views of the world with those of Americans. As you read through, make notes on how the Beng view their children and the differences between this and your own cultural background.

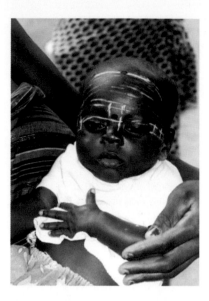

Figure 10   A Beng baby boy

Comment

This article points to profoundly different beliefs about child development from those found in the USA (and the rest of the minority world) where children are perceived as being born without skills such as language or understanding and are thought to acquire these skills gradually. In contrast, the Beng conceive the life course as a cyclical rather than a linear process. They believe that children are born with many skills and competencies but that they forget this knowledge as they get older. Growing up, for the Beng, is a process of losing rather than gaining knowledge and skills.

4.2   Anthropology and the United Nations Convention on the Rights of the Child

As the new social studies of childhood have developed, contemporary anthropologists have been heavily influenced by the United Nations Convention on the Rights of the Child (UNCRC). This was opened for signature in 1979, came into force in 1989, and is the most widely signed rights treaty in the history of international law, with only Somalia and the USA not ratifying it. It is made up of 54 legally binding articles which aim to protect and promote children's rights in the fields of health, education, nationality and the family. The UNCRC is based on the premise that children need special protection because of their age and emotional development, but clearly emphasises that children's rights spring from the inalienable fact of their humanity. Children's rights are human rights.

Figure 11   Bhutanese mandala representing children's rights and position within their community

The UNCRC states categorically that children are entitled to special protection, provision and rights of participation. It emphasises that all children have rights whoever they are and wherever they live, and that all children are equally entitled to these rights. The premise behind all such legislation is that concepts such as human rights or children's rights are not negotiable at a local level. Anthropologists, however, have had concerns about this. Because they have always stressed the importance of understanding local perspectives, anthropologists have been uneasy about the universal model of childhood presented in the Convention, especially as it is one based on chronological age and the insistence that everyone under the age of 18 is a child. In British society, people can marry, join the army and go to work from the age of 16, even though they are legally still children. In majority-world countries, the difficulties of setting a standard age of 18 are even more obvious; boys and girls marry much younger, often at puberty, they work as soon as necessary, and even have their own children at ages the UNCRC would still refer to as childhood. If custom and culture promote early marriage, then it is debatable whether international legislation could or should have any effect on this. There may well be grounds for legitimate concern about the possibility of abuse when children marry early or have children at a very young age, but even so, most anthropologists would argue that a child marrying at 15 – in full accordance with traditional norms and local customs – in India is very different from a child marrying at 15 in the UK. Once again, anthropologists have to deal with issues of cultural relativism, negotiating (not always successfully) a path between the understandings of local communities and international legislative standards.

The UNCRC is based on the principle that children are equal to adults and should be seen as rights-bearing citizens rather than immature beings. However, this view of adult–child relations is, in itself, a product of particular social, cultural and historical circumstances. We know from European history that children were not understood in this way 50 or 100 years ago and in the majority world, the idea of children as rights-bearing people and individuals in their own right can be even more contested.

Activity 6   Children's rights in Ghana

Allow about 20 minutes

Read through the following passage extracted from a longer journal article by an anthropologist from Ghana, Afua Twum-Danso. She has conducted research on children's rights in Ghana and how they are locally understood.

As you read through the passage, comment on:

*   how children's rights are viewed in Ghana
*   the relationship between rights and responsibilities.

> The stress by all informants on the importance of children's duties and the need to respect and obey parents and other adults can ultimately be attributed to the value of reciprocity, which underlines all social relationships in Ghana. The idea of

children having rights *a priori* was often met with rejection during the data collection process for this study ... several adults stated at various times during the research process that, 'we do not want Western children here in Ghana.' The implication behind this statement is that they believe that in Western countries children expect their entitlements, but do not give anything in return. What is evident here is the belief that rights, or better still entitlements, come along with duties ...

As reciprocity forms a central component of the socialization process in Ghana, children grow up very much aware that the caring that their parents provide for them is based on the belief of a pay-off. By bringing forth a child and taking care of him during his childhood a parent is issuing a contract, which he expects to be paid back once the child is in position to do this by fulfilling their expected responsibilities and behaving in an appropriate manner. A child who does that will have their rights fulfilled ...

It is because of the crucial role reciprocity plays in intergenerational relationships that children themselves emphasised values such as respect, obedience and the need to submit to parental control and discipline. They see these as crucial to ensuring that their needs are provided for by adults. Amongst the children interviewed for this study, there was a fear that if a child did not respect her parents, they may not pay school fees or even look after her. Comments made by children in FGDs [Focus Group Discussions] ... reflect the extent to which this is a factor in regulating their behaviour:

Children have the right to respect [elders] because if you do not respect your mother she will take you out of school or kick you out of the house.

If you are on the streets and you are respectful you could get someone to send you to school or help you in some way.

If you are disrespectful you will be sent out/kicked out of the house;

If you are disrespectful and you need help, you won't get it.

Children do not respect so they are not cared for.

> Children's rights provide an important backdrop to these discussions.

5 Conclusion

This chapter has identified some of the ways in which anthropologists have looked at children and shown the contributions that an anthropological approach can make to childhood studies. Anthropologists have a long history of studying children, especially those overseas, although nowadays they are just as likely to study them in the local classroom as in Samoa or Africa. The rise of child-focused anthropology and its insistence on child informants comes out of changing ideas about childhood in the minority world and the reconfiguration of adult–child relationships. The idea of children as equal participants in society, with a voice worth hearing, is now commonplace and widely accepted within anthropology. Many anthropologists contributed to the new social studies of childhood, but they are by no means the only ones and the next chapter will look in more detail at the theorisation that has gone on throughout the social sciences in this field.

References

Diener, M. (2000) 'Gift from the gods: a Balinese guide to early child rearing', in DeLoache, J. and Gottlieb, A. (eds) *A World of Babies: Imagined Childcare Guides for Seven Societies*, Cambridge, Cambridge University Press.

Eagleton, T. (2000) *The Idea of Culture*, Oxford, Blackwell.

Freeman, D. (1999) *The Fateful Hoaxing of Margaret Mead: A Historical Analysis of Her Samoan Research*, Colorado, Westview.

Geertz, C. (1973) *The Interpretation of Cultures: Selected Essays*, New York, Basic Books.

Hall, G. S. (1904) *Adolescence: Its Psychology and Its Relations to Physiology, Anthropology, Sociology, Sex, Crime, Religion and Education*, New York, Appleton.

Hammersley, M. (1990) *Classroom Ethnography: Empirical and Methodological Essays*, Milton Keynes, Open University Press.

Hardman, C. (1973) 'Can there be an anthropology of childhood?', *Journal of the Anthropological Society of Oxford*, vol. 4, no. 1, pp. 85–99.

James, A. and Prout, A. (eds) (1990) *Constructing and Reconstructing Childhood: Contemporary Issues in the Sociological Study of Childhood*, London, Falmer.

Korbin, J. (ed) (1981) *Child Abuse and Neglect: Cross-cultural Perspectives*, Berkeley, CA, University of California Press.

La Fontaine, J. S. (1986) 'An anthropological perspective on children in social worlds', in Richards, M. and Light, P. (eds) *Children of Social Worlds*, Cambridge, Polity Press.

La Fontaine, J. S. (1998) 'Are children people?', in La Fontaine, J. S. and Rydstrom, H. (eds) *The Invisibility of Children: Papers Presented at an International Conference on Anthropology and Children, May, 1997*, Linköping, Sweden, Linköping University.

Lancy, D. (2008) *The Anthropology of Childhood: Cherubs, Chattel, Changelings*, Cambridge, Cambridge University Press.

LeVine, R. and New, R. (eds) (2008) *Anthropology and Child Development: A Cross-cultural Reader*, Oxford, Blackwell.

LeVine, R., Dixon, S., LeVine, S., Richman, A., Leiderman, P., Keefer, C. and Brazelton, T. (1994) *Child Care and Culture: Lessons from Africa*, Cambridge, Cambridge University Press.

Malinowski, B. (1922) *Argonauts of the Western Pacific: An Account of Native Enterprise and Adventure in the Archipelagoes of Melanesian New Guinea*, London, Routledge.

Malinowski, B. (1967) *A Diary in the Strict Sense of the Term*, London, Routledge and Kegan Paul.

Mead, M. (1971 [1928]) *Coming of Age in Samoa: A Study of Adolescence and Sex in Primitive Societies*, London, Pelican.

Montgomery, H. (2009) *An Introduction to Childhood: Anthropological Perspectives on Children's Lives*, Oxford, Wiley-Blackwell.

Office of the Chief Rabbi (2009) *Covenant and Conversation – Tazria 5765* [online], www.chiefrabbi.org/ReadArtical.aspx?id=736 (Accessed 12 March 2011).

Opie, P. and Opie, I. (2001 [1959]) 'The lore and language of schoolchildren', New York, *The New York Review of Books*.

Twum-Danso, A. (2009) 'Reciprocity, respect and responsibility: the 3Rs underlying parent-child relationships in Ghana and the implications for children's rights', *International Journal of Children's Rights*, vol. 17, no. 3, pp. 415–32.

Wolf, M. (1972) *Women and the Family in Rural Taiwan*, Stanford, CA, Stanford University Press.

Reading A
Dealing with the dark side in the ethnography of childhood: child punishment in Tonga

Helen Kavapalu

Source: 'Dealing with the dark side in the ethnography of childhood: child punishment in Tonga', 1993, *Oceania*, vol. 63, no. 4, pp. 313–29.

Concepts and goals of socialisation in Tonga

The ideology and practice of child punishment is embedded within a more general theory of personhood and development. The two most salient features of Tongan personhood are *anga* or *'ulungāanga* (best glossed as nature/behaviour) and *loto* (heart/mind). Tongans emphasise the malleability of the person, and socialisation is perceived as a process of developing the individual's *anga* and *loto* correctly (to be 'good', 'nice', 'proper', 'appropriate', and so on). This development is necessary for the child to become *poto* – clever, capable, and socially competent. Becoming *poto* can be seen as the central aim of Tongan socialisation, and children are perceived as inherently *vale* (foolish, ignorant, 'crazy') – the opposite of *poto*.[1] Other negatively-valued qualities (naughtiness, laziness, aggression, disobedience, and so on) are also seen as 'natural' (*fakanatula*) and unsocialised, whereas socially-approved qualities – ideal aspects of *anga* and *loto* – must be learned. A great deal of emphasis is therefore placed on actively teaching children correct values and behaviour, and physical punishment is regarded as the most effective teaching method. Although children are not expected to understand properly what they are taught until late childhood, even until the end of primary school, this 'teaching' begins in infancy.

Three central values are associated with 'correct' *anga* and *loto*: *'ofa* (love, kindness), *faka'apa'apa* (respect) and *talangofua* (obedience). For children, the behaviour that expresses these values includes generosity, helpfulness, deference, unquestioning obedience, and submissiveness. This cluster of values and related behaviour are part of children's everyday lives, in the tasks they perform daily for their household, in their interactions with near and distant kin, and even in their play. They are also the key values associated with status relations in Tonga and,

---

[1]   Concern with social competence is a pervasive theme in Tongan discourse. Individuals of any age can be called *vale* when they have behaved foolishly or been 'socially inept' (Marcus 1978: 267), and the term is also used for insane and mentally handicapped persons.

indeed, understanding the intricacies of hierarchical relations is a crucial aspect of becoming *poto*. Physical punishment must be viewed within the framework of these hierarchical relations, since the motivations and justifications involved are inextricable from broader notions of status-appropriate behaviour.

'They punish me with their love'

For at least their first year, Tongan children are the focus of their households' attention, and they are treated with great concern and affection. Although much of the speech directed towards them consists of threatening, grumbling, scolding, and sharply-spoken orders, much of it is playful and affectionate, as when a nurse commented to a newborn baby, whose mother was feeding him, *'Taa'i koe, fa'a kai, e?'* ([I'll] hit you, eating all the time, eh?). When babies cry, every effort is made to soothe them, but loud and persistent crying is sometimes treated with annoyance and the baby is told sharply to *'Longo!'* (be quiet), *'Malolo!'* (rest) or *'Mohe!'* (sleep). By the end of the first year crying is increasingly treated as a nuisance, rather than a cause for concern, and babies are more likely to be shouted at or even punished for crying.[2]

Caregivers threaten to hit babies not only for crying, but for any behaviour that is annoying, dangerous or 'bad' (*kovi*). They are also threatened that other people (known or strangers) will come and hit them, or that animals or *tevolo* (ghosts/spirits) will come and harm them. Such threats are used with varying degrees of seriousness, from playful teasing to genuine warnings, though the proportion of the latter increases markedly toward the end of the first year. Children quickly learn to interpret the seriousness of threats, which is indexed in facial expression, vocal tone, gesture, and so on (see Ochs 1988: 153). Threats are also an element of the 'distracting routines' that are used to draw children's attention away from mischief or distress, or towards a particular person or object (see Watson-Gegeo and Gegeo 1986: 113).

As with threatening, smacking in early childhood can be playful or serious. A common game played with babies is to alternately cuddle and kiss, and then threaten and playfully smack them. Mock-punishment is also common: an exaggerated threat gesture followed by a light smack. The threat gesture is then repeated. This imitates more serious threaten-and-punish sequences, playfully introducing the baby to a routine that will later become both familiar and frightening. The typical response to

---

[2] There are numerous terms for kinds of crying, differentiated mainly by loudness and associated actions (e.g. *nga*: of a small child, to cry loudly; *tangituva'e*: cry and stamp foot). Loud, angry crying is especially discouraged.

a baby's crying after play-smacking is to laugh, and to kiss and cuddle her. Even when they have really been smacked, children up to about two years of age may be comforted and cuddled when they cry. This soothing is often delayed, though, as an attempt is made to make them restrain their crying by telling them to be quiet, threatening further smacks, or even covering their mouths. Older children are rarely comforted after punishment, and the emphasis on restraint becomes increasingly important.

The transition from play-smacking to more serious punishment occurs during the second year, and the frequency of punishment escalates until children are around four years old. By that age they are typically hit many times each day, ranging from single slaps to more severe beatings. As children get older there is usually some decline in frequency but an increase in the severity of punishment. Incidents involving physical punishment continue to occur throughout adolescence, and sometimes into adulthood. For women, there is often a movement from punitive parents to a violent husband. Girls tend to be punished more often than boys when they are young, because more work and better behaviour are demanded of them. As teenagers boys tend to be punished more often and more severely than girls. However, these gender differences are only slight, and are highly variable between households.

Children may be punished by anyone older than them within their extended family ... Mothers and female adolescents are typically the most frequently punitive within the household, largely because of their major caregiving role. Fathers are usually either uninvolved in physical punishment or deal out infrequent but severe beatings. Children are expected to punish younger siblings, and to assist adults' efforts to discipline them by reporting misdemeanours, catching children trying to run away from punishment, or fetching an object to be used for beating them. Brothers tend to be less punitive with sisters, particularly when the girls reach puberty and the relationship of respect/avoidance between brothers and sisters becomes significant. Also, boys of about ten and over are often absent from the home, doing agricultural work or socialising with peers, which reduces the frequency of their interactions with sisters and younger brothers. When children are too severe with younger ones, when they are perceived as *fakavalevale* (continually bullying), or especially when the crying of the younger child disturbs the adults, the young punisher may also be hit or at least scolded.[3] Outside the family, children receive corporal punishment at school, a practice strongly supported by most parents. ...

'Ofa (concern/love) is the central justification given for punishment. Parents are said to punish their children 'because of their love'; one boy said of his parents, 'They punish me with their love'. However, punishment is sometimes perceived by children as a withdrawal of love, and the explicit association between punishment and 'ofa clearly contributes to the ambivalence felt toward punishment, discussed shortly. There is no notion, as in Samoa, of a lack of punishment indicating a lack of love (Gerber 1975). The people who claimed they had never been hit by their major caregivers (often grandparents in these cases) interpreted this as a sign of special love. Pele, 'favourites', tend to be punished less often than their siblings. ...

Punishment forcibly teaches children behavioural and emotional control. Children are punished for inappropriate emotional displays, and for behaviour that does not conform to ideals of obedience and respect. They are expected to demonstrate restraint whilst being punished. An acceptable response to punishment is to plead and apologise, in a quiet, monotonous tone, such as repeatedly begging 'Fakamolemole' (please/ sorry). Children are also expected to remain still to show their submission to punishment.

Children begin, by the age of two or three, to attempt to dominate younger and same-age children by force. In play and in other interactions, they imitate the sequences of gestures and words used by adults and older children when threatening and punishing. Adults often give both covert and overt approval to violent and aggressive behaviour between children, and babies are frequently encouraged to hit, push, pull hair, and so on. Babies' first attempts to talk are often interpreted as 'pa' or 'ta' (hit). Since they are frequently encouraged to hit, and are themselves often threatened and play-smacked, they very quickly associate these sounds with their imputed meanings and begin to use them intentionally.

Children sometimes try to avoid punishment, by running away or by pretending not to hear when they are called to be punished. These ploys

---

[3] Older children are often punished when their younger siblings cry – whatever the reason – when they are responsible for supervising them. One man, the oldest of eleven children, complained, 'Every time one of my brothers or one of my sisters cried, I had to face the beating'.

can be successful, but for the most part any form of resistance to punishment, angry reactions to it, or claims of innocence, are regarded as *loto-lahi* – having a 'big heart/mind', that is being brave, bold, or in this context acting tough. Children who are defiant or ignore threats, warnings and lighter punishments are also *loto-lahi*. Although many children 'act tough', others respond to frequent punishment by becoming wary and nervous, and are called *mataila* (lit. 'awake eyes'), because they often flinch away from sudden movements as if expecting a blow.

Punishment is intended to make children feel *mamahi*. This term means physical pain as well as 'to be sorry, to feel sorrow or regret; to feel hurt (take offence); to be annoyed or angry, to harbour ill-feeling' (Churchward 1959: 328) … The ambiguity of the term *mamahi* reflects a general ambivalence towards physical punishment. Whilst regarding punishment as necessary and appropriate, the feelings of anger and resentment it engenders are also acknowledged. A thirteen-year-old girl commented:

> My dad tries talking to us and making us understand that what we did was wrong, but he knows it doesn't work because we don't learn, so he uses the belt, but he never does it with anger but with love and caring … When they punish me I honestly feel angry and hateful at first but after a while I understand them and see what they want from me. This makes me love them more.

Some people admitted to holding long-term grudges toward those who had harshly punished them. One man claimed that people often are not aware of such grudges: 'They think [punishment] is part of growing up, it's part of being Tongan, and it's part of being in a family'. However, he added, 'Underneath … you want to pay back when you get older … it explodes in different ways'. Many people remember particular incidents especially vividly, and with intense emotions. A man who was severely beaten by his uncle on one occasion said: 'Every time I think of that I can still feel the pain in my stomach, from being, you know, pounded in the stomach … I almost died'.

References

Churchward, C. (1959) *Tongan-English Dictionary*, Tonga.

Gerber, E. (1975) *The Cultural Patterning of Emotions in Samoa*, PhD Thesis, University of California, San Diego.

Marcus, G. (1978) 'Status rivalry in a Polynesian steady-state society', *Ethos*, vol. 6, no. 4, pp. 242–69.

Ochs, E. (1988) *Culture and Language Development: Language Acquisition and Language Socialization in a Samoan Village*, Cambridge, Cambridge University Press.

Watson-Gegeo, K. and Gegeo, D. (1986) 'The social world of Kwara'ae children: acquisition of language and values', in Cook-Gumperz, J., Corsaro, W. and Streek, J. (eds) *Children's Worlds and Children's Language*, Berlin, Mouton de Gruyter.

Reading B
Children's views of death

Myra Bluebond-Langner and Amy DeCicco

Source: 'Children's views of death', 2006, in Goldman, A., Hain, R. and Liben, S. (eds) *Oxford Textbook of Palliative Care for Children*, Oxford, Oxford University Press, pp. 85–95.

The literature on children's views of death is dominated by a developmental perspective, which focuses on the emergence of a 'mature concept of death.' Scholars have differed about the particular age or stage when a particular view emerges, and about the prevalence of particulars views at a given age or stage ... But, prevalent throughout developmental work is the assumption that at points in the maturation process the child casts aside immature notions for the elements of the adult or mature concept of death ... According to developmental thinking, there are five essential components to a mature concept of death: non-functionality (all life functions cease at death); irreversibility (being cannot come alive again); universality (all persons, indeed, all living things, die); causality (causes of death); personal mortality (the individual himself/herself will die) [Kenyon, 2001]. As children grow up, then, their view of death changes from that of death as a reversible occurrence, not unlike sleep or being transported to a different place, to a view of death as an irreversible and universal event, a consequence of physiological process, aging and disease, something that befalls everyone including oneself. 'Mature' views feature scientific notions and 'immature' ones draw upon fantasy. In the developmental model, then, the child's understanding of death is seen in terms of a linear process of development linked to age and a definite endpoint. ...

Terminally ill children and death

The need to look beyond an age-graded, developmental model for explanations of children's views of death was dramatically demonstrated for Bluebond-Langner [1978] in her research with terminally ill children, when she found that age was not at all predictive of the children's views of death, their awareness of their condition, or the ways in which they communicated that awareness. For example, the 5 year-old concerned with separation who talked about worms eating him, and who refused to play with the toys from deceased children, was the same 5 year-old who knew that the drugs had run out and demanded that time not be wasted. So, too, the 9-year-old who drew pictures of herself on blood red crosses and knew that the medication was damaging her liver was the same 9-year-old who never mentioned the names of deceased children, and could not bear to have her mother leave her for a moment.

In each of these children we find views that are expected for their age, as well as views one would not expect from children of that age. Yes, to hear a 5-year-old speak about worms eating him, and being concerned about separation, is predictable from the developmental perspective. But discussion of drugs running out is something that, according to these models, would not occur until much later, in middle childhood. Similarly, that a 9-year-old girl could state that drugs were damaging her liver is not terribly surprising, but a taboo on names of deceased children is more problematic in terms of the development model. In short, in both children all of the elements of a 'mature view' of death are there, as well as elements on an 'immature view.'

What is going on here? Why these contradictions? Have these children both gained in wisdom and regressed? We would suggest that children, like adults, are capable of simultaneously holding several views of death, even seemingly contradictory ones. The particular view that comes out at any one point in time reflects the child's concerns, thoughts, and feelings, not to mention the person the child is speaking to at that point in time.

Of primary concern to terminally ill children is separation: leaving everything and everyone behind. At the same time, they seek to protect those they care about—often their siblings, particularly their parents. For example, Jeffrey was a boy who often yelled at his mother. When asked why he simply replied, 'Then she won't miss me when I'm gone.' When Bluebond-Langner [1978] asked Jeffrey's mother, 'Why does Jeffrey yell at you so much?' She replied, 'He knows when I can't take it in that room anymore. He knows that if he yells at me I'll leave. He also knows I'll come back'. Displays of anger, banal chitchat, and silence were all distancing strategies, if you will, or, as some staff saw them, rehearsals for the final separation. As folks at St. Christopher's Hospice say, 'Withdrawal is not necessarily a hostile act'. They also were a part of mutual pretense.[1]

As noted above, death as a separate personality is often present in both adults' and terminally ill children's views. Bluebond-Langner found that the tendency to view death as a separate personality, or more

---

[1] For further discussion of mutual pretense—particularly with regard to ill children and their parents see Bluebond-Langner 1978.

commonly, to identify death with the dead, was notable among the ill children in two significant ways. First, it was through the death of a peer that the children internalized the terminal nature of their illness, which they would then present in conversation through comparisons of the deceased with themselves.

BENJAMIN: Dr Richards told me to ask you what happened to Maria. [Note: Dr Richards had said no such thing.]

MYRA: What do you think happened to Maria?

BENJAMIN: Well she didn't go to another clinic and she didn't go to another hospital or home.

MYRA: No. She was sick, sicker than you are now and she died.

BENJAMIN: She had nosebleeds. I had nosebleeds, but mine stopped.

Benjamin went through this conversation with everyone he saw that day. When asked why, he responded, 'I want to know who my friends are.'

Second, the identification of death with the dead was apparent in their reluctance to mention the names of deceased children, or to play with toys brought by the deceased's parents, or purchased in the child's memory—as if death were somehow contagious. These 'magical fantasy' views may be coupled with very real scientific views of death, as Tom's conversation with a nurse so dramatically illustrates.

TOM: Jennifer died last night. I have the same thing, don't I?

NURSE: But they are going to give you different medicines.

TOM: What happens when they run out?

NURSE: Well, maybe they will find more before then.

In this conversation, we see a notion of death as the time when the drugs (chemotherapies) would 'run out.' Following this interchange, his conversations about drugs and their side effects diminished. The drugs were not the answer that he and his parents once thought them to be. As with other children aware of the prognosis, he made little reference to his condition or progress. What was there to say? There were only indications of further deterioration and closeness to death. For these children, death is the result of a biological and inevitable process marked by steady deterioration. 'I just get weaker and weaker and soon I won't even be able to walk.'

With dying comes a loss of identity. Children with life-threatening and life-shortening illnesses feel that they are not like other children. For example, Bluebond-Langner noted that the children whom she studied spoke of not getting braces, clothes to grow into, or going to school. What is the identifying marker of childhood if not becoming? Looked at another way, to say these things meant that they knew that they had no future, that death is final. Death marks the end, the future is cut off. They did not mention what they would be when they grew up, and some became angry if others did.

One child who, when first diagnosed, said that he wanted to be a doctor, became angry with his doctor when she tried to get him to submit to a procedure with, 'I thought you would understand, Sandy. You told me once you wanted to be a doctor.' He screamed back at her, 'I'm not going to be anything,' and then threw an empty syringe at her. She said, 'OK, Sandy.' The nurse standing nearby said, 'What are you going to be?' 'A ghost,' said Sandy and turned over.

To these children, closeness to death also meant no future; consequently, conversations about the future declined noticeably. The future was limited to the next holiday or occasion. The children knew that holidays and events had a new significance for parents as well. Children would often talk about the way that holidays used to be celebrated and the way in which it was celebrated now that they were ill.

At the same time, the children also tried to rush these holidays or occasions, to bring them closer to the present. For example, one child asked for his Christmas presents in October; another wanted to buy a winter coat in July. In June, several children asked the physicians if they could go back to school in September.

Even doctors who doubted that a young child could know the prognosis without being told regarded these actions as indications that the child was suspicious, and perhaps even probing for how much longer he or she had to live. The child's lack of interest in future plans does not reflect a lack of interest in the passing of time.

Children with chronic life-shortening illnesses are very much concerned about the time that they have left, often pushing themselves to get things done. Bluebond-Langner reported how some became angry when people took too long to remember things, or to answer questions, or to bring things to them. The parents and staff often commented on such behavior. As one staff member commented, 'They demand because they know time is short. It's as if they know that if they wait too long, they might be dead by then. They're not just being difficult,' the staff person included, 'Those children know something.'

Some children verbalized their fear of wasting time directly with phrases like, 'Don't waste time,' or 'We can't waste time.' The staff often noted the activity and urgency that followed the death of a peer.

Time takes on meaning not usually found in young children. These children are having their time cut short, and they know it. Death and disease are constants in their lives. Images of death and disease fill disease related as well as non-disease-related play and conversations.

References

Bluebond-Langner, M. (1978) *The Private Worlds of Dying Children*, Princeton, NJ, Princeton University Press.

Kenyon, B. (2001) 'Current research in children's conceptions of death: a critical review', *Omega*, vol. 43, no. 1, pp. 63–91.

Reading C
The spiritual lives of Beng infants

Alma Gottlieb

Source: 'Do infants have religion? The spiritual lives of Beng babies', 1998, *American Anthropologist*, vol. 100, pp. 122–35.

Most Western folk models of child development imply a mute and uncomprehending newborn arriving for the first time in the world of humans from a restricted uterine life of minimal stimulation and no social interaction as such. Before that, the biological model underlying all this further implies, the fetus was a mere zygote of a few cells, and before those cells were joined, it had no existence whatsoever. Hence the Western caretaker of an infant, whether the mother or anyone else, usually attends to the bodily needs of the young tot with great care but may pay less attention to social relational concerns and virtually none to spiritual ones.

The Beng view of fetal development is quite different. Beng adults maintain that infants lead profoundly spiritual lives. In fact, the younger they are, the more thoroughly spiritual their existence is said to be. Affiliated with this spirituality is a set of infant care practices demanded of a caretaker. To understand this indigenous conception of infants' spirituality, we must investigate life before the womb.

In Beng villages, each baby is said to be a reincarnation of someone who died. By itself this ideology is by no means rare in Africa … But we anthropologists have rarely asked what the implications of this common ideology may be for the treatment of infants and their experiences. In the Beng context, let us trace their life course.

The Afterlife Is Where We Come From

In the Beng world, infants emerge not from a land of regressively diminishing life but from a rich existence in a place that adults call *wrugbe.* … The literal meaning of *wrugbe* is 'spirit village (or town).' In Western languages, with their roots in the Judeo-Christian tradition, a likely translation of *wrugbe* would be 'afterlife,' the place to which the *wru* (spirit) of a person travels once that person's body dies and the *nenen* (soul) transforms to a *wru*. But the term *afterlife*, while evocative, is not entirely accurate for two reasons. First, it implies that the ordinary or unmarked place and time of orientation are this human existence and that once one dies, one goes 'afterwards' to a space where one stays, presumably for eternity. In contrast, Beng souls go to wrugbe as a waystation; after some time (whose duration is variable), they are reborn as newborn humans. Yet even *waystation* is not ethnographically apt, as this suggests a liminal time and place of transit. In contrast, it is 'this life' that is seen by at least some Beng, certainly by religious specialists and others who think deeply about such eschatological matters, as the ephemeral site of transit whose ultimate goal is to reach the land of the ancestors ... Second, from the perspective of infancy, what is significant is that, in the Beng view, infants have just recently been living their lives in a previous and invisible existence. Thus for the Beng, what English speakers would term the *afterlife* might alternatively be termed a *beforelife*. Yet this term implies a finite end to one's life, whereas the doctrine of reincarnation is based on a cyclical trajectory, with no beginning and no end and death itself as a kind of life. ...

The call of *Wrugbe*

Once the umbilical stump drops off, the baby is said to start a long and difficult spiritual journey emerging from wrugbe, but the process takes several years to complete. Here is an excerpt from a conversation that I had with Kouakou Ba [a local diviner] on the subject:

KB: At some point, children leave *wrugbe* for good and decide to stay in this life.

AG: How do you know when this has happened?

KB: When children can speak their dreams, or understand [a drastic situation, such as] that their mother or father has died, then you know that they've totally come out of *wrugbe*.

AG: When does that happen?

KB: By seven years old, for sure! At three years old, they're still in-between: partly in *wrugbe* and partly in this life. They see what happens in this life, but they don't understand it.

During the liminal time of early childhood, the consciousness of the baby or toddler is sometimes in wrugbe and sometimes in this life. Parents ought to do all they can to make this life comfortable and attractive for their infant, to ensure that their child is not tempted to return to wrugbe. For help with the bodily needs, a mother regularly consults her mother, her grandmother, or any other experienced mother around her (Gottlieb [1995]). But sometimes an infant appears miserable for no obvious reason. In this case, the Beng say the baby is endeavoring to communicate a spiritual need that the parents are unable to understand. Such an infant is probably homesick for wrugbe. This is where diviners enter the picture, for these specialists are seen as intermediaries between the living and the ancestors, as well as between the living and bush spirits (Gottlieb 1992: ch. 2; Gottlieb and Graham 1993). …

Almost invariably, when diviners are consulted by parents, usually mothers, they recommend that the new mother give a cowrie shell to their baby. [One informant] put it this way:

> All babies must be given a cowrie shell as a first gift, when the baby is born, because the cowrie was important as currency for the ancestors; it was the second most important thing, after gold. The newborn had contact with the ancestors before birth, and the cowrie shell reminds the baby of the previous life in wrugbe.
>
> Nowadays not all women contact a diviner immediately after the birth; they may wait for a day when the baby is in distress. Other mothers may give a cowrie shell to the baby as a personal gift, though they weren't told to do so by a diviner.

… A diviner's instructions to parents to buy jewelry for their crying child may serve to remind parents that the infant, while seemingly helpless and unable to communicate, was recently living a full life elsewhere and thus needs to be respected as a fellow person rather than being viewed as a suffering, wordless creature.

The language of *Wrugbe*

One day I was playing This Little Piggy with the toes of [a six-month-old Beng girl called] Amwe. As the last little piggy went home, I laughed aloud at myself, acknowledging that the baby couldn't possibly understand the words of the ditty, all the more because they were in English. The baby's Beng mother Amenan objected strongly to my remark, which she took as an insult. Amenan insisted that [her] daughter understood perfectly well all that [I] was saying. When I asked somewhat skeptically, 'You think so?', Amenan explained the linguistic situation of wrugbe. Unlike life in this world, she pointed out, different ethnic groups do not live apart from one another in the afterlife. Rather, members of all the world's ethnic groups live there together harmoniously. Associated with this ethnic mixture is a striking degree of linguistic ecumenicism. When the residents of wrugbe speak to each other in their own languages, everyone understands, with full mutual comprehension.

In the minds of many middle-class Western parents, young infants are seen as lacking linguistic abilities. As popular British author Penelope Leach writes unequivocally, 'At the beginning a new infant has no language other than crying' (1983: 62). The Beng model could not pose a starker contrast, for it posits a baby who is anything but 'prelinguistic.' In fact, among the Beng, infants are said to be as *multilingual* as imaginable. Having only recently emerged from wrugbe, where everyone understands every language, Beng newborns have full comprehension not only of Beng but of every language spoken on this earth.

Furthermore, Beng infants are said to begin gradually to leave their previous existence behind. This includes gradually giving up their knowledge of languages other than the one spoken around and to them daily. But as we have also seen, this emergence from wrugbe is a very slow process that takes several years. Until it is complete, the child continues to understand the many languages spoken in wrugbe, though with only sporadic and diminishing comprehension. In sum, Beng infants are doing the opposite of learning new languages subsequent to a prelinguistic phase, as a popular Western folk model posits. Instead, they are *losing* old languages in order to strip away excess linguistic baggage, as we might put it, and leave room for the languages that are most appropriate for this life.

References

Gottlieb, A. (1992) *Under the Kapok Tree: Identity and Difference in Beng Thought*, Bloomington, IN, Indiana University Press.

Gottlieb, A. (1995) 'Of cowries and crying: a Beng guide to managing colic', *Anthropology and Humanism*, vol. 20, no. 1, pp. 20–8.

Gottlieb, A. and Graham, P. (1993) *Parallel Worlds. An Anthropologist and a Writer Encounter Africa*, New York, Crown/Random House.

Leach, P. (1983) *Babyhood*, 2nd edn, New York, Knopf.

Chapter 5

Childhood: a sociocultural approach

Lesley Gallacher and Mary Jane Kehily

Contents

In this chapter, you will:

- examine the key features of a sociocultural approach to childhood
- explore the ways in which sociocultural researchers have studied children and contributed to understandings of childhood
- consider the main features of the 'new' social studies of childhood and explain why they are important in childhood research
- critically evaluate some of the strengths and limitations of sociocultural approaches to childhood.

1   Introduction

Sociocultural research encompasses a variety of fields and academic disciplines including, but not limited to, sociology, cultural studies, anthropology, social psychology, social and cultural geography, and education. The interdisciplinary scope of this work means that sociocultural researchers draw upon, adapt and produce a diverse and eclectic mix of different approaches for exploring and analysing childhood and youth, or children and young people's lives. This chapter looks at how sociocultural researchers have studied children and young people in the past, and how these approaches have been developed, extended and transformed in various ways over time.

Children and childhoods, young people and youth

The terms 'children', 'young people', 'childhood' and 'youth' are used throughout this chapter and, indeed, throughout this book. 'Childhood' refers to a part of the human life course which, following the definition used in the UN Convention on the Rights of the Child (1989), can refer to the period from birth to 18 years of age. 'Children' are those individuals who fall within this age range. The term 'youth' also refers to a portion of the life course. It does not correspond exactly to the latter part of childhood, and usually encompasses at least parts of both adolescence and early adulthood. Individuals who fall into this age range are often referred to as 'young people'. While anyone under the age of 18 can be referred to as a 'child', it is common to refer to adolescents as 'young people' rather than 'children'. However, childhood and youth do not exist unproblematically as age-defined portions of the human life course. They are sociocultural ideas rather than absolute facts, and come to have very different meanings in different places and at different times. The association between 'childhood' and the age range from birth to 18 is not universally accepted; in some societies or cultures 'childhood' is believed to start later than birth, and to end earlier than 18. However it is defined, being placed within the category of 'childhood' affects how children are treated and the expectations placed upon them. In this way, the terms 'childhood' and 'youth' are used both to understand children and young people's lives and to regulate them.

2 Making the familiar strange

Children and young people are a ubiquitous feature of social and cultural life: you may be a parent or a grandparent, an aunt or an uncle; you may work with children and young people, directly or indirectly; you are likely to encounter children and young people in public spaces as you go about your daily business; and you probably see or hear about children in the media on a regular basis. Whether or not you have ever formally studied childhood, you almost certainly already know a great deal about children and young people. Indeed, before you started reading this book, you had probably formed a variety of ideas and opinions about what children and young people do – and what they should do – and the issues that affect them. The sociologist Chris Jenks explains that childhood is a 'totalising concept'. By this he means that all humans have, at some point in their lives, been a child: 'it is the only truly common experience of being human, infant mortality is no exception' (Jenks, 2005, p. 6). Yet, the universality of childhood as a feature of human experience can make it difficult to study childhood because it can cause us to overlook the peculiarity of individual childhoods.

Chapter 2 explored how childhoods have varied over historical time. Chapter 4 discussed how anthropologists have studied the distinctive character of children and young people's experiences within particular cultures and in different places. As a stage within the life course, childhood may be a universal feature of human experience, but it is far from homogenous in its manifestations. Indeed, even within cultures, individual experiences of childhood can vary markedly. For example, Mary Jane Kehily's (one of the authors of this chapter) own childhood experience differed in a variety of subtle but important ways from her sister's experience of childhood even though they grew up within the same household. The everyday and mundane character of childhood in everyday life can also make it a difficult topic to study. Chris Jenks (2005) explains that the ubiquity of childhood can actually work to obscure its analytic importance. Childhood is such a commonplace and *visible* aspect of everyday life that the sociocultural worlds of children may not seem like an important area for research. This is a problem that would be familiar to many sociocultural researchers, not only those concerned with the study of childhood. Sociocultural researchers are often charged with the task of 'making the familiar strange' (Mills, 1959). As James W. Carey explains:

> the social sciences can take the most obvious yet background facts of social life and force them into the foreground of wonderment. They can make us contemplate the particular miracles of social life that have become for us just there, plain and unproblematic for the eye to see … Dewey knew that knowledge most effectively grew at the point when things became problematic, when we experience an 'information gap' between what circumstances impelled us toward doing and what we needed to know in order to act at all. This information gap, this sense of the problematic, often can be induced only by divesting life of its mundane trappings and exposing our common sense or scientific assumptions to an ironic light that makes the phenomenon strange.
>
> (Carey, 2008, pp. 19–20)

Sociocultural research should challenge us to recognise and explore how our thoughts and experiences are shaped by the world around us in various ways. This allows us to better understand ourselves and our societies, so as to make better decisions and to evaluate processes of sociocultural change more effectively.

Figure 1   Childhood is imbued with memories

Activity 1   Childhood memories

Allow about 30 minutes

In Chapter 1, you carried out an activity in which you made some notes about your memories of your own childhood. Reread these notes now and consider the following questions:

- How close do you think this account is to your 'real' childhood experience?

- What factors might have influenced the account you've given?

- What changes would you make to this account of your experience of childhood? Would it be more 'accurate'?

Comment

It is unlikely that your notes present an entirely objective account of your experience at the time you were a child. You are likely to have forgotten many of the details, and some aspects of your memories may have become confused with stories told by other people, with other memories from other points in your childhood, or with stories you have read elsewhere. Your account is also likely to have been shaped by the fact that you are no longer a child. You may have described the experience using language that you probably didn't know, or at least didn't use, at the age you are remembering. Similarly, your subsequent experiences in life, and the opinions you hold, are likely to have coloured your account in various ways. Accounts of our own personal histories can be described as a kind of 'self work' (Plummer, 1995) through which we assemble the various elements of our lives into a coherent, if ongoing, narrative through which we can understand ourselves. This kind of account will also be shaped by what Elizabeth Tonkin (1992) refers to as 'genres' of storytelling; accounts of personal histories are always produced for a particular purpose and will be shaped by the implied audience of the account as much as by the interpretive practices of their tellers. For this reason, you cannot ever be 'truly objective' or give a factual account of your own childhood, but this does not mean that the exercise is worthless. Tonkin explains that accounts of this type are useful in illuminating the interconnections between memory, cognition and sociocultural forces in shaping individual selves.

As a postgraduate student Mary Jane Kehily (one of the authors of this chapter) engaged in group-work to explore how individuals narrate personal experience and develop a sense of identity through stories about themselves (Kehily, 1995). Recognising the stock of ready-made narratives we all tell about ourselves, each member of the group generated their own well-worn story for discussion in the group. Considering the components of the story as well as their omissions, embellishments and varying points of emphasis in different contexts, highlighted the identity work we all do in the narration of personal stories. It is possible to glimpse something of how the past is continually being reworked in the context of the present, and the role of memory as a selective process that can conjure up the past and reconfigure it for the present. Our childhood stories can be seen as condensed moments of experience that exist as personal *constructions* of self – who we were, who we are and how we wish to be seen.

Extrapolating from how the self may be constructed, childhood can be seen as a collective construction that is both known and unknown to us. The sociocultural worlds of childhood are not necessarily as familiar as we might believe them to be. In Chris Jenks's words, 'the child is familiar to us and yet strange, he or she inhabits our world and yet seems to answer to another, he or she is essentially of ourselves and yet seems to display a systematically different order of being' (2005, p. 3). Stainton-Rogers and Stainton-Rogers describe the problem of having at one time been a child but being unable as an adult to gain direct access to that experience as 'one of the deep paradoxes of finding out about childhood' (1992, p. 19). Stuart Aitken (1994) has also reflected on the irony that humans are generally unable to reflect upon the experience of being a child, and particularly the experience of being a young child, until they are so far removed from the experience itself – in both a temporal and a developmental sense – that it becomes very difficult to properly empathise. In the process of 'growing up', we undergo such dramatic cognitive and sociocultural changes that adults find it difficult to imagine a child's world at all. This means that, even though the majority of us have some store of memories of our own childhoods, we cannot simply rely upon these memories as unproblematic and authentic experiences of childhood. As Owain Jones explains:

> We have all been 'children', or at least biologically young, so, perhaps uniquely in this concern for a form of otherness, we have all been that other once, and may still contain some form or traces of it. This raises the question of whether it, or elements of it, are retrievable through memory, or whether the illusion that it is in fact makes the other/other even more inaccessible and invisible. Once childhood is superseded by adult stocks of knowledge, those adult filters can never be removed to get back to earlier states. Adult constructions and memories of what it is/was to be a child are inevitably processed through *adultness*.
>
> (Jones, 2001, p. 177)

While Jones (2001) argues that the gap between the experiences of adults and children is so profound as to be unbridgeable (in both a theoretical and a practical sense), others studying childhood are more optimistic about the possibilities for adults to maintain some 'fragment of connection' to childhood because they have all been, at some more or less distant point in the past, 'younger, bodily smaller, experientially deficient and largely dependent upon, provided for and regulated by adults' (Philo, 2003, p. 11). Indeed, Chris Philo believes that this simple fact is an advantage to childhood researchers over those studying groups within society in which they have never, and never will be, included.

Like all sociocultural research, childhood research is never entirely straightforward, and researchers have to think carefully about how they understand childhood, and the consequences of thinking in this way. In the remainder of this chapter, we explore how ideas about how to study children and childhoods have developed over the course of the last century, and the different approaches that have emerged as a result.

Summary of Section 2

Sociocultural approaches explore how our thoughts and experiences are shaped by the world around us.

Childhood is constructed through everyday social practices, including memories and stories of being a child.

3 Development and socialisation

Sociocultural approaches suggest that, in conducting research on children, researchers also produce a version of 'the child' and indeed a version of childhood. The recognition that there may be different ways of being a child and different kinds of childhood is important to the development of this approach, which is framed by the understanding that childhood is not universal; rather, it is a product of culture and as such will vary across time and place.

The disciplines of psychology and sociology have made a significant contribution to contemporary understandings of childhood. In general, psychological research has focused upon the individual child, while sociological research has been interested in children as a social group. In the early twentieth century, developmental psychology became established as the dominant paradigm for studying children (Woodhead, 2003), documenting the stages and transitions of minority-world childhood. Within this framework, childhood is seen as an apprenticeship for adulthood that can be charted though stages relating to age, physical development and cognitive ability. The progression from child to adult involves children in a developmental process wherein they embark upon a path to rational subjectivity. Sociological approaches by contrast have been concerned with issues of socialisation; ways of exploring how children learn to become members of the society in which they live. The differences between the two approaches are outlined and discussed in an academic intervention that sets out the parameters for a 'new sociology of childhood' (James and Prout, 1997). James and Prout propose that 'the immaturity of children is a biological fact of life but the ways in which it is understood and made meaningful is a fact of culture' (1997, p. 7).

3.1   Childhood socialisation

Traditionally, the sociocultural study of children and childhood has been dominated by two concepts: 'development' and 'socialisation'. These concepts understand the child as incomplete – both biologically and socially – at birth, and explore the processes through which they develop and are socialised into fully formed adults.

The term 'childhood socialisation' is often associated with Talcott Parsons' work on the American family in the 1950s. Parsons believed that children were born completely ignorant of social values and that growing up was a process whereby they gradually learned about and internalised social conventions in order to become a full member of their culture or society. Socialisation is the name given to the process through which children acclimatise to and internalise the culture of the society into which they are born (Parsons, 1951). Parsons views socialisation as a positive thing that is important for the individual (who would be otherwise unable to find their place in society) and for society (which would otherwise fall into ruin and decay). Socialisation is, therefore, an important topic for sociocultural research, and one which necessarily concentrates on childhood. As Parsons explains:

> There is reason to believe that among the learned elements of personality, in certain respects the stablest and most enduring are the major value-orientation patterns and there is much evidence that these are 'laid down' in childhood and are not on a large scale subject to drastic alteration during adult life.
>
> (Parsons, 1951, p. 101)

Norman K. Denzin agrees with Parsons that the notion of socialisation makes childhood an important focus for sociocultural research, but he views the process as far more reciprocal than Parsons. For Denzin, socialisation neither ends at adolescence nor passively moulds individuals. Rather, he views socialisation as 'a fluid, shifting relationship between persons attempting to fit their lives of action together into some workable, interactive relationship' (Denzin, 2010, p. 2). Children are shaped by the socialisation process, but they are also active in their own socialisation.

Figure 2   The family as a site of socialisation

3.2   Gender identities

A significant feature of the socialisation process is the learning of gender. How children come to understand themselves as girls or boys and inhabit a gender identity is a feature of sociocultural approaches to childhood. Gender is one of those properties which seems to be a fixed attribute that is intrinsic to human experience, but which is, in fact, a product of socialisation. Gender is something that individuals come to acquire in and through the interactions that take place within their sociocultural environments. Sociocultural researchers can, therefore, study how children come to acquire gender through their processes of socialisation. Barbara Risman and Kristen Myers (1997) argue that there are three main ways in which sociocultural researchers have approached the acquisition of gender identities in childhood.

Risman and Myers' analysis can be summarised in the following points:

1   Approaches which view children as actors in the gendering process, who are able to seek information and appropriate it into their patterns of behaviour in order to make sense of their worlds.

Figure 3 Learning gender

2 Approaches which view gender as an attribute imposed on children from outside, which becomes encoded into their future behaviour.

3 A middle ground of approaches which view children as constrained by gender norms, but active participants able to renegotiate their enactment nonetheless.

(Risman and Myers, 1997)

Risman and Myers adopted this third approach in a study about how children were socialised within feminist households in the USA. They explored the consequences of what they refer to as 'fair' child-rearing techniques with regards to the development of children's gendered identities. These 'fair' families attempted to adopt more equal gender roles for the parents than was usual in American families in the 1990s, and to bring their children up to believe in gender equality. The study explored the effects of their parenting practices in terms of how successful they were in producing 'post-gendered' children, or at least in altering dominant gender relations in society.

They found that most of the children (aged between four and 18) in the study consciously identified with their parents' feminist ideas; they believed that men and women should be treated equally in society and be afforded the same opportunities. In this regard, the parents had been successful in transmitting different norms and values to their children. However, Risman and Myers found that the children's experiences often contradicted their apparent beliefs and values, and that those experiences were often more powerful in shaping their attitudes and actions. The children who had not yet started school did not make any intrinsic difference between boys and girls, but the older children, for whom family influences played a diminished role in their lives, had begun to adopt more conventional and stereotyped attitudes towards gender, despite the statements they made in support of their parents' feminist views to the researchers. As the researchers explain:

> When family experiences collided head-on with experiences with peers, the family influences were dwarfed. For example, one 6 year old boy told us that if a magician were to turn him into a girl, he'd be different because he'd have long hair. This boy's father had a long straight black ponytail which went to the middle of his back, and his mother's hair hardly reached below her ears. A four year old boy told us that if a magician were to turn him into a girl, he'd have to do housework—despite his father's flexible work schedule, which allowed him to spend more time in domestic pursuits than his wife. Children knew that *women and men* were equal; it was *boys and girls* who were totally different. It almost seemed as if these children believed that boys and girls were opposites, but men and women magically transformed into equal and comparable people.
>
> (Risman and Myers, 1997, p. 242)

Risman and Myers explain these inconsistencies as arising from the many different sources of gender socialisation in the children's lives. They only found one case where the children lived completely gender-neutral lives. This was a family with two children under four years old who were never referred to as 'girls', always as 'people'. The researchers wondered if and how these apparently non-gendered young children would change when their parents were no longer the primary socialising influence in their lives. There are many sources of gender socialisation in children's lives – including, but not limited to, the family, the education system and children's peers – and they do not all 'do gender' the same way (Risman and Myers, 1997, p. 249). Children must choose from and adapt the gendered roles available to them in particular contexts.

Risman and Myers argue that children from 'fair' families tended to encounter more inconsistency in gender roles and meanings that most children. The children were also better able to recognise different formulations of gender roles, which allowed them to choose and negotiate gendered meanings and identities more effectively than children with more conventional upbringings. The children in the study were both subject to societal norms and active in their response to them:

> They pick and choose gendered meanings and identities; some conform without knowing it, others crossover dramatically, and most do a little of each. Life for these children is one in which they must negotiate new meanings. They not only 'do gender' they must 'make' it too.
>
> (Risman and Myers, 1997, p. 249)

Parenting practices are not absolute determinants of children's socialisation, both because children are subject to a wide range of other influences and because children are active participants in the socialisation process.

Summary of Section 3

Socialisation refers to the process by which children learn to become members of the society in which they live.

Learning gender is an important part of a child's socialisation and a significant feature of sociocultural approaches.

---

4 The 'new social studies of childhood'

As mentioned in Chapter 4, by the 1980s, a growing number of sociocultural researchers were becoming dissatisfied with the dominance of 'development' and 'socialisation' in approaches to children and childhood within the social sciences. They criticised these approaches for always viewing children and young people as inferior to adults, and for only attending to their interests or activities because of how they related to the adults they would eventually become (see James and Prout, 1997; James et al., 1998; Holloway and Valentine, 2000). Over time, sociocultural researchers in a range of disciplines began to attend more and more to children and young people's views and experiences, and to the peculiarities of childhoods in different times and places. By the early 1990s this work had begun to reach a kind of critical mass and some sociocultural researchers were able to draw out prominent themes from this body of research, which they described as constituting a 'new paradigm' that was emerging in childhood research. This new paradigm formed the basis of a movement that is often referred to as the 'new social studies for childhood' (see Section 4 of Chapter 4).

A paradigm is a dominant pattern of thought within a field of study at a particular time (Kuhn, 1996). Scholars involved in the new social studies of childhood criticised developmental approaches for assuming that all children proceed through a universal set of stages before they reach the fully developed end point known as adulthood. They also criticised models of childhood socialisation for rendering children passive in relation to the forces of (adult) socialisation through which they would be transformed into adults. These approaches are problematic because they subordinate childhood to adulthood, and seek only to attend to the processes and practices through which children are transformed into adults. Traditionally, children were viewed as immature, irrational, incompetent, asocial and acultural in contrast to adults who were mature, rational, competent, social and cultural beings. As such, their everyday activities and concerns could only be of interest insofar as they revealed the progression of development or socialisation; they could not have any intrinsic value in their own right. Similarly, children themselves could only have value as 'future adults'. As the previous section indicates, these criticisms of developmental and socialisation approaches were somewhat caricatured and certainly overstated. This strategic caricature could be contrasted with and opposed to the principles embedded within the new paradigm, which described an emerging body of research that sought to explore children and young people's interests and activities, and to value their contributions to society. In this way, the position of the new social studies of childhood relative to more traditional understandings of 'socialisation' and 'development' could be presented and understood in terms of a paradigm shift.

Figure 4   The new social studies of childhood set out principles for studying children

The researchers involved in the new social studies of childhood rallied around the contention that children are people too, just as adults are, and urged those studying (and working with) children to take them seriously in their own right. In 1997, Alan Prout and Alison James wrote a position paper in which they set out what they believed to be the 'central tenets' of the (at the time) emerging paradigm for the social study of childhood. This paper did not reinvent the sociocultural study of childhood; rather, Prout and James attempted to draw out various ideas and principles that had been growing in importance in sociocultural approaches to childhood since the 1970s, which they saw as characteristic features of this new paradigm. They summarised these features as follows:

1   Childhood is understood as a social construction. As such it provides an interpretive frame for contextualizing the early years of human life. Childhood, as distinct from biological immaturity, is neither a natural nor universal feature of human groups but appears as a specific structural and cultural component of many societies.

2   Childhood is a variable of social analysis. It can never be
    entirely divorced from other variables such as class, gender, or
    ethnicity. Comparative and cross-cultural analysis reveals a
    variety of childhoods rather than a single and universal
    phenomenon.

3   Children's social relationships and cultures are worthy of study
    in their own right, independent of the perspective and concerns
    of adults.

4   Children are and must be seen as active in the construction and
    determination of their own social lives, the lives of those
    around them and of the societies in which they live. Children
    are not just the passive subjects of social structures and
    processes.

5   Ethnography is a particularly useful methodology for the study
    of childhood. It allows children a more direct voice and
    participation in the production of sociological data than is
    usually possible through experimental or survey styles of
    research.

6   Childhood is a phenomenon in relation to which the double
    hermeneutic of the social sciences is acutely present (see
    Giddens, 1976). That is to say, to proclaim a new paradigm of
    childhood sociology is also to engage in and respond to the
    process of reconstructing childhood in society.

                                        (Prout and James, 1997, p. 8)

In producing this list, Prout and James hoped to influence the way in
which sociocultural researchers approached childhood in their work by
gathering momentum around these ideas. It was not intended to be a
prescriptive programme or a set of instructions, but rather a set of
loose principles which researchers could use to work towards
sociocultural approaches which value children's contributions to society
on their own terms. Different scholars have taken on these principles in
a variety of different ways in their own work and developed the new
social studies of childhood into a vibrant and important field of
scholarship. The list does not adequately summarise all of the diverse
work in the sociocultural study of childhood, but it does provide a
useful summary of some key ideas within the field. In the remainder of
this section, we examine how sociocultural researchers have explored
the social construction of childhood as a sociocultural phenomenon and

how they have attended to children and young people's everyday lives, activities and interests.

4.1   The social construction of childhood

Chapter 4 introduced the idea that childhood is a social construction and explored the different ways in which infants are approached in particular societies. The idea that a sociocultural phenomenon, like childhood, can be socially constructed – that is, constituted in and through the ideas and practices prevalent within a specific historical and sociocultural context – can be difficult to understand at first. After all, the stage of biological immaturity we refer to as childhood is real and this creates very real differences between adults and children. Sociocultural researchers do not seek to deny this. By asserting that childhood is a social construction, researchers are arguing that childhood cannot be seen as a straightforward description of a natural, and intrinsically biological, stage of the life course. Childhood always refers to a 'particular cultural phrasing' (James and James, 2004, p. 13) of this biological immaturity, which is produced in different ways in particular times and places. Cultural ideas about what children are and how they should be treated affect the ways in which we behave towards them. This shapes their experiences of being a child and also how they engage with the world and respond to what they encounter in it. As such, childhoods vary according to cultural context, both in how they are articulated in law, policy and custom, and in the everyday interactions between adults and children. As James and James go on to explain:

> childhood is a developmental stage of the life course, common to all children and characterised by basic physical and developmental patterns. However, the ways in which this is interpreted, understood and socially institutionalised for children by adults varies considerably across and between cultures and generations, and in relation to their engagement with children's everyday lives and actions.
>
> (James and James, 2004, p. 13)

Chris Jenks (2005) argues that the idea that childhood is socially constructed is important in sociocultural research because it allows us to move away from the kinds of common-sense reasoning that pervade the ways in which we think about childhood. This allows us to begin to understand how children are shaped and produced through a variety of forms of discourse. In this sense, the term 'discourse' refers to systems of thought, which are made up of ideas, attitudes, courses of action, beliefs and practices. These discursive systems of thought actively construct our sociocultural worlds (Foucault, 1972). Jenks explains that it is vital that sociocultural researchers are able to critically interrogate the assumptions and practices within particular societies (including their own) as it is only through doing so that sociocultural research 'can prise itself free of a commitment to bolstering up the "old order" in society' (2005, p. 51). This matters because of what Prout and James refer to as 'the double hermeneutic of the social sciences' in the sixth point on their list. That is, the knowledges we hold about the world and particular phenomena within it do not simply, and neutrally, describe or reflect the world; they work to alter and construct the world and the specific phenomena they purport to portray.

It is not sufficient to simply assert that a sociocultural phenomenon like childhood is socially constructed; sociocultural researchers must investigate *how* childhood is constructed in particular contexts, and the societal consequences of this. As Nikolas Rose explains:

> It is now commonplace, of course, to refer to the objects of the scientific imagination as 'socially constructed'. This is especially common where the social or human sciences are concerned. We have studies of the social construction of intelligence, of the emotions, of mental illness, of child abuse and so forth. Many of these studies are extremely valuable. But the language of social construction is actually rather weak. It is not very enlightening to be told repeatedly that something claimed as 'objective' is in fact 'socially constructed'. Objects of thought are constructed in thought: what else could they be? So the interesting questions concern the ways in which they are constructed. Where do objects emerge? Which are the authorities who are able to pronounce upon them? Through what concepts and explanatory regimes are they specified? How do certain constructions acquire the status of truth – through experimental procedures, demonstrations and other interventions, through the production of effects and the

reflection on effects, through the rhetorical deployment of evidence and logic and so forth?

(Rose, 1999, pp. x–xi)

In *Governing the Soul: The Shaping of the Private Self* (1999), Rose attempts to trace what he refers to as a *genealogy* of how human subjectivities – that is, how we think of ourselves and act upon ourselves – have been constructed by the human sciences, especially psychology and other endeavours which can generally be termed 'psy' (p. vii). This genealogical approach is heavily influenced by the work of the French historian and philosopher, Michel Foucault. Foucault used this approach to show that a particular way of thinking was not inevitable (however much it may seem to be to those caught within a discursive regime), but was always the result of contingent processes and procedures (see Foucault, 1977, in particular). The appeal of this approach, for Rose, is that it offers 'a kind of destabilisation or de-fatalisation of our present' by showing 'that things have been different, could have been different' (1999, p. xii).

Drawing on a Foucauldian framework, Rose argues that the emergence of the science of child development and developmental psychology as an academic discipline (afforded by the institutional frameworks of the clinic and the nursery school) enabled the production of a set of standards and norms against which children could be measured and assessed in a whole range of contexts. With this came what he calls 'the rise of a normative expertise of childhood' (1999, p. 154), supported by a whole range of technical apparatuses – tables, scales and charts – through which childhood (and parenthood) could be governed and controlled in new ways.

4.2 Constructing childhood through consumer culture

James et al. (1998) productively sketch out a field for childhood studies in an academic intervention that offers ways of theorising childhood and developing new work. The growing significance of consumerism and the market in the construction of childhood, however, is largely overlooked by the new paradigm. The authors reiterate the need to understand childhood as a social construct without acknowledgement that so much of modern childhood materialises through a global market. A growing body of sociocultural studies suggests that contemporary minority-world childhood cannot be read outside of

Figure 5   The material child?

market forces, but is constituted in and through relations of capital
(Cook, 2004; Cross, 2004; Buckingham, 2011). Moreover, processes
of globalisation are by no means restricted to the minority world, and
any meaningful idea of childhood and youth in late modernity needs
to be understood through the varied complex engagements with
consumer culture, retail and global media. As Buckingham affirms,
'From the moment they are born children today are already consumers'
(2011, p. 5).

Activity 2   Reading A

Allow about 35 minutes

Reading A is an extract from Buckingham's (2011) study of children in
the commercial world. The book draws upon Buckingham's experience
as Chair of a government initiative in the UK that responded to concerns
of a crisis in childhood by commissioning an independent report to
'assess the impact of the commercial world on children's well-being'. As
you read through the extract, make notes about how the figure of the
child is constructed in consumer culture, and how these ideas might

affect parents and society as a whole. Based on your notes and responses to the views expressed, answer the following questions:

- How has consumerism changed the experience of childhood?
- How might a social constructionist perspective explain the 'problem' of children and consumption?
- Write a short description of your own ideas in relation to these themes. Pay attention to the strength (or otherwise) of your emotional response and where you think these feelings come from.

Comment

Buckingham documents the contemporary reality of minority-world childhood as a consumer-saturated experience, beginning before birth and playing an increasing role in all aspects of childhood. There is no commercial-free environment, as the market develops new ways to talk to children, and children, in turn, have an impact on parental consumption, becoming consumers in their own right. This growing presence of consumer culture in children's lives is regarded by many as a significant shift in the experience of childhood and seen largely in negative terms. Consumer culture is charged with contributing to the growth of social problems such as childhood obesity, early sexualisation and a pervasive sense of childhood being damaged or lost. A social constructionist perspective suggests looking behind the headlines. Rather than taking a moral position, social constructionists ask questions such as, 'How is this social problem generated?', 'Where does it come from?' and 'Whose interests does it serve?' Viewed in these terms, the assumptions underpinning social problems are called into question; the idea of *all* childhood as despoiled and all consumption as *bad* breaks down into other ways of thinking that create space for diversity, difference and multiplicity of experience.

In response to the third question, Mary Jane Kehily (one of the authors of this chapter) writes: 'As someone who has always had trouble with authority, that is to say a general tendency – my whole family has it – to resist being told what to do or what to think, I'm unlikely to be swept up by a media generated social problem that sociologists would call a moral panic. Social constructionist perspectives speak to my lingering sense of resistance to the normative, to the anarchy of my childhood and the experience of adulthood as blissfully non-unitary. So my feelings are bound up with constructions of self and identity referred to at the beginning of this chapter. There are also some intangible and contradictory feelings/desires about the market and childhood being self-determining and adult-free. I realise the impossibility of this position but also recognise the significance of self-regulating peer group practices and activities that may be facilitated by the market.'

Figure 6   The proliferation of goods aimed at children

In the remainder of this section, we examine the imperative within the new social studies of childhood to attend to children and young people's experiences and to listen to their own accounts.

4.3   Children's everyday experiences

Although the new paradigm views childhood as a social construction, it does not view individual children and young people as passively constructed through the ideas and practices of the adults around them, or moulded in more diffuse ways by societal forces. One of the foundational principles of the new social studies of childhood is that children should be taken seriously as actively involved in shaping their own lives and the societies around them. As James and Prout explain:

> The third important feature of the emergent paradigm is that childhood and children's social relationships and cultures are worthy of study in their own right, and not just in respect to their social construction by adults. This means that children must be seen as actively involved in the construction of their own social lives, the lives of those around them and of the societies in which they live. They can no longer be regarded as simply the passive subjects of structural determinations.

(James and Prout, 1997, p. 4)

Figure 7   Children's cultures are worthy of study in their own right

Sociocultural researchers working within the new paradigm have not only been concerned with the social construction of the child as an idea or childhood as a category of human existence, they have also been concerned with individual children's experiences of childhood. Much of this research is concerned with what might, at least at first, seem to be mundane and unimportant matters. The following activity invites you to consider some examples of research with children and young people that have pursued the ordinary in order to gain insights into the social worlds of young people themselves.

Activity 3   Why would you want to research that?

Allow about 35 minutes

Claudia Mitchell and Jacqueline Reid-Walsh note that they sometimes meet with bemusement and occasionally even outright hostility when they explain that they carry out research into children's popular cultures. Popular culture in general has a low status legacy as the trivial and ephemeral paraphernalia of working-class life. Commonly regarded as unworthy of serious study or evidence that the masses were being duped, the study of popular culture gained some recognition through cultural studies and related perspectives seeking to understand the significance of the *ordinary*. The hostile reception Mitchell and Reid-Walsh remark on can be summarised in the response: 'Cabbage Patch dolls or pogs, why would you want to research that?' (2002, p.10).

The following examples provide a cameo of studies on children and popular culture. Answer the questions after reading the examples:

- How do you feel about this kind of research?
- Why might researchers choose to explore children and young people's popular cultures?

Example 1: Claudia Mitchell and Jacqueline Reid-Walsh (2002)

A study of children's engagement with film, toys, comics, fashion, games, etc. It devises methodological approaches for getting close to children, and documenting their play and interactions with these forms of popular culture, in order to develop a fuller understanding of childhood.

Example 2: Valerie Hey (1997)

A study of girls' friendship that includes analysis of the notes and drawings girls pass around in the classroom. Hey treats the notes as social texts that communicate how girls develop a community of practice for 'doing' friendship and femininity.

Example 3: Mary Jane Kehily (2002)

An ethnography of gender and sexuality in a secondary school that includes an analysis of the sexual content of girls' magazines in order to understand the different ways girls learn and talk about sex.

Comment

The geographers John Horton and Peter Kraftl argue that much of the sociocultural world is all too often neglected, lost and even disparaged in the dominant academic and political understandings of the world. Children's interests and activities, and perhaps particularly their popular cultures, can seem 'too mundane, too obvious, too pointless, or too insignificant, to write about or even think about' (2005). However, while popular cultural phenomena like pogs or cabbage patch dolls can seem mundane and straightforward to those around them (as well as faddish and highly commercialised), they are, at the same time, frequently opaque to those not directly involved. Discussing his study of English schoolchildren's reaction to the release of a single by the pop band S Club 7 in 2000, Horton explains: 'Frequently, in discussions with children about their popular cultural lives, I felt "out of my depth"; frequently, too, parents and teachers admitted that they felt this way. Frequently, moreover, children evidently revelled in being able to talk "over the heads" of adult onlookers' (2010, p. 392). It is useful to attend to those aspects of children's lives that might be dismissed as 'frivolous' or 'inconsequential' both because they matter to the children involved and because we, as adult onlookers, do not necessarily know what is going on in children's popular culture, even when we find it taking place in our own homes or those of our friends.

Drawing upon feminist influences, Berry Mayall (2002) advocates an overtly political sociology *for* childhood, rather than *of* it. She considers children and young people as a minority social group (see also James et al., 1998). Like other minority groups – such as women; gay, lesbian, bisexual and transgendered people; people with disabilities; and minority ethnic groups – children and young people are often marginalised in various ways, and their views are not always sought or listened to. Mayall argues that sociocultural researchers should endeavour to 'look up from childhood' – they should draw upon children's own accounts and attend to their interests – rather than 'look down at' children and young people.

Since the 1970s, sociocultural researchers have concerned themselves with exploring children and young people's lives in a range of everyday contexts. For example, the anthropologist Alison James (1982) carried out a study of children and young people's consumption of cheap sweets or 'kets' in north-east England in the late 1970s, and the geographer Willam Bunge (1971, 1973) studied young people's experiences of the urban environment in Detroit and Toronto. In doing so, they have interrogated both the external forces that shape children and young people's experiences, and their own ways of shaping their lives. The new social studies of childhood built upon this foundation of scholarship and provided a framework in which sociocultural researchers could situate this work. Childhood researchers have tended to concern themselves with what matters to the children and young people involved, rather than making assumptions based on what seems important to adults (particularly policy makers).

4.4   Documenting the children's perspective: Tikyan street cultures

Figure 8   Understanding the experience of street children

Hazel Beazley (2003) studied street children on the Indonesian island of Java. She carried out fieldwork with boys who lived on the streets of the city of Yogyakarta, aged between seven and 18, who refer to themselves in their own language as Tikyan. Street children are a topic of concern for policy makers and other groups both within Indonesia and internationally. However, Beazley's focus was not on the 'problem' of street children; instead, she concentrated on their experiences and attempted to understand the issues that were important to them. In one part of the paper, she discusses practices of bodily modification among Tikyan boys, which seem to exacerbate their marginalisation in Indonesian society.

Mainstream Indonesian culture dictates that boys should wear their hair short and neat; it also disapproves of bodily modifications like tattoos and piercings (even if these bodily modifications are traditional to Javanese culture). Despite this, the boys in Beazley's study often cultivated different kinds of hair style – such as dreadlocks, or shaved patterns on the sides of their head – and adorned their bodies with a range of tattoos and piercings. Indeed, gaining a tattoo was seen as a rite of passage for many Tikyan boys. Beazley explained that the Tikyan style is a way in which street boys are able to defy the mainstream society from which they are excluded, and to control their own bodies and express their own meanings. Nonetheless, the choice to modify their bodies is not without repercussions. Street boys often found themselves in trouble with the authorities for having long hair, which the police would shave off in order to mark them out as a criminal (a traditional punishment in Java). Other Tikyan boys would shave off their own hair as a sign of solidarity and to invert the logic of state control over their hair. Similarly, having tattoos would limit the work opportunities available to street boys who would find they could only sell goods at traffic lights at night when the tattoos were less visible. In this way, the bodily modifications and fashions of Tikyan street culture perform an ambiguous function. They allow socially marginalised street boys to feel that they belong to a subculture but, by having these bodily modifications, the boys find themselves further excluded from mainstream society.

By focusing on the practices, interests and agendas of the Tikyan street boys, Beazley was able to approach the issues of street children without reinforcing stereotypical views of street children as either antisocial delinquents or pitiful victims in need of adult intervention. In doing so, she was able to present a far better picture of the complexities of life for street children in Indonesia.

Summary of Section 4

The new social studies of childhood have been influential in setting out a framework for the way childhood is shaped and understood.

Central to this new framework is the socially constructed nature of childhood that can be extended to include the way consumer culture constructs childhood.

Close observation of the cultural worlds of children and young people, including engagement with popular culture, can be a productive way of understanding the experience of childhood.

5 After the new paradigm

By the turn of the twenty-first century, the new social studies of childhood had become the established framework for the sociocultural study of childhood. It could no longer reasonably be referred to as a 'new' or 'emergent' paradigm, struggling against dominant models of 'socialisation' or 'development'; it had become the dominant paradigm in the field. As a result, a set of critiques of this, now dominant, paradigm began to emerge, and scholars began to investigate ways of proceeding in the light of them. Indeed, Alan Prout, who had been intimately associated with the movement throughout the 1980s and 1990s, remarked in 2005 that 'productive though the new social studies of childhood have been, the intellectual limits of the programme are increasingly apparent' (Prout, 2005, p. 2).

In articulating his growing concerns about the movement, Prout situates the new social studies of childhood within the broader history of modernist thought and, indeed, he notes that it occupies a somewhat anomalous position within sociocultural research as a result. The central project of modernist thought had been the search for the principles of social order, which was often explained in terms of dichotomies or binary oppositions – mutually exclusive categories which cleave the world in two, such as structure and agency, male and female, and adult and child. Socio-economic shifts during the twentieth century – for example, the move towards flexible working in an increasingly globalised economy and the loss of certainty in social roles that accompanied shifts in gender relations as a result of the feminist movement (Lee, 2001) – had begun to expose the limits of modernist thought and researchers turned towards new 'late modern' or 'postmodern' social theories as a more adequate means of explaining sociocultural phenomena. In comparison, the new social studies of childhood seemed to be asserting and reinforcing the dichotomous oppositions of modern thought. As Prout explains:

> At the very time when social theory was coming to terms with late modernity by decentring the subject, the sociology of childhood was valorizing the subjectivity of children. While sociology was searching for metaphors of mobility, fluidity and complexity, the sociology of childhood was raising the edifice of childhood as a permanent social structure. The sociology of childhood arrived, then, on the cusp of modernity when the social theory adequate to the transformations underway in modernity was in the process of being constituted. Childhood sociology, then, seemed to need to run in order to catch up with modernist social theory that was itself becoming disorganized by social changes that exceeded and defeated its conceptual range. So to sum up, one could say that sociology's encounter with childhood is marked by late modernity – but primarily in an ironic sense: at the very time that sociological assumptions about modernity were being eroded they arrived, late, to childhood.
>
> (Prout, 2005, p. 62)

The new social studies of childhood had sought to make space for children and childhood in sociocultural thought, but it had done so by inverting a set of established dichotomies, principally adult/child, nature/culture and becoming/being. Until the late twentieth century, children and childhood had largely been given up to 'nature' and were viewed as the concern of the biological or medical sciences. When they were considered socioculturally, it was through notions of 'socialisation' and 'development', which accounted for children's transition from 'natural' beings to 'social' or 'cultural' ones. The new paradigm produced a reverse discourse to this by emphasising the social construction of childhood; it replaced a biological reductionism with a sociological reductionism. At the time, this was a useful strategy, but Prout explains that it was ultimately an overstatement which caused as many problems as it solved.

Similarly, the binary opposition becoming/being has long been implied in the distinction between adults and children. Traditionally, children are understood as 'growing up', that is they are in the process of becoming adult. It is for this reason that they are so often theorised in terms of 'development' (the process of becoming a mature human) and 'socialisation' (the process of becoming social). In contrast, adults could be understood as stable, complete, independent human beings. The new social studies of childhood sought to abandon this concentration on children as adults-in-the-making and instead sought to take them seriously as 'beings in their own right rather than pre-adult becomings' (Holloway and Valentine, 2000, p. 5). However, Nick Lee argues that, while the distinction between being and becoming may remain an important means of regulating children and childhoods, it is increasingly unhelpful as a means of understanding them. Due to the socio-economic shifts discussed above, it is increasingly untenable to view humans of any age as stable, independent and complete. Instead, Lee sets out to explore approaches which view both children and adults 'as fundamentally dependent and incomplete' (2001, p. 103); that is, approaches which make no distinction between being and becoming at all, and instead view them as one and the same thing.

Both Lee and Prout are concerned with moving beyond the 'reverse discourse' of the new social studies of childhood, both by reconnecting with the valuable contributions of 'development' and 'socialisation' as a concept, and by making new connections with theories being developed elsewhere in the social sciences. Lee sets out what he, somewhat provocatively, refers to as an 'immature sociology' based in associational rather than binary thinking. He draws upon and combines a range of theoretical resources in setting out this project, including 'actor-network theory' or ANT (see Latour, 2005) and the concept of 'assemblages' (Deleuze and Guattari, 1988), and ethnomethodology (Garfinkel, 1967). He identifies three key principles of this approach.

1 'Agency as dependency' (Lee, 2001, pp. 129–31)

The concept of 'agency' is traditionally used within sociocultural research to explain processes of change within societies. It is often attributed to individual humans who are understood to possess some property of 'agency' which allows them to act as agents of change in the world. The new paradigm in childhood research led to a great number of studies that were concerned with demonstrating children's agency in a range of different contexts and situations. In contrast, Lee does not view agency as an attribute that can be 'possessed' by individual human actors independently of their surroundings. Instead, he turns to an approach developed within science and technology studies known as 'actor-network theory' or ANT (Latour, 1992, 2005). Bruno Latour makes no distinction between humans and non-humans, and views social life as the outcome of networks of connections and associations between actors of all kinds: humans, animals, plants, objects, and so on. The actors within these networks are only able to act because of the network of connections in which they are engaged. Humans – both adults and children – are always incomplete because they are necessarily dependent on a range of material 'extensions' and 'supplements' on which their powers and abilities rely. Approaching children and childhood in this way forces sociocultural researchers to attend to what children and young people do, rather than focusing on what they intrinsically are. The task for researchers, then, is to trace the patterns and networks of extension and supplementation in which children and childhoods are embroiled, and to account for how they emerge from these networks. Thinking in this way opens the question of how agency is achieved to empirical study and analysis; it is not the end of the analysis, but the beginning.

2 'Incomplete convention' (Lee, 2001, pp. 131–33)

Where the concept of 'agency' has traditionally been used to account for social change, notions of 'structure' or 'convention' are often relied upon to account for the stability of social life. The approaches to socialisation discussed in Section 2 are based upon a concept of stable social structures into which children and young people can be socialised. As with the notion of agency within ANT, 'structure' or 'convention' have no explanatory power in and of themselves. Latour (2005) views social structure or convention as a contingent outcome of networks of associations in exactly the same way as agency. The task remains for researchers to explain how conventions or structures arise within networks of socio-material relations and to account for the processes and practices through which they are sustained. Lee turns to an area of sociology known as ethnomethodology as a means of exploring the production of social convention without assuming that those conventions are ever complete or stable. Harold Garfinkel explains that social order is achieved and produced as an 'endless, ongoing accomplishment' (1967, p. 1) through the everyday practices of members of a society. Ethnomethodologists attempt to account for and explain the methods through which members of a particular sociocultural group produce social conventions and orders through their ordinary practices. In this sense, social orders must be explained in relation to social practices, which necessarily encompass discursive and material elements.

3 'Ethics in motion' (Lee, 2001, pp. 133–34)

The 'new paradigm' contends that children deserve recognition because they are 'beings'; we, as adults and researchers, should listen to them and seek out ways to afford them 'a more direct voice and participation in the production of sociological data' (James and Prout, 1997, p.8). However, Lee argues that there cannot be any unmediated access to the child, for adults or for the child; there is no 'authentic' child to be found. The task for sociocultural researchers, then, is 'to mediate children well' (Lee, 2001, p. 134). Rather than thinking of ethics as a set of stable positions, Lee urges us to consider ethics as 'motion'. The relevant question is not whether a particular approach is more 'ethical' than another, but to ask 'whether particular patterns of the extension or mediation of children open movements and transfers of voice that are desirable' (Lee, 2001, p. 134).

In setting out these principles of an 'immature sociology', Lee seeks to build an alternative picture of the process of 'growing up' and of the differences between adults and children. As he explains:

> growing up is what happens as networks or assemblages of extension expand and incorporate more and more elements. The bigger the assemblage, the slower it can change or be changed. From this perspective, growing up is a slowing down, a decrease in the rate at which a person can pass from one social order to another. Slowing down or growing up has a cost. It sets limits to the pace of personal and social change. But it also has a benefit. The more extensive one's network, the more elements included in one's assemblage, the more powerfully agentic one can be.
>
> (Lee, 2001, p. 137)

In this way, Lee sets out to explain the differences between adults and children in terms of the reach and complexity of the socio-material networks or assemblages in which they are enmeshed. Lee urges childhood researchers to explore, describe and analyse the socio-material encounters from which children and childhoods emerge. In the remainder of this section we look at how this kind of approach affects sociocultural accounts by considering ideas of 'embodiment' and 'assemblage' – two themes that have contributed to the theoretical development of childhood studies.

Figure 9 Childhood studies encourage us to pay attention to children's embodied activity

5.1 Bodies

Chris Shilling (1993) has identified two ways in which sociocultural researchers have tended to approach the human body, which he refers to as 'foundational' and 'anti-foundational' approaches. Foundational approaches view the body as a natural and biological entity through which humans are able to experience and interpret the world. Sociocultural researchers adopting this type of approach are interested in exploring how this pre-given, biological body is given meaning through sociocultural practices and how it is experienced in different sociocultural contexts. In contrast, anti-foundationalist approaches view the body as socially constructed. Researchers subscribing to extreme forms of this position might assert that there is no natural or biological body at all, only social constructions and representations of it. Most sociocultural researchers take a less extreme view of the body but insist that, although humans do have a biological and material body, we are only able to access or experience it through the discourses which structure and shape our experiences. This group of sociocultural researchers set out to explore how the body is represented and to analyse the social processes through which bodies are constructed in particular ways.

Shilling sets out another possible position, which attempts to move beyond and bridge between these views of the body as either inherently natural (the foundational approaches) or cultural (the anti-foundational approaches). He asserts that the human body is both socially and biologically unfinished. It changes throughout the life course in ways that are both social and biological. Shilling describes a reciprocal and symbiotic relationship between the body and society; the human body constrains and enables sociocultural relations and, at the same time, it is shaped by them.

Alan Prout sees this approach as particularly promising for childhood studies because 'once we grant the body a biological/physical existence we can begin to see how it is worked upon by society' (2005, p. 104). It allows sociocultural researchers to approach children's bodies by tracing through the materials, practices and processes implicated in the production and maintenance of bodies.

5.2   Assemblage

Gilles Deleuze (a French philosopher) and Félix Guattari (a French psychoanalyst turned philosopher) (1988) view humans as constitutionally unfinished. Humans (whatever their chronological age) are always becoming otherwise by entering into new relations and alliances with each other, things and animals. Deleuze and Guattari argue that it is impossible to think of humans in isolation because we must always take into account the various borrowings through which human existence is mediated. Instead, they advocate thinking in terms of assemblages.

They develop this concept of assemblages through an account of the domestication of horses and their use in warfare and agriculture. In the Bronze Age, humans began to ride horses; they 'were able to extend their powers to cover geographical distance by borrowing the legs, hearts and lungs of horses' (Lee, 2001, p. 114). By entering into '[hu]man–horse' assemblages, riders could travel faster and over longer distances than they could alone. But, by entering into this assemblage both humans and horses were changed: horses were captured, trained and transformed into mounts; by learning about horses and developing the skills to ride them, humans became 'riders'. The 'human–horse' assemblage was enrolled into wider patterns of extension and borrowing through which metals are mined, refined and worked to produce tools and weapons. In warfare, daggers were too short to be of use to riders and so they were equipped with swords or lances. The 'human–horse–sword' assemblage altered the practices and strategies of warfare, just as the 'human–horse–plough' assemblage altered the practices of agriculture and enabled European societies to change, as they could rely on greater agricultural yields. Lee explains that each of these assemblages forms a temporary order, an alliance in which humans, materials and animals combine, and through which all involved are changed. Humans are, therefore, not 'naturally' or inherently riders, warriors or farmers, but they can become so through their encounters with materials and animals.

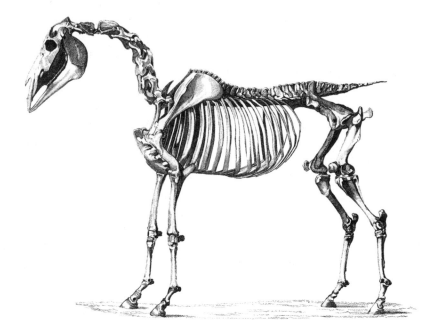

Figure 10   Assemblages bring human and non-human together

Activity 4   Reading B

Allow about 35 minutes

Reading B is an extract from Valerie Walkerdine's (2009) book chapter, 'Developmental psychology and the study of childhood'. The extract reviews the approaches and considers research possibilities for 'doing childhood differently' (Walkerdine, 2009, p. 118).

Read through the extract from Walkerdine's chapter and complete the following tasks:

- Make a list of the three ways in which children become subjects in Walkerdine's account.
- Explain how the concept of 'situated cognition' is helpful for understanding childhood.
- Explain how 'actor-network theory' and the concept of assemblage might be useful in studying children's experiences.

Comment

Valerie Walkerdine's chapter aims to think about the place of psychology in the understanding of childhood. She notes that developmental psychology has played a central role in the scientific study of children since the end of the nineteenth century. The sociological critique of this body of literature has had the effect of purging psychology from childhood studies, only to replace it with forms of neuroscience. Walkerdine suggests that psychology can contribute to our understanding of childhood and can be understood within the context of a historically specific political moment of minority-world democratic societies. She explores the experience of schooling in nineteenth-century England as a process designed to address national problems of crime and pauperism. Education would teach moral values and good habits. This investment in pedagogy produced a new way to understand the *nature* of children. From this perspective, developmental psychology provides valuable insights into childhood as a process of adaptation marked by the staged progression towards adulthood. Walkerdine points out that childhood is always produced as an object in relation to power. Moreover, the modern minority-world conceptualisation of the child exists in circuits of exchange between the minority and majority worlds. Walkerdine suggests that it is important to move beyond dualisms to understand how people become subjects within specific local practices and, further, to understand how subject positions and practices operate within complex circuits of exchange. In conclusion, Walkerdine outlines three approaches to rethinking the place of psychology in childhood: situated learning and apprenticeship; actor-network theory; and Deleuze and Guattari's notion of assemblages.

Summary of Section 5

The new social studies of childhood have been followed by further studies that develop and expand approaches to understanding childhood.

Actor-network theory and the concept of assemblage offer exciting ways of theorising childhood.

6 Conclusion

The late twentieth century is marked by an interest in forms of reflexivity. Sociocultural researchers reflect on the nature and status of academic inquiry in questions such as 'How do we know what we know?' and 'How far does research bring into being the subject it purports to study?' The argument could be made that, in conducting research on children, researchers also produce a version of 'the child' and indeed a version of childhood. The recognition that there may be different ways of being a child and different kinds of childhood is a touchstone of sociocultural approaches to childhood, underlining the premise that childhood is not universal; rather, it is a product of culture and as such will vary across time and place.

Sociocultural research in childhood and youth is a very diverse, interdisciplinary field, which makes it difficult to provide an overview or to set out anything that might reasonably be referred to as a singular sociocultural approach to childhood and youth. In this chapter, we have discussed some ways in which sociocultural researchers have approached children and childhood. The concepts of 'socialisation' and 'development' that dominated sociocultural approaches to children and childhood for most of the twentieth century did not disappear with the advent of the new social studies of childhood, and were never as incompatible with the new paradigm as its proponents often made out. Nevertheless, the principles of this new paradigm have been hugely influential in shaping the sociocultural study of childhood, particularly with regards to the notion of childhood as a social construction and the emphasis placed on children and young people's everyday experiences, interests and views. Scholars seeking to move beyond the dichotomies embedded within the new social studies of childhood have sought to revisit some aspects of more traditional approaches to childhood and youth. In doing so, they have sought to build upon, rather than abandon, the achievements of childhood research in the last century and to connect with developments elsewhere in the social sciences through a focus on practices, bodies and materials.

References

Aitken, S. C. (1994) *Putting Children in Their Place*, Washington, DC, Association of American Geographers.

Beazley, H. (2003) 'Voices from the margins: street children's subcultures in Indonesia', *Children's Geographies*, vol. 1, no. 2, pp. 181–200.

Buckingham, D. (2011) *The Material Child: Growing Up in Consumer Culture*, Cambridge, Polity.

Bunge, W. W. (1971) *Fitzgerald: Geography of a Revolution*, Cambridge, MA, Schenkman.

Bunge, W. W. (1973) 'The geography', *The Professional Geographer*, vol. 25, no. 4, pp. 331–7.

Carey, J. W. (2008) *Communication as Culture: Essays on Media and Society*, 2nd edn, New York, Routledge.

Cook, D. (2004) *The Commodification of Childhood*, Durham, NC, Duke University Press.

Cross, G. (2004) *The Cute and the Cool: Wondrous Innocence and Modern American Children's Culture*, Oxford, Oxford University Press.

Deleuze, G. and Guattari, F. (1988) *A Thousand Plateaus: Capitalism and Schizophrenia*, London, The Athlone Press.

Denzin, N. K. (2010) *Childhood Socialization*, 2nd edn, New Brunswick, NJ, Transaction Publishers.

Foucault, M. (1972) *The Archaeology of Knowledge*, New York, Pantheon Books.

Foucault, M. (1977) *Discipline and Punish: The Birth of the Prison*, London, Penguin.

Garfinkel, H. (1967) *Studies in Ethnomethodology*, Englewood Cliffs, NJ, Prentice-Hall.

Giddens, A. (1976) *The New Rules of Sociological Method*, London, Hutchinson.

Hey, V. (1997) *The Company She Keeps: An Ethnography of Girls' Friendships*, Buckingham, Open University Press.

Holloway, S. L. and Valentine, G. (2000) 'Children's geographies and the new social studies of childhood', in Holloway, S. L. and Valentine, G. (eds) *Children's Geographies: Playing, Living, Learning*, London, Routledge.

Horton, J. (2010) '"The best thing ever": how children's popular culture matters', *Social and Cultural Geography*, vol. 11, no. 4, pp. 377–98.

Horton, J. and Kraftl, P. (2005) 'For more-than-usefulness: six overlapping points about children's geographies', *Children's Geographies*, vol. 3, no. 2, pp. 131–43.

James, A. (1982) 'Confections, concoctions and conceptions', in Waites, B., Bennett, T. and Martin, G. (eds) *Popular Culture, Past and Present: A Reader*, London, Croom Helm/Open University Press.

James, A. and James A. L. (2004) *Constructing Childhood: Theory, Policy, and Social Practice*, Basingstoke, Palgrave Macmillan.

James, A. and Prout, A. (eds) (1997) *Constructing and Reconstructing Childhood: Contemporary Issues in the Sociological Study of Childhood*, London, Falmer Press.

James, A., Jenks, C. and Prout, A. (1998) *Theorizing Childhood*, Cambridge, Polity Press.

Jenks, C. (2005) *Childhood*, 2nd edn, London, Routledge.

Jones, O. (2001) '"Before the dark of reason": some ethical and epistemological considerations on the otherness of children', *Ethics, Place and Environment*, vol. 4, no. 2, pp. 173–8.

Kehily, M. J. (1995) 'Self narration, autobiography and identity construction', *Gender and Education*, vol. 7, no. 1, pp. 23–31.

Kehily. M. J. (2002) *Sexuality, Gender and Schooling: Shifting Agendas in Social Learning*, London, Routledge.

Kuhn, T. (1996) *The Structure of Scientific Revolutions*, 3rd edn, Chicago, IL, University of Chicago Press.

Latour, B. (1992) 'Where are the missing masses? The sociology of a few mundane artifacts', in Bijker, W. and Law, J. (eds) *Shaping Technology/*

Building Society: Studies in Sociotechnical Change, Cambridge, MA, MIT Press.

Latour, B. (2005) *Reassembling the Social: An Introduction to Actor-Network-Theory*, Oxford, Oxford University Press.

Lee, N. (2001) *Childhood and Society: Growing Up in an Age of Uncertainty*, Buckingham, Open University Press.

Mayall, B. (2002) *Towards a Sociology for Childhood: Thinking from Children's Lives*, Buckingham, Open University Press.

Mills, C. W. (1959) *The Sociological Imagination*, Oxford, Oxford University Press.

Mitchell, C. and Reid-Walsh, J. (2002) *Researching Children's Popular Culture: Cultural Spaces of Childhood*, London, Routledge.

Parsons, T. (1951) *The Social System*, London, Routledge.

Philo, C. (2003) '"To go back up the side hill": memories, imaginations and reveries of childhood', *Children's Geographies*, vol. 1, no. 1, pp. 7–23.

Plummer, K. (1995) *Telling Sexual Stories: Power, Change and Social Worlds*, London, Routledge.

Prout, A. (2005) *The Future of Childhood*, London, RoutledgeFalmer.

Prout, A. and James, A. (1997) 'A new paradigm for the sociology of childhood? Provenance, promise and problems', in James, A. and Prout, A. (eds) *Constructing and Reconstructing Childhood: Contemporary Issues in the Sociological Study of Childhood*, London, Falmer Press.

Risman, B. J. and Myers, K. (1997) 'As the twig is bent: children reared in feminist households', *Qualitative Sociology*, vol. 20, no. 2, pp. 229–52.

Rose, N. (1999) *Governing the Soul: The Shaping of the Private Self*, 2nd edn, London, Free Association Books.

Shilling, C. (1993) *The Body and Social Theory*, London, Sage.

Stainton-Rogers, R. and Stainton-Rogers, W. (1992) *Stories of Childhood: Shifting Agendas of Child Concern*, Hemel Hempstead, Harvester Wheatsheaf.

Tonkin, E. (1992) *Narrating Our Pasts: The Social Construction of Oral History*, Cambridge, Cambridge University Press.

Walkerdine, V. (2009) 'Developmental psychology and the study of childhood', in Kehily, M. J. (ed) *An Introduction to Childhood Studies*, Maidenhead, McGraw-Hill/Open University Press.

Woodhead, M. (2003) 'The child in development', in Woodhead, M. and Montgomery, H. (eds) *Understanding Childhood: An Interdisciplinary Approach*, Chichester, Wiley/Milton Keynes, The Open University.

Reading A
Exploited or empowered?

David Buckingham

Source: *The Material Child: Growing Up in Consumer Culture*, 2011, Cambridge, Polity, pp. 5–12.

Constructing the child consumer

From the moment they are born, children today are already consumers. Contemporary childhoods are lived out in a world of commercial goods and services. Marketing to children is by no means new, but children now play an increasingly important role, both as consumers in their own right and as influences on parents. They are exposed to a growing number and range of commercial messages, which extend far beyond traditional media advertising. They are surrounded by invitations and inducements to buy and to consume; and commercial forces also increasingly impact on their experiences in areas such as public broadcasting, education and play.

Consumer culture offers children a wide range of opportunities and experiences that they would not have enjoyed in earlier times. Yet, far from being welcomed or celebrated, children's consumption has often been perceived as an urgent social problem. Politicians, religious leaders, child welfare campaigners and consumer rights groups – not to mention armies of newspaper columnists and media pundits – routinely express concern and outrage at the harmful influence of advertising and marketing on children. Such concern is not confined to a single moral or political perspective: traditional conservatives and anti-capitalist activists, feminists and religious fundamentalists, all join forces in a chorus of condemnation. Children, they argue, should be kept away from harmful commercial influences: advertising and marketing to children should be banned, and parents should seek to raise their children in a 'commercial-free' environment. In these debates, consumerism is often tied up with a series of other social problems. Advertising and marketing are blamed for causing obesity and eating disorders, for encouraging premature sexualization, for promoting materialistic values, and for inciting conflict within the family and the peer group. Consumerism, it would seem, is destroying the fundamental values of childhood – and, in the process, it is making children's and parents' lives a misery.

And yet the focus of the objections here is often far from clearly defined. 'Junk food' advertising, sexy underage fashion models and deceptive marketing online are all precise enough as targets. But the criticisms of consumerism and the commercial world often range much more broadly: indeed, the debate often seems to be about the wholesale destruction of childhood itself. So are we only talking about advertising and marketing here, or about the economic system as a whole? Is 'consumption' just about buying stuff, or about using it too? Where does 'the commercial world' begin and end – and where might we find a 'non-commercial world'? Does the act of consumption inevitably involve sets of values or ideologies, such as 'consumerism' or 'materialism' – and how are these to be identified? Why are certain kinds of consumption implicitly seen to be acceptable – buying books or classical music CDs, or paying for your children to attend ballet classes – while others are not? Is the problem one of *excessive* consumption, or of people having *too much* money to spend – and, if so, who defines what counts as 'too much'?

Such arguments are certainly applied to adults, yet they seem to carry a unique force when it comes to children. Parents are frequently urged to resist consumerism *on behalf* of their children: only then, it would seem, will children be able to experience a good or proper childhood. Yet on what basis are some consumer products perceived to be inappropriate for children in general, or for children at particular ages? Why are some things deemed acceptable for adults, and not for children? Are children in general somehow more vulnerable than adults to the harmful behaviours and values apparently promoted by consumer culture? In what sense is it even possible, in a modern capitalist society, for children to be kept away from commercial influences – and what might be the negative consequences of seeking to do so? What are the alternative values that somehow stand outside the commercial world, and which might enable children and parents to resist its influence?

The construction of social problems

These questions point to the fact that the 'problem' of the child consumer is typically defined in quite particular ways. At stake are assumptions both about consumption – about what consumption is, and about 'good' and 'bad' consumption – and about children – about what children essentially are or should be, and about 'good' and 'bad' childhoods. These assumptions are not given statements of fact, and they are not neutral. On the contrary, the figure of the child consumer is framed and constructed in specific ways, which thereby marginalize or prevent other ways of thinking about the issue.

In recent years, analyses of social problems have explored such questions from a 'social constructionist' perspective. Broadly speaking, social problems can be defined as phenomena that are believed to be morally wrong, and that are seen to require positive intervention. Yet the things we identify and categorize as social problems are not stable or fixed. On the contrary, problems are defined in different ways in different social and cultural settings, and people often disagree about how they should be understood. Problems or issues are not simply given, but actively constructed. Groups of people have to identify, select and name them: problems must be categorized and typified in particular ways in order to become the focus of public attention. The metaphor of 'framing' is often used here: putting a problem into a frame serves to define it and focus attention on it, but it also detracts attention away from what lies outside the frame, and thereby limits the ways in which we can understand the problem in the first place.

Social constructionists suggest that in the more diverse and fluid context of contemporary societies, there is less consensus about right and wrong; and, accordingly, the construction of social problems is often a contested process, in which feelings may increasingly come to count for more than logic or evidence (Loseke, 2003). The actions of 'claims-makers' play a central role in this process. Studies have explored how key claims-makers – campaigners, politicians, experts, media commentators – work to define a social problem and increase its public visibility, often in pursuit of their own sectional interests. This typically entails mobilizing forms of rhetoric. Claims-makers compete with each other for media attention, often by overstating the scale of the problem, focusing on dramatic or spectacular manifestations, and occasionally drawing on dubious expert or scientific evidence (Hilgartner and Bosk, 1988). Such claims are often cumulative and mutually reinforcing, and so the scope of the problem tends to expand. The claims with most power to persuade are those that reflect other dominant themes – and indeed stereotypes and prejudices – within the culture. Simple claims are more effective than complicated ones; and formulaic stories featuring 'goodies' and 'baddies' – often involving melodramatic narratives of corruption and decline – are less likely to be challenged, not least because they can invoke powerful emotions. This is most evidently the case with the generation of 'moral panics' – a phenomenon that has, of course, been the focus of a great deal of sociological and historical analysis (e.g. Barker, 1984; Cohen, 2002; Springhall, 1998).

The figure of the child – or perhaps a certain idea of childhood – is often crucial here. As Joel Best (1990, 1994) and others have noted, the contemporary rise to prominence of child abuse as a social issue can be analysed in this way. Child abuse in various forms has always existed: but the processes through which it is defined – and indeed what *counts* as child abuse – have changed significantly over time. During the 1980s and 1990s in particular, various concerns about 'threatened children' – from homeless children to 'crack babies' to the victims of paedophiles – came to dominate the public agenda. Children were increasingly presented as endangered and vulnerable to harm; and parents were urged to take responsibility for their protection, and for the development of a healthy personality. As Best argues, contemporary images of children as victims resonate very effectively with the idealized, sentimental image of childhood that became culturally dominant in the nineteenth century, initially among the middle class. Children themselves are also relatively low in the hierarchy of claims-makers: they are rarely consulted – for example in media or policy debates – thus leaving the way clear for adults to make claims on their behalf (Loseke, 2003).

Indeed, making children the focus of claims often provides a powerful means of pressing emotional 'buttons', and hence of commanding assent, even when the actual target is much broader. If harmful influences in society can be shown to impact specifically on children, the argument for controlling those influences comes to appear much stronger. For example, Philip Jenkins (1992) provides a detailed study of the role of claims-makers and 'moral entrepreneurs' in the moral panics around child abuse – from sexual violence to paedophilia to Satanic rituals – which became so prevalent in Britain during the 1980s. As Jenkins shows, campaigns against homosexuality were redefined as campaigns against paedophiles; campaigns against pornography became campaigns against child pornography; and campaigns against immorality and Satanism become campaigns against ritualistic child abuse. Those who had the temerity to doubt spectacular claims about the epidemic proportions of such phenomena – or to question the need for censorious or authoritarian forms of action – could thereby easily be stigmatized as hostile to children. While some of the campaigns Jenkins identifies have faded, others have replaced them, and some have become steadily more prominent: concerns about childhood have become a powerful dimension of much broader assertions about the unravelling of the social fabric, and the moral collapse of what the Conservatives call 'broken Britain'.

The point here is not that these problems are merely illusory, or just a matter of irrational panic – although that probably is the case with some of the examples analysed by Jenkins. Rather, the focus of analysis is on how the problem is socially defined and constructed, and by whom; on the assumptions and emotional responses that are invoked in the process; and on the ways in which alternative perspectives are thereby excluded. In particular, as Jenkins (1992), Sternheimer (2010) and others argue, there is a risk that the construction and framing of specific social problems may divert attention away from more complex, more intractable issues – notably those which relate to the economy, and to social deprivation and inequality.

The problem of the child consumer

To what extent might we see the 'problem' of children and consumption in these terms? In recent years, there has been a flurry of popular critical publications about children and consumer culture, following in the wake of Naomi Klein's influential *No Logo* (2001). Prominent examples include Juliet Schor's *Born to Buy: The Commercialized Child and the New Consumer Culture* (2004), Susan Linn's *Consuming Kids: The Hostile Takeover of Childhood* (2004), Alissa Quart's *Branded: The Buying and Selling of Teenagers* (2003), Daniel Acuff and Robert Reiher's *Kidnapped: How Irresponsible Marketers are Stealing the Minds of Your Children* (2005) and, in the UK, Ed Mayo and Agnes Nairn's *Consumer Kids: How Big Business is Grooming Our Children for Profit* (2009). To be sure, there are some important differences among these publications. For example, Schor's is the most academic, and presents detailed statistical evidence from a psychological study of the links between consumption and 'materialism'; while Quart's is essentially a journalistic exposé of the teen marketing industry. As 'claims-makers', the authors also speak from different positions: Mayo, for example, is the director of a consumer pressure group, while Linn is a child psychiatrist, and Acuff and Reiher are both marketing consultants. However, these books share a highly critical view of the negative influence of advertising and marketing on children's lives: they all have a strong campaigning edge, and several of them conclude with a 'manifesto' and a series of links to activist organizations.

On one level, the arguments being made here are far from new. One can look back to similar assertions about the harmful influence of advertising being made in the 1970s, for example by campaigning groups like Action for Children's Television in the United States (see Hendershot, 1998; Seiter, 1993). However, there is a new tone of urgency here: these critics argue that contemporary marketing is significantly more sophisticated, and that children are now caught up in a powerful, highly manipulative form of consumer culture that is almost impossible for them to escape or resist. They accuse advertisers and marketers of using increasingly devious and deceitful techniques in order to target children, and of flouting legal regulations on the promotion of harmful products. They argue that children are being targeted at a younger and younger age, and that the boundaries between childhood, youth and adulthood are being progressively eroded, as children increasingly gain access to sexual and violent material. According to these critics, this new commercial culture is actively opposed to children's wellbeing and their best interests.

While there are certainly truths in some of these claims, all these books link the issue of consumerism with other time-honoured concerns about media and childhood, thereby broadening the scope of the problem and creating a picture of wholesale decline. Thus, as well as turning children into premature consumers, the media are accused of promoting sex and violence, junk food, drugs, tobacco and alcohol, gender stereotypes and false moral values, as well as contributing to an 'epidemic' of mental health disorders, anxiety, stress and harmful addictions (including the addiction to consumption itself). Today's children suffer from what Linn calls 'impulsivity' or Acuff and Reiher call 'Invisible and Intangible Information Overload' (IIIO). Children's play has been devalued, and their capacity for creative experience has been destroyed, in favour of conformity and superficial, materialistic values.

Of course, this is a familiar litany, which tends to confuse very different kinds of effects and influences; and it is informed by a much wider critique of 'consumerism', which sees it as fundamentally opposed to positive moral or human values. Linn (2004), for example, describes consumerism as an attack on democracy and family values, and on 'the spiritual, humanistic, or ineffable splendors of life' (p. 185). This ties in with a broader account of social and cultural decline, which sees children as increasingly threatened and endangered. Thus, Acuff and Reiher (2005) begin their book by declaring: 'Parents, your children today are in greater physical, psychological, emotional, and ethical danger than during any other era of modern civilization' (p. xii).

Perhaps paradoxically, the most vehement of these texts is that written by the two marketing consultants, Acuff and Reiher, whose biographies boast an extensive list of high-profile corporate clients. These authors employ the full range of rhetorical strategies that are characteristic of social problems claims-makers. Parents are addressed – via the collective 'we' – as partners in a crusade. A large collection of authorities is enlisted in support, by means of short (and frequently platitudinous) quotations that scatter the text, seemingly at random, from Billy Graham and Martin Luther to Albert Einstein, James Baldwin and Eleanor Roosevelt. Scientific evidence, principally drawn from infant neuroscience ('brain science') and developmental psychology, is presented as undisputed truth. The core chapters of the book present lists of 'basic needs', 'core developmental elements' and 'key vulnerabilities' relating to children at each of Piaget's developmental stages. Yet these apparently scientific arguments about the 'wiring' of the brain and about 'developmental blind spots' are used to justify what are clearly *moral* judgements, particularly about the influence of sexual and violent content in the media – for example about 'age-inappropriate sexuality' and the promotion of 'irresponsible attitudes'.

Lurking behind these judgements are further prejudices about taste and cultural value. Commercial marketing is acceptable, it would seem, if it promotes products that are 'healthy' or 'wholesome', but not if it relates to things that the authors deem to be harmful. For each age group, Acuff and Reiher present 'a week in the life' of an ideal and a dysfunctional family, arranged in two parallel columns. While the good parents set boundaries, preserve quality time and generally promote a healthy learning environment, the bad parents are permissive and neglectful (they send their children to daycare!), and allow their own enjoyment of popular culture to act as a model for their children. The contrast here is so absolute and stereotypical as to be comical – indeed, it rather resembles a meeting between the Brady Bunch and the Bundy family from *Married with Children*. While the teenagers from the good family are at their church group meeting, listening to 'soft rock' and reading poetry, the bad ones are wearing trench coats and miniskirts, playing violent computer games and generally living the life of sex, drugs and gangsta rap.

Collectively, these texts tell a simple story of the struggle between good and evil. Children are represented here as essentially innocent and helpless, unable to resist the power of commercial marketing and media. They are seduced, controlled, manipulated, exploited, brainwashed, bamboozled, programmed and branded. They are seen as fundamentally passive, vulnerable and defenceless – as 'passive commercial fodder', 'cogs in a wheel' or, in the words of Acuff and Reiher, 'sitting ducks' and 'easy prey' for marketers. Yet, as with other such campaigns invoking children, these books rarely include the voices of children themselves, or try to take account of their perspectives: this is essentially a discourse generated by adults *on behalf of* children.

The marketers, meanwhile, are the original Hidden Persuaders of popular legend (and indeed Vance Packard's classic Cold War paranoia about the thought-controlling power of subliminal advertising is quoted approvingly by several of these books: Packard, 1957). Marketers are seen to be engaged in a 'war on children': they bombard, assault, barrage, and even subject them to 'saturation bombing'. They 'take children hostage', invade, violate and steal their minds, and betray their innocence and trust. Even Mayo and Nairn (2009), who tend to represent children as more sceptical and resistant to the appeals of advertising, nevertheless present marketers in highly melodramatic terms. The subtitle of their book effectively equates marketers with paedophiles, while terms such as 'grooming' and 'stalking', and the metaphor of the 'child-catcher', recur throughout (on publication, an extract from the book was published in *The Times* newspaper accompanied by a large image of the evil Robert Helpmann character from *Chitty Chitty Bang Bang*).

As the social constructionists would put it, this story resonates very powerfully with the dominant 'feeling rules' of contemporary society (Loseke, 2003). Children reside in the highest moral category: they are constructed as blameless victims, innocent and morally pure. The marketers represent their moral counterpart: they are the smug, evil villains of the piece, deserving of our most vehement condemnation.

However, the intervening role of parents here is somewhat more ambivalent and problematic. 'Good' parents – those implicitly addressed by these books – exercise proper protection and control over their children, while 'bad' parents are liberal and permissive, indulging their own and their children's consumer desires. Ultimately, parents appear strangely powerless in the face of the 'onslaught' of commercial marketing; and yet they are also somehow to blame for what is happening to their children. In this context, 'good' parents can all too easily slip into being 'bad' parents, whether as victims of ignorance or of their own lack of self-discipline. Acts of consumption – whether by children or parents themselves – require constant vigilance and supervision, ideally armed with the checklists and 'toolboxes' such publications provide. Thus, while all of these books call for some kind of ban on marketing to children, or at least for much tighter regulation, much of the onus for dealing with consumer culture ultimately falls to parents: and indeed much of the rhetoric appears designed to inflame parental anxiety and guilt. The only solution, it seems, is for parents to engage in counter-propaganda, to censor their children's use of media, or keep them locked away from corrupting commercial influences. Only then, it would seem, when their lives are wholly supervised and controlled, will children truly be free to be children once more.

References

Acuff, D. S. and Reiher, R. H. (2005) *Kidnapped: How Irresponsible Marketers are Stealing the Minds of Your Children*, Chicago, IL, Dearborn.

Barker, M. (1984) *A Haunt of Fears*, London, Pluto.

Best, J. (1990) *Threatened Children*, Chicago, IL, University of Chicago Press.

Best, J. (ed) (1994) *Troubling Children: Studies of Children and Social Problems*, New York, Aldine de Gruyter.

Cohen, S. (2002) *Folk Devils and Moral Panics*, 3rd edn, London, Routledge.

Hendershot, H. (1998) *Saturday Morning Censors: Television Regulation before the V-chip*, Durham, NC, Duke University Press.

Hilgartner, S. and Bosk, C. (1988) 'The rise and fall of social problems: a public arenas model', *American Journal of Sociology*, vol. 94, no. 1, pp. 53–78.

Jenkins, P. (1992) *Intimate Enemies: Moral Panics in Contemporary Great Britain*, New York, Aldine de Gruyter.

Klein, N. (2001) *No Logo*, London, Flamingo.

Linn, S. (2004) *Consuming Kids: The Hostile Takeover of Childhood*, New York, New Press.

Loseke, D. R. (2003) *Thinking about Social Problems: An Introduction to Constructionist Perspectives*, New Brunswick, NJ, Aldine Transaction.

Mayo, E. and Nairn, A. (2009) *Consumer Kids: How Big Business is Grooming Our Children for Profit*, London, Constable.

Packard, V. (1957) *The Hidden Persuaders*, New York, McKay.

Quart, A. (2003) *Branded: The Buying and Selling of Teenagers*, London, Arrow.

Schor, J. (2004) *Born to Buy: The Commercialized Child and the New Consumer Culture*, New York, Scribner.

Seiter, E. (1993) *Sold Separately: Parents and Children in Consumer Culture*, New Brunswick, NJ, Rutgers University Press.

Springhall, J. (1998) *Youth, Popular Culture and Moral Panics*, London, Macmillan.

Sternheimer, K. (2010) *Connecting Social Problems and Popular Culture*, Boulder, CO, Westview.

Reading B
The social production of children as subjects

Valerie Walkerdine

Source: 'Developmental psychology and the study of childhood', 2009, in Kehily, M. J. (ed) *An Introduction to Childhood Studies*, Maidenhead, McGraw-Hill/Open University Press, pp. 121–3.

Understanding the social production of children as subjects

I argue that the study of childhood must be able to understand the discourses and practices in which childhood is produced and the way that the positions within those practices are experienced and managed to produce particular configurations of subjectivity ... However, we need to develop tools for the microanalysis of practices and their place in the positioning of subjects. I want to point finally and briefly to three approaches to this that already exist and which might be developed to assist in this work. The first is work on situated learning and apprenticeship (Cole and Scribner 1990; Haraway 1991; Lave and Wenger 1991); the second is actor network theory (Law and Moser 2002); and the third is the idea of assemblages (Deleuze and Guattari 1988; Lee 2001).

Work on the idea of learning being situated rather than general comes from two sources. The first is the work of feminist theorist Donna Haraway (1991), who questioned the idea of a 'god-trick' of large macro stories told by science as universalized accounts freed from context. The other trajectory comes from the work in the 1970s of Michael Cole and Sylvia Scribner (1990), who aimed to demonstrate that reasoning is not a generalized accomplishment but something produced in specific and local practices. This idea has been taken up by many psychologists and anthropologists in the last 30 years, perhaps the best-known of whom is Jean Lave. This body of work, known as situated cognition, has developed the study of apprenticeship (Lave and Wenger 1991) as a way of thinking about specific accomplishment of competences without having to look to a generalized developmental model. Lave and Wenger report a number of studies of traditional and modern apprenticeship. What they demonstrate is the way in which apprentices participate peripherally in the practices of the craft or skill they are learning. They argue that learning involves an inculcation into the culture of the practices being learned:

From a broadly peripheral perspective, apprentices gradually assemble a general idea of what constitutes the practice of the community. This uneven sketch of the enterprise (available if there is legitimate access) might include who is involved; what they do; what everyday life is like; how masters talk, walk, work, and generally conduct their lives; how people who are not part of the community of practice interact with it, what other learners are doing; and what learners need to learn to become full practitioners. It includes an increasing understanding of how, when, and about what old-timers collaborate, collude and collide, and what they enjoy, dislike, respect, and admire. In particular it offers exemplars (which are grounds and motivation for learning activity), including masters, finished products, and more advanced apprentices in the process of becoming full practitioners.

(Lave and Wenger 1991: 95)

This approach gives us a clear way of thinking about how children both are and become outside a developmental framework. The approach does not locate learning within the child but within the culture of practice. It is not at all incompatible with one which draws upon an idea of the production of children as subjects within particular practices as I discussed earlier. However, the approach which I proposed did also stress the importance of power in terms of understanding the kind of subject needed by liberalism. In addition, I stressed the importance of the complex emotional economies which form part of the production of the child as subject within a practice.

Other approaches, which are also compatible, are the reference by Lee (2001) to Deleuze and Guattari's (1988) idea of assemblages in which, for example, horse and rider as an assemblage manage to produce more than, or a supplement to, what either could accomplish alone. For Lee, the child learns by supplementation to take their place within the adult world. Finally, it is worth also considering the work of Bruno Latour and what is often described as actor network theory (Law and Moser 2002). Law and others have developed Latour's approach to science studies to take in the idea that organizations work to produce subjects in quite complex ways, so that what we might classically think of as power and agency are distributed.

So, for example, when exploring how the subjectivity of a manager of a science laboratory is created, Law and Moser (2002: 3) demonstrate that all actions within the organization are joined in a complex network so that 'it is no longer easy to determine the locus of agency, to point to one place and say with certainty that action emerges from that point rather than from somewhere else'. The manager only knows where 'he' is because his subjectivity as manager is an effect of a performance that is distributed in a network of other materials and persons, jobs and activities. It is these which produce the manager as an effect of power, power distributed in the complexities of networks, the 'intersecting performance of multiple discourses and logics' (Law and Moser 2002: 6). Like Lee, Law and Moser propose that the manager is an assemblage. In this approach, as in the others explored, the subject (in this case the manager) is not an essential psychological beingness. Rather, it is created as a nodal point at an intersection of complex discourses and practices. Could it be that children as subjects are created as both beings and becomings through the production of them as subjects who are created in practices, through what Law et al. call intersecting performances of discourses and practices, yet also in a way which means that they are constantly apprenticed into new practices?

Could we also say that the practices themselves involve complex circuits of exchange between children and between adults and children, which not only link locals to globals in Castenada's sense but also make connections within emotional economies in which, as with the case of the little girls I explored, girlhood does work for both adults and children and catches them up emotionally through the emotional investments in the contradictory positions which they enter? I am proposing that all these approaches potentially offer us ways of approaching childhood which take us beyond development but which do not throw out the psychological, but then also attempt to go beyond a number of dualisms, thus displacing the binaries of interior and exterior, individual and social, psychology and sociology.

Childhood, within these approaches, is mobile and shifting. Yet, potentially, change and transformation can just as easily be studied as within the developmental approach. But we are no longer in the terrain of an essential childhood with a fixed and universalized psychology of development. Rather, the practices in which we are produced as subjects from birth to death, and the ways in which they produce our subjectivity as both being and becoming, always in relation, always at once interior and exterior, provide us with a different way of studying and understanding the many and varied childhoods in their local variants and global forms.

References

Cole, M. and Scribner, S. (1990) *The Psychology of Literacy*, Cambridge, MA, Harvard University Press.

Deleuze, G. and Guattari, F. (1988) *A Thousand Plateaus: Capitalism and Schizophrenia*, London, Athlone.

Haraway, D. (1991) 'Situated knowledges: the science question in feminism and the privilege of partial perspective', in Haraway, D. (ed) *Simians, Cyborgs and Women: The Reinvention of Nature*, New York, Routledge.

Lave, J. and Wenger, E. (1991) *Situated Learning: Legitimate Peripheral Participation*, Cambridge, Cambridge University Press.

Law, J. and Moser, I. (2002) *Managing Subjectivities and Desires*, Lancaster, Centre for Science Studies, University of Lancaster.

Lee, N. (2001) *Childhood and Society*, Milton Keynes, Open University Press.

Chapter 6

**How is knowledge about childhood produced?
The issue of methodology**

Martyn Hammersley

Contents

In this chapter, you will:

- consider the main sorts of evidence that can be used in exploring issues about childhood
- examine some of the different ways in which researchers in various disciplines carry out their work
- be introduced to some of the methodological issues surrounding the production of knowledge about childhood
- be able to assess research findings about childhood issues, and develop your own conclusions on the basis of these.

1   Introduction

This chapter adopts a somewhat different approach from earlier ones. Rather than focusing upon substantive issues about childhood, it is more concerned with examining how we should go about the task of addressing these issues – in order to find better answers to questions such as whether or not childhood is currently in crisis; why there are very different ideas about how to bring up children across societies, and even within the same society; whether conceptions of childhood have changed significantly over the course of history; and so on. So, the focus in this chapter is on how we go about developing arguments that can answer questions like these, and assessing evidence relevant to them.

In doing this, we will want to know whether or not the available evidence is reliable and whether it offers sufficient support for any conclusion. In broad terms, these are questions about social research methodology: what is an issue is how we can come to know what we wish to know about the various topics addressed in childhood studies. In this chapter we will try to get some sense of the range of methods used in studying childhood – as regards ways of formulating research questions, types of data employed, modes of analysis adopted, and so on. We will also consider some of the fundamental debates that have taken place about these matters.

2 Types of data

A common way of thinking about social research methodology is to distinguish among various conflicting approaches, using labels like 'positivism' and 'post-modernism'. While this certainly highlights important disagreements and differences in orientation amongst researchers, such labels can be misleading; not least because they are used in a variety of ways. Instead, we will begin by adopting a more concrete focus on the sorts of data that social researchers employ and how they analyse these.

In reading earlier chapters, you may have noticed that many kinds of data can be used as a basis for drawing conclusions about childhood issues. In part, differences in the sort of data employed derive from variation in the character of the questions addressed. However, these differences also reflect divergent orientations among the disciplines and approaches that have explored this field.

Activity 1   Sources of data

Allow about 40 minutes

Look back over earlier chapters, and your notes on these, and identify five or six different types or sources of data mentioned. Try to make sure that your list includes at least one example that employs numerical data and at least one that relies on qualitative or textual data.

When you have done this, briefly answer the following questions for each item, as far as this is possible on the basis of the information that is available:

- Who produced the data or evidence, and for what purpose?
- By what methods did they produce it?

Finally, consider what the main differences are among the types of evidence you have found.

Comment

There are many examples of data referred to in earlier chapters that you could have listed. These include:

- Chapter 1: Personal memories of childhood; a letter to a national newspaper in the UK; government reports and legislation; survey data commissioned by a charity; boys' comics; observations of children's birthday parties and interviews with their mothers; pregnancy and childcare magazines; interviews with new mothers carried out as part of a research project; manuals of childcare.

- Chapter 2: Archived historical documents of various kinds, including illuminated manuscripts and coroners' records; published reports of government commissions; different types of literary sources, including novels and autobiographies; visual materials, including paintings and photographs; archaeological data; information from court records; diaries; letters; scientific and medical books on childhood illnesses; published poetry; religious and philosophical writings.

- Chapter 3: A book about a boy found living in the wild; anthropological interviews in Bangladesh and among the Navajo people in North America; UN documents on the rights of the child; textbooks on childhood psychology; a father's (Charles Darwin) biography of his son's development; data about child-rearing practices from a comparative study of an urban community in Boston, USA and a rural Gusii community in Kenya; a UK government report on education (Plowden); Piaget's experiments.

- Chapter 4: Reports of early anthropologists about their work, including Malinowski's diary; Mead and Freeman's published accounts of their anthropological research on Samoa; data collected in longitudinal studies of infant care; data from child informants; data on views about infants and childhood in Bali, Taiwan and Côte d'Ivoire; data from a study of views about children's rights in Ghana.

- Chapter 5: Adult memories of childhood; interview data from a study about how children were socialised within feminist households in the USA; texts on children's consumption practices; notes and drawings that girls passed around in the classroom; girls' magazines; interview data about children and young people's consumption of cheap sweets or 'kets' in north-east England in the late 1970s; interview data about young people's experiences of the urban environment in Detroit and Toronto.

In many of these cases we have little detailed information about how the data was produced, though we gain a general sense of their nature. I singled out the following examples where it was possible to say a little more about how the data was produced:

1   The survey data from UNICEF (2007) mentioned in Chapter 1, where the aim was to compare children's levels of well-being in different countries.

2   Evidence from the 1851 census about employment of children used in Chapter 2. Here the aim was to document the proportion of children in paid work.

3   The experiments mentioned in Chapter 3, carried out to test Piaget's previous results about cognitive development.

4   The observational material from Kavapalu's study of childhood in Tonga, used in Chapter 4 to illustrate cross-cultural differences in child-rearing.

5   The data about the hairstyles, tattoos and piercings among Tikyan boys in Indonesia, obtained by direct observation in the course of an ethnographic study. This was used to understand their distinctive subculture and how they relate to mainstream Indonesian society.

In the remainder of this chapter, I will use a couple of these examples (those numbered 1 and 4 above) for further illustration, and in the process I will draw on additional information about them.

Perhaps the most commonly mentioned methodological division to be found within social science is between research that relies primarily upon quantitative data (e.g. of the kind supplied by UNICEF (2007) – referred to in Chapter 1 – and the census figures used in Chapter 2), and that which depends mainly on qualitative data (most of the other sorts of data listed in the 'Comment' on Activity 1). Disciplines and areas of study in the social sciences generally, vary in the emphasis they give to these two types of data. For instance, much psychology relies upon quantitative data – notably, from experiments and tests – though there has also been an increasing amount of qualitative work in this discipline in recent years. By contrast, anthropology, history and cultural studies have tended to rely primarily, though not exclusively, upon qualitative methods. Within sociology, in Europe and the USA, there has been more of a balance, both quantitative and qualitative data being frequently used.

In the next section we will try to get a clearer sense of the difference between quantitative and qualitative data, how they are produced, and some of the distinctive threats to validity that inferences from them typically involve.

Summary of Section 2

A variety of kinds of data are used in research relating to children and young people, as in the rest of social science.

A broad distinction can be drawn between quantitative and qualitative data, and the different sorts of method used to produce these types of data.

> The use of methods varies significantly across social science disciplines and approaches within these.

3 Quantitative data

Quantitative data takes the form of numbers that are intended to indicate the frequency of various types of event and/or the degree to which objects (including people) possess some type of attribute. For instance, the census data used in Chapter 2 provide frequencies (number and proportion of children in work), whereas the data in the UNICEF study referenced in Chapter 1 is concerned with the degree of well-being of individual children, on average, within various societies.

Researchers generate numerical data in their research by a variety of means, but before considering how they do this we should remember that a large amount of numerical data is readily available to them, for example, published in 'official statistics' by governments and other formal organisations, including commercial companies. This data includes: demographic information about births, deaths, migration, illness, and so on; economic data about income, wealth, prices, unemployment, company balance sheets, profit levels, and sales; information about households: for example, about the number of people they contain, the kind of accommodation they have, how they spend their disposable income; data about education systems, such as numbers of different types of school, achievement levels; and so on. There is also much quantitative data, stored in archives, produced by previous research projects, which can be subjected to 'secondary analysis'. In addition, it is worth noting that published material of textual kinds – whether in print or online – can be analysed in quantitative terms, through applying categories distinguishing between different kinds of content (for instance, 'positive' or 'negative' representations of youth in the news media), or by using corpus linguistic techniques that identify (within some text or set of texts) the frequency with which particular words and their synonyms are used or with which one word or phrase is used in association with others (e.g. the frequency with which child/children/childhood and innocent/innocence co-occur within single paragraphs).

Where researchers set out to generate new quantitative data they can use several strategies. The main distinction here is between experimental and survey research. For example, the work based on Piaget's experiments – mentioned in Chapter 3 – produced quantitative data about the frequency with which children within particular age groups correctly recognised that the volume of liquid transferred from one container to another remains the same. What is distinctive to experiments is that some control is exerted by the researcher over variables relevant to the research. Thus, in the case of Piaget's experiments, and subsequent work building on it, control was exercised over the age of the children participating (and perhaps other attributes they had too), and over the 'cognitive level' of the tasks they were required to carry out.

Survey research usually involves the distribution of questionnaires, though there are also observational surveys (see Croll, 2001). And questionnaires are normally distributed to a relatively large number of people. The primary concern is with how particular attributes are distributed within this sample or a larger population, and how possession of these attributes, or different degrees of them, may be causally related. For example, research might investigate whether there is an association within a population between parental level of income and children's level of educational achievement; and, if so, whether this indicates that the first is causally related to the second. Questionnaires may be administered face-to-face (e.g. in homes or to whole classes of children in school), sent by post, carried out by phone, or done via email or the internet. Surveys can include a variety of types of question, from those seeking factual information, for instance asking people to report on their own lives (an illustration would be asking mothers whether they breast-fed or bottle-fed their babies), to those designed to measure attitudes (such as people's views about 'young people today').

It is important to remember that numerical data, like all data, is the result of a production process. This is true even when it is already available in government or organisational statistics: here it will have been generated by members of the relevant organisation rather than by researchers, but many of the same decisions will have been involved – about what to count and how to count it, what to measure and how to measure it. Furthermore, these decisions may have been shaped by somewhat different aims and concerns than when academic social scientists generate their own data, and this may affect its reliability and the purposes for which it can be used.

Activity 2   Children's well-being

Allow about 40 minutes

The UNICEF research discussed in Chapter 1 examined children's well-being under a number of headings. Three of these were 'material well-being', 'educational well-being' and 'subjective well-being' (referred to as 'young people's own perceptions of well-being' in Chapter 1), which were measured by the following means.

The conclusions about material well-being relied on information about: variation in household income; percentage of households without an employed adult; percentage of children reporting low family affluence; percentage of children reporting few educational resources; and percentage of children reporting fewer than ten books in the home.

The conclusions about educational well-being were based on information about: average achievement in reading literacy; average achievement in mathematical literacy; average achievement in science literacy; percentage aged 15–19 remaining in education; percentage aged 15–19 not in education, training or employment; and percentage of 15 year olds expecting to find low-skilled work.

The conclusions about subjective well-being relied on information about: the percentage of young people rating their own health no more than 'fair' or 'good'; the percentage of young people 'liking school a lot'; the percentage of children rating themselves above the mid-point on a *'Life Satisfaction Scale'*; and the percentage of children reporting negatively about personal well-being.

Carry out the following two tasks:

- Pick two of the dimensions of well-being listed above and, for each, outline what you think the researchers would have needed to do in order to produce quantitative data about the various features listed as measuring it.

- On the basis of your answer to the task above, what is your assessment – on a scale from 'unlikely to be true' through 'may be true' to 'very likely to be true' – of the conclusions about international differences in children's well-being produced by the UNICEF researchers?

Comment

The UNICEF researchers seem to have used a mixture of sources of data, drawing on official statistics and questionnaire surveys within the various countries covered. In both cases, this will have involved identifying and counting the relevant units (households, employed adults, children, etc.) plus identifying specified features and/or measuring relevant attributes (income, educational resources, reading literacy, etc.).

Completing the second task requires a personal judgement, but my own view is that, at least in the case of educational and subjective well-being, the validity of the conclusions is very uncertain.

The reasons for this will become clear from the rest of the discussion in this section.

As mentioned earlier, quantitative data take two basic forms. First, it may be the result of counting things. For instance, the UNICEF researchers used 'percentage of children in families without an employed adult' as one of their measures of the material well-being of children in different countries. In principle, this involves counting, within each country, the number of children in families without an employed adult in the household, and then calculating this as a proportion (in the form of a percentage) of the total number of children in the country. In practice, the data the UNICEF researchers used often involved drawing conclusions from samples of children or households in each country, but the basic process is the same whether or not sampling is involved. We will address sampling issues later.

Alternatively, numerical data may result from a process of measurement aimed at capturing the varying degrees to which a set of objects possesses some property, or the amount of time that something has existed or persisted. Thus, the UNICEF researchers used 'average achievement in reading literacy' as one measure of educational well-being. This data relies on the administration of a test of literacy, involving a range of tasks on the basis of which the degree of literacy of each child, measured on some scale, is recorded. These scores are then used as a basis for calculating the average literacy level, on the same scale, for children in each country. In practice, the research relied upon different tests, in different languages, in each country, but the data is presented as measuring literacy *across* countries.

In producing numerical data we need some means of identifying and characterising what it is that we are counting or measuring. Moreover, the concepts involved can often be troublesome or contentious. This is certainly true of the concept that is central to the UNICEF study – well-being (see Bailey, 2009; Morrow and Mayall, 2009) – but also of some of the concepts involved in the various indicators used to measure dimensions of well-being. For example, we saw that one of the UNICEF indicators was concerned with the percentage of children in households without an employed adult. In many respects, and contexts, this may be a useful indicator of poverty – though this would not always be true because, for example, there may be people with inherited wealth who do not need to take employment but are certainly not in poverty. Even where this is an appropriate indicator, there are often problems in determining what counts as a household, who does and does not belong to a particular household, and who is and is not employed (and perhaps even who is and is not an adult). Especially where data is being collated from many different sources relating to many countries, we can guess that there will be some deviation in how these concepts have been interpreted in order to produce counts. Sometimes the result will simply be minor variations in the data that do not lead us astray in our overall comparisons. However, if it were the case that how a household is defined, or how an employed person is identified, varied in a consistent way between countries, then this would affect the validity of any comparisons we make among those countries on this measure.

Similar, and often more severe, problems arise with measurement data. Here, again, we are dependent upon concepts that may not be easy to operationalise effectively. For instance, literacy is not a straightforward notion: what exactly would count as being literate? In terms of reading, measures here could range from, at one end of the scale, being able to read a written sentence aloud with some level of accuracy to, at the other, comprehension tests in which the focus is on assessing different levels of understanding. Furthermore, if we are to measure average literacy in a country, we must, first of all, be able to identify all children of the relevant age (not a straightforward matter in countries where comprehensive records of birth and age are not kept), and then find some test that will measure variation in literacy (defined in a particular manner) accurately in ways that are appropriate *within* each country and language, and yet that also allow comparison *between* countries. It should be clear that there is considerable scope for disagreement about what literacy is and how it varies, and there are practical problems in devising manageable tests that capture variation in literacy (however it is defined) accurately in different countries using different languages. How serious the potential for disagreement and the problems are is itself a matter of degree, and may be open to dispute.

One of the advantages of quantitative data is that they allow various sorts of arithmetical operation that enable us to summarise patterns or trends. For example, we saw that the UNICEF researchers turned frequencies of children in households without an employed adult into percentages of the total number of children, thereby allowing comparisons to be made across countries which have very different total numbers of children. Other kinds of rate are also possible. Thus, as a measure of the relative health and safety of children, the UNICEF researchers use 'number of infants dying before age 1 per 1,000 births' and 'deaths from accidents and injuries per 100,000 aged 0–19'.

Measurement data may allow even more complex forms of calculation to be carried out, starting with the production of averages (especially means and medians), but going beyond this to the use of other kinds of descriptive and inferential statistics (on these techniques see, for example, Bryman, 2008). We saw that in relation to literacy the UNICEF researchers used the scores of individual children to produce an average literacy level for each country. Averages are an extremely useful way of summarising the measurement scores of a population or sample. However, we should remember that they do not tell us everything we might want to know about the distribution of scores. For instance, two countries can have the same average level of literacy even though one has a much bigger proportion of the population with low levels of literacy (see Figure 1).

In order to get a better sense of the meaning of a particular average, quantitative researchers generally use measures that provide information about the spread and shape of the distribution. There are some technical means of measuring this, notably 'standard deviation', but also simpler, more crude, methods. For example, if we are interested in differences in income level between countries, in addition to comparing average levels of income we could compare the proportion of people within each society whose income is above some relatively high threshold and/or the proportion whose income is below a relatively low threshold. Thus, Norway and the USA have similar average levels of income, on some measures, but if we look at the distribution of levels of income across their populations we find that the USA is further away from an even distribution than Norway, with a greater proportion of very rich people and also a much larger proportion below what might be taken to be a poverty threshold.

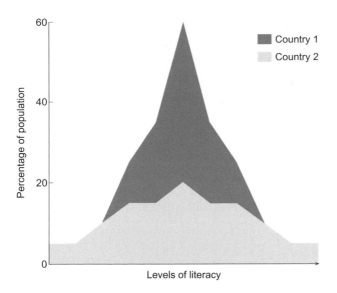

Figure 1   A fictional representation of variation between two countries with the same average level of literacy

It is also worth noting that the UNICEF researchers turn all of their data about each dimension of children's well-being into measurement on a single scale, which they use both to give different countries a ranking, and also to show the degree of variation among countries on the dimension. Figure 2 is the summary they provide of their findings about subjective well-being. The graph is scaled to show each country's distance above or below the OECD average of 100 and shows each country's standing in relation to the average for the OECD as a whole.

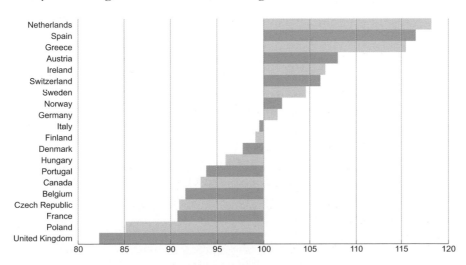

Figure 2   Subjective well-being of young people, an OECD overview (UNICEF, 2007)

At first sight, this sort of graphical representation may seem convincing, providing apparently clear-cut comparisons of levels of children's subjective well-being in different countries. They can undoubtedly be very useful in giving us a general sense of differences between countries. However, caution needs to be exercised in interpreting them: they certainly should not be taken at face value.

Activity 3   International differences in children's well-being

Allow about 20 minutes

Look at Figure 2 and answer the following questions:

- What does the order in which the countries are listed in the left-hand column claim to tell us?

- What are the shaded horizontal lines representing Germany and Italy intended to indicate?

Comment

The list of countries claims to tell us their rankings relative to one another in terms of subjective well-being. Rankings indicate which country came top, which came second, and so on. However, they do not tell us, in themselves, how much greater subjective well-being is in, say, the Netherlands as compared with Spain, or with the UK. The countries could all be quite close together and the gaps between them relatively even, or they could be spread out with gaps that are very uneven; so that, for example, the difference between the Netherlands and Spain could be much greater than that between Spain and the UK, or all of the countries could be very close together at a very low (or a very high) level of subjective well-being.

The shaded lines allow us to tell how far above the average of all the countries Germany was, and how far below that average Italy was. In this way, the lines enable us to judge, in principle, how far apart the countries were in terms of children's subjective well-being – in a way that a ranking could not. However, it is important to recognise that we are not being told here how far apart the countries are on some scale of children's subjective well-being, but rather how far apart they are *from one another*. Once again, they could all be clustered in low (or high) levels of subjective well-being rather than spread out across the whole scale. Furthermore, we need to remember the caution mentioned earlier about the limitations of averages in telling us about the spread and shape of a distribution: we cannot assume that the pattern of distribution of children's subjective well-being (e.g. across social classes, ethnic groups, genders, etc.) is the same in all the countries. Some may involve greater variation around the average than others.

We should also remember that, for reasons outlined earlier, the data may be unreliable and the transformations of the data (to produce the averages) may have introduced distortions.

As noted earlier, much of the data on which the UNICEF report is based relates to samples drawn from the populations of each country, rather than to the whole populations about which conclusions are presented. This is quite usual with survey data – it is characteristic, for example, of the opinion polls that are commonly reported in the news media.

One use that is made of mathematical statistical theory by social scientists is to provide a basis for assessing the likelihood that a frequency or a measure calculated for a sample will be a reasonably accurate estimate for the whole population from which it was drawn. This requires that the sample has been selected randomly, which means that each member of the population had an equal or known chance of being chosen. If this is the case, and the sample is of sufficient size, there is a strong chance that it will be representative of the population in many respects, and statistical calculation can tell us the likelihood that it is misleading.

However, assessing the likely validity of inferences from sample to population becomes more uncertain and much more difficult when, as is often the case, a complete listing of all the cases in the population was not available (this being essential for random selection), or data could not be collected on some of the sample initially selected because respondents could not be found or because they refused to fill in the questionnaire. It is not easy to get information about these sampling issues in relation to many of the surveys on which the UNICEF research is based, but we can be fairly sure that problems of inaccurate listings and non-response will have been present, as they are in most surveys. This is another reason for exercising caution in interpreting the findings. (The authors of the study recognise many of these problems, see Bradshaw, 2007. For other assessments of this research, see Ansell et al., 2007, and Morrow and Mayall, 2009.)

The UNICEF study is a particularly complex piece of descriptive quantitative research because it collates data on a range of dimensions each measured by several indicators and methods, relating to many countries. Nevertheless, it exemplifies one major use of quantitative research: to provide us with general information about large populations, and to enable comparisons amongst them.

This does not, however, represent the character of *all* quantitative research. Very often, the aim is not only to describe but also to *explain*. For example, we might try to address the question of why, according to the data presented in Figure 2, the UK has a much lower level of subjective well-being on the part of young people than the Netherlands. This sort of explanatory aim is frequently pursued in both experimental and survey research; indeed, the former is specifically designed for this purpose.

In the case of experimental research, the number of cases studied is usually much smaller than the number covered in official statistics and survey research. The partial exception to this is a form of experimental research called the randomised controlled trial (RCT). This was developed in the field of medicine to test the effectiveness of new drugs, but in the past few decades its use has been extended to other areas, including education, in order to try to discover which policies or practices are effective in producing improvements in educational achievement – for example, which methods of teaching reading work best. In such trials, relatively large numbers of people are randomly assigned to 'treatment' and 'control' groups, or between groups receiving different 'treatments'. Because the allocation is random, the differences between the groups in terms of background characteristics will be small (on average) so that background variables are controlled, giving us a better chance, in principle, of discovering whether or not there is a causal relationship between treatment and desired outcome.

Many non-experimental quantitative studies relying on survey data are also concerned not just with providing descriptions, in the manner of the UNICEF research, but also with discovering causal relationships, or measuring the causal contribution of particular factors. As an illustration, we might be interested not only in seeking to document the extent to which childhood has come to be sexualised in some countries in recent decades, but also to identify the *causes* of this – for example, commercial companies targeting children and playing on their desire to be 'grown up', increased permissiveness on the part of parents, etc. Addressing this causal question is a complex and difficult task. For one thing, we need to explore exactly what 'sexualisation' means, and we should take care not simply to rely on the evaluative implications that tend to be associated with that term, and the associated assumptions about the process involved; for example, that any interest in sexual matters on the part of children must be a product of external and 'unnatural' influences. On top of this, if some change broadly corresponding to 'sexualisation' has occurred, we must then think about how to try to identify possible causes of this and then to check our hypotheses. For instance, is 'sexualisation' more likely to occur where children have relatively high disposable incomes (themselves or through the influence they can exert on their parents) and where they are targeted by commercial companies in ways that appeal to 'sexual themes'? We may be able to compare cases where these factors are present, or operate at a high level, with those where they are absent, or are at a low level – at the same time controlling for other potential causes. Analysing such contrasting cases might enable us to reach a conclusion, though in the case of survey research it is rare to be able to make all of the comparisons required to come to strong conclusions about the validity of causal claims. Thus, even when we find a pattern (an association or correlation between the suspected cause and the outcome we are trying to explain), we cannot assume that it indicates a causal relationship. It may have been a product of some other variable(s) that we have not taken into account in our investigation. Furthermore, even if we can be confident that this is not the case, there may still be an issue about the direction of causation. For example, even if surveys have shown that children who watch a lot of television tend to be more materialistic in attitude than children who watch less (i.e. demanding the latest toys or clothes), there would still be a question about whether it is watching television that leads to materialism or the other way round.

While I have raised some questions about the capacity of quantitative research to achieve both descriptive and explanatory goals, this does not mean that it fails completely. The point is simply that we should not be beguiled by the apparently definitive character of the numerical conclusions it generates, for example, of the kind presented in Figure 2. Quantitative work can provide us with a relatively sound basis for generalising to large populations. And in some forms it has considerable capacity to identify causal relations, particularly where we are able to carry out an experiment in which we vary the hypothesised causal factor, and hold constant most other possible factors through random allocation to treatment and/or control groups. In such an experiment, if there is a corresponding change in the outcome variable, this would give us relatively strong evidence that our hypothetical cause operates; especially if the same thing occurs when we repeat the experiment. However, it is rare to be able to approximate perfect implementation of experimental procedure, and attempting this usually makes the experimental situation rather different from the 'real world' situations that we are trying to understand through doing the research.

The difficulties faced in carrying out quantitative research, and the uncertain validity of some of the findings produced, are among the reasons why the use of qualitative methods increased across many social science disciplines in the second half of the twentieth century. Moreover, these methods were central to the new field of childhood studies that emerged at that time.

Summary of Section 3

Quantitative data consists of numbers representing counts, rankings or measurements.

This data can come from a variety of sources. There is much data of this kind already available, produced by governments and other large organisations, for example. In addition, researchers carrying out surveys and experiments usually generate quantitative data.

It is important to remember that data is always the outcome of a process of production that involves a variety of decisions about how phenomena and features of them are to be identified and measured. These decisions may involve threats to validity.

One of the advantages of quantitative data is that some of the resources of mathematics can be used to describe and draw inferences from them.

Very often, surveys involve studying a sample of cases – with a view to generalising to a larger population – and mathematical statistics provide guidance in maximising the likelihood that the sample will be representative, as well as allowing calculation of the likelihood that it is unrepresentative. However, it is not easy to meet the requirements of sampling theory.

Quantitative studies can be descriptive, but they can also be explanatory, concerned with explaining why something happened. Here, control must be exercised over relevant variables, either through experimental design (e.g. random allocation to treatment and control groups) or through comparative analysis of large numbers of cases.

4 Qualitative data

It is often said that qualitative data consists of words rather than numbers. While there is truth in this, there is rather more to the distinction, as we shall see. Furthermore, qualitative data can take a wide variety of forms.

Activity 4   Comparing qualitative and quantitative data

Allow about 15 minutes

Building on your work in Activity 1, look at the example(s) of qualitative data you found and consider how they differ from the quantitative example(s), and also how they *differ from one another*. On the basis of this, and any other knowledge of qualitative research you have, map out some broad types of qualitative data.

There is no specific comment on this activity; the remainder of this section of the chapter will cover the relevant issues.

We will distinguish here between the following types of qualitative data: documents produced by people and organisations which may be available to, or elicited by, a researcher; field notes written by researchers to record data from observation or interviews; electronic recordings (both audio and video), and transcripts produced from these recordings.

In looking through earlier chapters, you could have found many references to *documents*, of various kinds. In Chapter 1, for example, there is mention of a letter published in a newspaper, of Enid Blyton's stories about *The Famous Five*, and of books by Palmer and Furedi. Use is also made of documentary data from parenting magazines. This illustrates the fact that published texts are a major form of data used by researchers in the field of cultural studies, but they are also used in other disciplines too. Historians rely particularly heavily on documents – both those belonging to archives and other kinds – as Chapter 2 indicates. Mentioned are reports of Royal Commissions and other official sources, personal letters and diaries, and also Ariès' analysis of paintings. One dimension of variation here relates to whether the document concerned has been published, circulated in a more restricted way (such as internal government documents), or whether it was intended solely for personal use; for example, some diaries.

All the examples of documents I have mentioned up to now have been paper based (or, in the case of the paintings, perhaps, canvas based), but, of course, today many documents are available in electronic form, including via the internet. In recent years, researchers have made increasing use of such evidence as data.

We can distinguish a variety of types of material in documents:

(a) **Text**. This refers to writing of some kind, which could be written in many languages and formats.

(b) **Diagrams and maps**. These are, of course, usually accompanied by written text, but it is important to recognise the rather different kind of representation that diagrams and maps involve, and the various functions they can serve.

(c) **Photographs and video-recordings produced independently of the research process**. There was an explosion in the amount of this type of material produced during the twentieth century, and this has increased over the past decade or so with the emergence of relatively cheap and easy-to-use digital cameras, including those built into mobile telephones. In addition, there has been a proliferation of television channels producing large amounts of video material, and a huge growth in the number of photographs in newspapers and magazines.

(d) **Drawings and paintings**. These types of data have long been available, from cave paintings to modern art and architectural designs. They are less commonly used than other types in social research generally, though they have been quite significant in the study of young children – not only in investigating changing images of children across historical periods, but also, for example, in examining children's drawings produced in school to learn about their capabilities or experiences.

In discussing documentary data up to this point we have focused primarily on those kinds that have been produced independently of the research process. However, it is important to remember that anthropologists, sociologists and others quite often actively elicit documents from people; for example, asking children to write diaries, or getting them to take photographs or shoot videos. On occasions children have also been asked to produce drawings, because these are sometimes seen as providing important insights into aspects of their state of mind, such as the effects of traumatic events on them.

The second broad form of qualitative data used by researchers that we mentioned was field notes. These are written by researchers based on participant observation or in order to provide a record of what informants say in interviews. This was the main source of data for anthropologists and many other ethnographers in the past (before the availability of cheap and portable audio-recorders), and field notes still play a crucial role in much qualitative research, if only as a complement to other kinds of data. The role of field notes is mentioned in Chapter 4 as central to the work of anthropologists, and these were the main kind of data used by Margaret Mead in her study of Samoa.

Today, qualitative researchers frequently use audio- and video-recording devices to produce an electronic record of naturally occurring events, and especially of interviews; and they usually produce transcripts from these. Audio-recording provides more detailed and accurate records of speech than field notes but, of course, there is much that they do not include. Video-recordings provide information about physical context and movement, as well as words, though it is a mistake to assume that they can present everything that is occurring in a scene   they only provide what was 'within shot', and there is almost always much going on outside of this. In addition, the use of video-recording may prevent ordinary observation, and/or significantly alter people's behaviour.

Both field notes and electronic recordings usually require processing in one way or another before they can be analysed and used as a basis for drawing research conclusions. Field notes are usually written in jotted form in the field, because of time constraints, and then written up in fuller form later. As already mentioned, audio- and video-recordings will usually need to be transcribed. Furthermore, transcribing audio-recordings is not always straightforward – notably where there is much background noise and/or where the talk is in a language of which one is not a native speaker – while transcription of video-recordings raises challenging issues about how to 'transcribe' the content and form of moving images. Transcription is very time-consuming, and this may place limits on the length of time and range of contexts in which data can be collected if researcher overload is to be avoided. In some cases the result of such restrictions may be that the data produced is insufficient for answering the research questions posed.

Analysis of qualitative data often involves simultaneously developing conceptual categories relevant to the research focus that make sense of the data – assigning data to these categories so as to provide a basis for producing descriptions and explanations. This contrasts sharply with the case of quantitative research, where, generally speaking, the categories into which data are to be coded are pre-defined: they are established before the data collection process begins. Qualitative analysis may also sometimes require detailed analysis of particular sequences of interviews or observational material, for example, looking at narrative structure.

Activity 5   Child-rearing in Tonga

Allow about 40 minutes

Read again the short extract below from Kavapalu's ethnography of child-rearing in Tonga (this is just one paragraph from the extract that you read for Chapter 4). As you read this, answer the following questions:

- Are the claims being made here qualitative or quantitative in character?

- If someone were to carry out further research in Tonga about patterns of child-rearing and the results were significantly different from those of Kavapalu, how might this be explained?

Here is the extract:

> For at least their first year, Tongan children are the focus of their households' attention, and they are treated with great concern and affection. Although much of the speech directed towards them consists of threatening, grumbling, scolding, and sharply-spoken orders, much of it is playful and affectionate, as when a nurse commented to a newborn baby, whose mother was feeding him, '*Taa'i koe, fa'a kai, e?*' ([I'll] hit you, eating all the time, eh?). When babies cry, every effort is made to soothe them, but loud and persistent crying is sometimes treated with annoyance and the baby is told sharply to '*Longo!*' (be quiet), '*Malolo!*' (rest) or '*Mohe!*' (sleep). By the end of the first year crying is increasingly treated as a nuisance, rather than a cause for concern, and babies are more likely to be shouted at or even punished for crying.
>
> *(Kavapalu, 1993, p. 318)*

Comment

Answering the first question is not as straightforward as it might seem. No numbers are used in this extract, or in most of the rest of the article; the description is entirely in words, so we might conclude that the data here is qualitative. This would be the generally accepted view. However, we should note that there can be a difference between the form that data takes and the nature of the claims it is making. These claims are actually quantitative in character, to a large extent: they are about frequencies and degrees of properties. Examples include: the proportion of actions displaying 'great concern and affection'; the amount of speech consisting of 'threatening, grumbling, scolding and sharply-spoken orders' and the proportion of this that is 'playful and affectionate'; the amount of effort made to soothe babies when they cry; the frequency with which 'loud and persistent crying is [...] treated with annoyance'; and the estimate that 'by the end of the first year crying is increasingly treated as a nuisance'. Furthermore, the author is generalising from observations of the behaviour of a relatively small number of Tongan parents to draw conclusions about what is common behaviour in Tonga. What this highlights is that quantitative judgements are often formulated in qualitative, rather than numerical, terms. This is true in everyday life as well as in much research (the word 'much' in this sentence is another example!). We can see from this that the difference between quantitative and qualitative data is not quite as simple as sometimes assumed.

You may be tempted to infer from this that it would have been better if Kavapalu had produced numerical rather than qualitative information about Tongan behaviour, or you might even draw the conclusion that her study would necessarily be inferior to a survey of child-rearing practices that relied on parents reporting in numerical terms how frequently they scolded young babies for crying, etc. However, such conclusions are too hasty, at best. There is a continual danger with numerical data of over-precision; for example, of presenting specific counts and measurements when verbal estimations using words like 'high' and 'low', 'more' and 'less', etc. would be more accurate. To some degree there is an inverse relationship between accuracy and precision: for example it would be easier to identify whether the majority of Tongan parents have a particular view about children than it would be to provide a precise and accurate estimate of what percentage share this view. Verbal descriptions that do not pretend to be precise may be superior to inaccurate numerical data.

Turning to the second question, this relates to a more general issue regarding how we should go about assessing competing accounts of the same phenomenon. The account presented by Kavapalu is based on a variety of kinds of evidence: notably, reports from some Tongans about their child-rearing practices and observations of their interactions with their children. These same sources of data could be used in any restudy. However, we should note that, because the description is framed in terms that are less precise than would be the case if numbers were used, there would be scope for disagreement between the original researcher and our imaginary second researcher carrying out a restudy about what typically goes on. What one person means by words like 'typically', 'common', 'much', 'frequently', and so on, can differ from what another means by these terms.

One reason for this is that those producing the descriptions are operating with different implicit comparisons. We can imagine that two anthropologists whose home societies differed sharply in the degree to which, and seriousness with which, babies are reprimanded and punished could vary in their estimates of prevailing patterns of behaviour in Tonga. In a later monograph produced on the basis of her research, the author reports being shocked when, prior to becoming an anthropologist, as an Australian who had married a Tongan, she saw her nieces lined up and beaten with a stick on their legs and hands for disobedience. She reports: 'By the time it was the youngest girl's turn she was sobbing with fear, but her mother, sitting cross-legged on a mat, resolutely administered her punishment' (Morton, 1996, p. 1). As this makes clear, severe punishment of this kind was shocking to her, and therefore very noticeable; so that, despite her best efforts, she may have overestimated its frequency. The point here is not whether or not this is true in the case of Kavapalu/Morton – she had developed in-depth knowledge of Tongan society over a long period of time – but rather a more general one that our informal estimates are shaped, and sometimes distorted, by our background expectations and feelings about what we are observing.

Another source of potential variation between the original study and a restudy concerns the different samples of people on which the two anthropologists are likely to be relying (if they are not simply reusing the original data). In other words, they will almost certainly employ testimony from and observation of different Tongans. Equally important, the data will have been collected at different times, and this too may generate discrepancies. For instance, the later collection of data may take place under a different balance of conditions; for example, at a time when economic and political conditions are better or worse than previously. So, in assessing the descriptions produced by the two anthropologists we would need to ask: how far does the sample of people, settings, etc., that constitutes the sources of information provide us with a basis for generalising to what all or most Tongans do, or to what they typically did in some particular time period?

The above Comment identifies some of the issues that need to be addressed in evaluating the likely validity of findings from qualitative research. However, there are others too. For instance, where studies rely heavily on interview data, there is the problem that what people tell us may not be entirely accurate, and can sometimes be seriously misleading. As we saw in Chapter 4, this became a major issue in connection with Margaret Mead's study of Samoa (1928). Many years later, on the basis of his own lengthy fieldwork in that society, Freeman (1983, 1999) challenged some of the main findings of her study; for example, that there was a relaxed attitude towards adolescent sexual activity among Samoans, and that such activity was commonplace. Freeman claimed that Mead had been misled ('hoaxed') by the young girls who had acted as her informants (see Bryman, 1994; Shankman, 2009).

There is a variety of reasons why people may not tell the truth to researchers. One is that they wish to present their own society, or themselves, in a good light. We should note that what this leads to may vary according to what assumptions informants make about the researcher, and especially about what he or she would expect, approve of, etc. What people say may also reflect their own desires about how their lives should be. Another reason why information from informants might be misleading is that their estimates of what they typically do may not be very accurate; they could be distorted in similar ways to those mentioned in the Comment on Activity 5. Often we cannot make very accurate estimates of our routine behaviour because this is below the level of consciousness – most of the time we do not give it close attention, and certainly do not engage in counting or measurement. Nor should we assume that people's interpretations of their own motivations will always be accurate.

Another reason for error, which Freeman claims was true in the case of Mead, is that informants may play tricks on the researcher, providing false information, or that they may be embarrassed about the topic of discussion and joke about it as a way of dealing with this embarrassment. Of course, much the same questions could be raised about Freeman's interviews in Samoa, including that with one of Mead's informants (Freeman, 1999).

Generally speaking, qualitative researchers will check the accounts from informants against their own observations, and/or check accounts against one another. Even where they are not be able to carry out very extensive observations – for example, because they are unable to gain access to all of the settings that might be relevant, or they are unable to observe over a time period that would allow them to make judgements about changing practices – their observations will serve as a means of assessing the likely reliability of informants' accounts. Similarly, being able to talk to multiple informants in the same context will often allow checks on the accuracy of data and provide a fuller picture of the phenomena being studied. The potential for comparing data from different sources in these ways is an important strength of qualitative research, by comparison with quantitative work where neither of these sorts of checking, via observation or the use of multiple accounts, is usually possible. For example, in the UNICEF study many of the indicators relied entirely upon responses to questionnaires, with no other data about what the respondents were reporting being available.

At the same time, qualitative research has weaknesses that mirror the potential strengths of quantitative work. For example, most qualitative studies only tell us directly about one or a few cases, they do not cover the large number of people and situations that surveys usually do. Furthermore, generally speaking, in research we are not interested in the particular people and situations studied for *themselves* but rather for what they can tell us about the attitudes and behaviour of some type of person or larger group of people, or the patterns of social relationships to be found in some society or culture. For example, as already noted, in her work in Tonga, Kavapalu worked with a relatively small number of families but drew conclusions about Tongan society more generally; both about particular patterns of parental behaviour towards children and about the motivations for this. Her generalisations may well be correct, but it is important to remember that there is a process of inference involved here (from sample to population), and it is quite possible to draw false conclusions about what goes on generally from what is observed in some particular situation, or to make false inferences from what a few people say to what most would say. Imagine doing a study of parental practices in your own society based on close investigation of just a few families. How accurate the conclusions would be depends a great deal on *how many* and *which* families are studied. Furthermore, even if studying a small number of families might give us a sense of some of the variation that occurs in the population of parents within the society more generally, it would not allow us to get a clear and reliable sense of what *proportions* of the population display particular patterns of behaviour.

Another weakness of qualitative inquiry concerns its capacity to identify causal relations. Many qualitative researchers today deny that this is their aim, but in practice they are usually engaged in producing explanations that assume causal relations of some kind. For example, an earlier study of Tonga sought to explain the use of punishment by Tongan parents in terms of the wider functional requirements of Tongan society, and also claimed that the treatment of children generated psychic stress that shaped their behaviour as adults, including the treatment of their own children (Beaglehole and Beaglehole, 1941). In relation to these causal claims, we must ask: what kinds of evidence are needed to establish their validity beyond reasonable doubt?

There are two kinds. First, there is information about what happens *within* particular cases that might indicate possible causal relations. This is sometimes referred to as 'process tracing' (George and Bennett, 2005) and is similar to what historians do when they are seeking to find an explanation for some historical event (Roberts, 1996). The second is comparative analysis: the search for patterns or associations between the presence or absence of an outcome and that of various potential causal factors. Both these kinds of evidence are of great value, though it is rare for them to be entirely conclusive. While it is certainly true that being able to observe what happens over time in particular contexts, and to talk to the people directly involved, provides important and distinctive data that can be very useful in causal analysis, qualitative research still relies on inference: it is not possible to directly 'see' causal relations. Furthermore, unless qualitative researchers are able to employ systematic comparisons of cases that differ in the key respects that are relevant, it will be almost impossible to determine whether an outcome was produced by the causal factor suspected rather than by some other feature of the particular context being investigated (see Cooper et al., 2012) – as we saw in the example of the relationship between television watching and materialistic attitudes among children. However, much the same is true of quantitative survey research.

Up to now we have examined the nature of quantitative and qualitative data and how they are produced. We have also considered some of the threats to the validity of inferences from them designed to answer research questions about childhood issues. In the next section we will consider some of the arguments that have been put forward by social scientists regarding the superiority of one or other of these two approaches, and about their compatibility or incompatibility.

Summary of Section 4

Qualitative data consists of words rather than numbers.

It can take a variety of forms, notably: documents of various kinds (including visual as well as textual, electronic as well as paper based), field notes written by researchers, and audio- and video-recordings, plus transcriptions of these.

The distinction between qualitative and quantitative data is not quite as straightforward as often assumed: we often use words to refer to number and frequency ('a few', 'some', 'many', 'frequently', 'rarely', etc.) and measurement ('more powerful/less powerful', 'more vulnerable/less vulnerable', etc.).

Like quantitative data, qualitative data is the outcome of a production process and involves various threats to validity.

Some of these arise from estimating quantities, but it is a mistake to assume that precise figures about frequency or amount are automatically more accurate than less precise verbal descriptions.

Qualitative researchers are able to check the validity of their descriptions and interpretations through comparing data of different types relating to the same case – for example, observations with accounts from informants – in a way that quantitative researchers are not usually able to do.

It is more difficult for qualitative researchers to generalise from a sample to a population, and to control variables, because they generally study small numbers of naturally occurring cases in depth.

This illustrates a general point that all methodological decisions involve trade-offs between advantages and disadvantages; there is no perfect method.

5 The choice between using quantitative and qualitative data

Researchers have to make decisions about what sorts of data are required in order to try to answer the questions they are addressing. Similarly, in reading and assessing research reports we need to consider whether the best sort of data was used for investigating the topic, and whether the data was adequate to support the conclusions reached. In some cases, the research question may seem to more or less determine what sort of data is required, at least in terms of whether it should be quantitative or qualitative. For example, if the aim is to discover whether incidents of bullying are increasing within a particular school or school system, quantitative data would seem to be essential. By contrast, if we are interested in how children identify and interpret bullying, then a qualitative approach might appear more appropriate. In many cases, though, the same research question can be addressed by either or both approaches.

In the discussion up to now we have examined quantitative and qualitative methods in terms of the strengths and weaknesses of each, treating neither as superior to the other. This attitude towards the two approaches is quite common amongst social scientists today in many fields; indeed, there has emerged a 'mixed methods' movement over the past couple of decades that argues for the benefits of *combining* quantitative with qualitative data, on the grounds that by doing so the complementary weaknesses of each approach can be overcome and thereby sounder conclusions reached (see, for example, Tashakkori and Teddlie, 2010).

However, there are some researchers, especially in the qualitative tradition, who take a very different view. They often regard quantitative method as inappropriate in studying the social world, not least when the focus is on the views and activities of children and young people. There is a variety of reasons for taking this position. These usually reflect fundamental assumptions about the nature of research, and often also about the character of the social world itself.

For instance, it may be argued that only by first-hand contact with people, in which the researcher adopts an open-ended approach designed to learn about their perspectives and practices, can sound knowledge of social phenomena be produced. In Chapter 5, it was noted that many of those involved in the new social studies of childhood suggested that adults face great difficulty in understanding children, even though all adults have themselves been children. It is often argued that only qualitative method allows the barriers to be reduced, and thereby facilitates understanding, enabling researchers to see the world differently from the way they normally do.

Qualitative researchers also sometimes argue that the very character of social phenomena – the creative, dynamic and contextually variable nature of people's attitudes and actions – means that these cannot be measured, or even categorised in the fixed way that is required if they are to be counted. In other words, it is suggested that attempts at both counting and measuring involve serious distortion of social phenomena, whereas qualitative methods are more flexible and thereby able to adapt to the distinctive and variable character of these phenomena. Similarly, it is frequently claimed that the assumptions about social causality built into quantitative method are at odds with the nature of the social world – where causal relations are complex and non-linear – and particularly with the socially constructed character of human activities and institutions, whereby people exercise agency in following one course of action rather than another. Finally, there are sometimes ethical and political arguments mounted against quantitative research: to the effect that, for example, it filters people's views of themselves and their worlds through an 'objective' structure rather than allowing them to speak for themselves – effectively subjecting them to the information requirements of state administration, commercial organisations or professional surveillance.

Activity 6   Difficulties facing adults in studying children
Allow about 30 minutes

Look back at the discussion in Chapter 5 about the difficulties facing adults in studying children. First, list the arguments mentioned, identifying the source of these difficulties, and add any further ones that you can think of. Secondly, consider how convincing each of these arguments is.

Comment

There are at least two arguments here.

1 Since children have not yet been fully socialised, because of their earlier 'developmental stage', or because of their distinctive conditions of life, they are alien or 'other' in relation to adults. This means that in order to understand them, adults need to put aside what seems to them normal and obvious – they need to learn to see and feel things differently. They may not be able to do this, or only be able to do it partially and with considerable difficulty. There is a parallel here with arguments about the difficulties of understanding people living in past historical periods. While it was once assumed that there is a common human nature – that all human beings are more or less the same, and can therefore understand one another – from the eighteenth century onwards in the West, the dominant view was that historical differences constitute significant barriers to understanding. While it was usually argued that these could be overcome if the right approach were adopted, there have always been some sceptics who have doubted this. As the discussion in Chapter 5 makes clear, there are some of these in the field of childhood studies. Thus, Owain Jones is quoted as arguing:

Once childhood is superseded by adult stocks of knowledge, those adult filters can never be removed to get back to earlier states. Adult constructions and memories of what it is/was to be a child are inevitably processed through *adultness*.

(Jones, 2001, p. 177)

2 Since all adults have been children, and most of us have at least some dealings with children, there is a danger of assuming too readily that we can understand them, adopting familiar assumptions that fail to recognise how distinctive the experience and lives of particular children are. As part of this, we may also assume too much homogeneity among children, neglecting differences arising from gender, class, ethnicity, locale, and so on. In addition, we may forget the extent to which different generations can have very different life experiences. The category 'children' does not pick out a single homogeneous set of beings, but a loosely defined and heterogeneous set. Moreover, some of the ways in which they differ, as well as some of what they share, will parallel variation in the experience of adults.

Both these arguments have some force. It is fairly clear that young children, especially, tend to have a very different mode of existence from that of most adults; this is partly shaped by distinctive capabilities and motivations, and how they are treated. This clearly poses a challenge to adult understanding. It is also true that many adults, much of the time, tend to assume that they even know what babies and young children want and need, why they behave the way they do, etc. Indeed, to some extent they must assume this in caring for them. There is a huge vocabulary of explanations available at hand, designed to make sense of the behaviour of children, but while these may capture some aspects of childhood, they are generally designed to facilitate adult handling of children, and very often are not well attuned to understanding the latter's experience and perspectives.

There are also some potential problems with these two arguments. For one thing, they both seem to assume that what is required in order to explain children's behaviour is, in effect, for adults to become children again: to be able to grasp children's experience directly and see the world from their point of view. Implicit here is the idea that children themselves have direct knowledge of what it is like to be a child. However, this idea relies upon a questionable theory of knowledge. Knowledge, in the form of social scientific understanding at least, is not simply a reflection or embodiment of experience, but rather a processing of data in which interpretation and judgement are required, drawing upon theoretical resources, in order to answer particular research questions.

The issue we have just been discussing, about the difficulties involved in understanding children's behaviour, is just one of many fundamental disputes that now characterise the field of social research methodology. There have been almost exactly the same arguments about understanding in other areas; for example, about whether men can understand women's experience and lives, and about whether we can understand other cultures. In these cases, by contrast with that of adults understanding children, there is not even any past shared experience to give us confidence in the possibility of understanding.

Other methodological disagreements among social scientists relate to the extent to which all accounts of the world, including those of social scientists, create what they purport to represent. We cannot necessarily rely upon a particular language, and the cultural resources in which it is embedded, to formulate those accounts. This argument arises most obviously in anthropologists' accounts of religious views and practices, though it extends far beyond these. To take an extreme example, the anthropologist Marvin Harris explains the sacredness of cows in the Hindu religion as arising from the fact that they are essential to the agricultural system in India, being the source of oxen which are 'the Indian peasant's tractor, thresher and family car combined' (1995, p. 202). This clearly conflicts with the way that Hindus themselves explain the sacredness of cows. Do we have a contrast here between a genuine explanation and a spurious one, or between a minority-world and a Hindu construction of reality?

In the next section I give attention to a further methodological dispute, one that is raised directly by Kavapalu's work, but is also relevant to the work of the UNICEF researchers, and much of social science.

Summary of Section 5

Some research questions seem to specifically require quantitative or qualitative data, but most can be investigated using either or both.

There is a growing movement that advocates combining or mixing the two methods of collecting data.

However, many qualitative researchers regard quantitative methods as inappropriate for investigating social phenomena, and perhaps especially for studying children and young people. They emphasise, for example, the difficulties facing adults in trying to understand the perspectives and activities of children, suggesting that only a qualitative approach, if anything, can overcome these.

There are other fundamental disagreements to be found within social science that are relevant here; for example, about whether researchers produce accounts of the world that simply reflect their own preconceptions, preferences and sociocultural backgrounds, rather than documenting reality.

6 Evaluative versus documentary orientations

In a part of her article that is not included in the reading for Chapter 4, Kavapalu refers to Beaglehole's earlier study of Tonga, and his negative reaction to the way children were treated, noting that it was similar to hers. She observes, however, that while he recorded negative evaluations in his diary, in his published account, written with his partner, he employed a non-evaluative, or what might be called a 'documentary', approach. In other words, he sought simply to describe and explain the behaviour he observed, how it arose out of the wider cultural context, and also to consider its consequences for adult personality amongst the Tongans. Broadly speaking, Kavapalu also adopts this documentary, non-evaluative approach in her work – albeit with some misgivings – and it is characteristic of much social science work, especially in anthropology.

One way of formulating this approach, used in Chapter 4, is to say that anthropologists have a commitment to cultural relativism: to denying that there is any overarching set of criteria, or underlying basis, on which we can judge cultural practices. For this reason, anthropologists generally resist the temptation to evaluate other cultures, fearing that this amounts to ethnocentrism – judging other cultures by the standards of their own. From this point of view, common practices and beliefs within a society must be treated as justified within the culture to which they belong, and any negative evaluation of them is regarded as simply expressing the criteria of some other culture. A similar kind of orientation can also be found on the part of many qualitative researchers outside of anthropology. Thus, researchers in sociology and cultural studies often emphasise the need to listen to the voices of the people they study – especially those belonging to marginalised groups – and to try to understand their perspectives and practices in their own terms, rather than adopting a 'correctionalist' stance in which they are evaluated from some purportedly correct point of view (Matza, 1969). Similarly, historians are often hesitant about condemning the practices of the past when they offend current sensibilities, viewing this as anachronistic.

There is much to be said for cultural relativism, in the sense that it dissuades researchers from becoming preoccupied with evaluative judgements. By adopting this approach, Kavapalu helps us to understand something of the nature of the disciplinary practices used by Tongans in child-rearing, why they adopt them, and how those practices relate to other aspects of Tongan society. However, at the same time, she is concerned about Tongans' treatment of children, as most readers probably would be, and in the course of her article raises the question of whether it should be labelled as 'child abuse'. (For studies in which anthropologists specifically address the issue of child abuse, see Scheper-Hughes, 1987.) Of course, to apply this label would break away from cultural relativism, and it might carry the danger of reframing Tongans' treatment of their children in a way that prevents us from seeing what they actually do, or asking why they do it; the concept of child abuse brings with it a characterisation of the behaviour concerned and implicit explanations in terms of inherent evil, psychological defect, and so on.

There may be a way out of this dilemma. It is important to emphasise that adopting a documentary stance does not require us to accept a culturally relativist view, in the sense of denying that people from other cultures can make legitimate evaluations of practices within Tonga, or vice versa. It is quite possible to insist that the task of research is to document – not evaluate – the world, while recognising that making evaluations can be a quite reasonable, and sometimes unavoidable, practice. When it comes to making practical judgements and decisions about how to bring up children, how to respond to parents' and others' treatment of children, etc., we cannot adopt a purely documentary stance; we must engage in evaluation, and this may include evaluating practices found in cultures other than our own, whether excessive punishment of children or other contentious practices. However, we are not required to do that in carrying out research, or in reading research reports.

In other words, in carrying out research it is possible to use a set of values to frame an investigation but then to concentrate entirely upon documenting the features of the world that this value perspective picks out as relevant, and to set about explaining these features rather than evaluating or criticising them. And there is much to be gained by refraining from evaluation in this way, as Kavapalu's work demonstrates. Most important of all, this restricted focus forces us to make sure that we have accurately documented the features of the world in which we are interested. The danger with an evaluative stance is that we take the accuracy of the documentary assumptions built into evaluations for granted – for example, reducing what we see and hear to a stereotypical picture of the people whose behaviour we are evaluating; or in explaining what we have found, resorting to stock explanations associated with those evaluations. Furthermore, by trying to suspend our own evaluative reactions and trying to find out how the people we are studying view things – for instance, 'Tongan parents' attitudes towards children – we may find that this forces us to recognise assumptions built into our own evaluative stance that are not quite so obviously true as we had previously assumed. For example, we might raise questions about whether verbal reprimands are always better than physical punishment.

Activity 7   Documentary versus evaluative stance
Allow about 15 minutes

Did the UNICEF research adopt a documentary or an evaluative stance? Indicate what features of the study led you to your conclusion. Are there any aspects of the study that count against your interpretation?

Comment

The UNICEF research sets out to *document* the relative levels of well-being in different societies. At the same time, on most interpretations 'well-being' is just as evaluative a concept as 'child abuse'. This does not mean, however, that this research cannot avoid being evaluative. We could view the UNICEF researchers as having adopted a particular definition of well-being, and a set of ideas about what are indicators of this, and then setting about discovering the relative level of well-being, so defined, across different societies within the OECD. From this perspective, the UNICEF research is not evaluative, it does not tell us about relative levels of well-being *per se*, only about relative levels of well-being *under a particular definition*. However, this is not actually how these researchers present their work. They seem to treat their measures as capturing well-being in all its forms. Given this, they do adopt an evaluative stance. Yet, other researchers could carry out a similar study using a different definition of well-being – for example, one informed by religious ideas or by secular ideas about well-being based on some notion of human flourishing (see, for instance, Nussbaum, 2011) – and produce very different results. Furthermore, research cannot tell us which definition of well-being is the right one, if indeed it makes any sense to assume that there is a single right one. What it *can* do is to provide us with documentary evidence relevant to particular definitions of well-being.

Summary of Section 6

A fundamental issue in the field of childhood studies, and elsewhere, is whether the task of research is to produce knowledge documenting how things are and why they are that way, or whether it is to engage in critical evaluation of how things are and to contribute to change.

Traditionally, social scientists have limited their task to the production of knowledge, but a more critical, evaluative and interventionist approach has become increasingly influential, not least in the field of childhood studies.

Studies of the treatment of children in other cultures dramatise the tension between these orientations: is the task simply to document how children are treated and why they are treated this way, or should what is happening be evaluated, for example, as a case of child abuse?

One formulation of the older position used by anthropologists is to suggest that researchers should adopt a culturally relativist position, refusing to judge other cultures, since there is no overarching scheme in terms of which this can be done.

There is an alternative way of supporting a documentary orientation that does not assume cultural relativism: this argues that while cross-cultural evaluations can be legitimate, these are not the task of research – to engage in evaluation as part of the research process is likely to introduce bias into our understanding of what is going on and why.

7 Conclusion

We began this chapter by looking at the kinds of evidence that social scientists use to try to answer questions in the field of childhood studies. We adopted the common contrast between quantitative and qualitative data, and looked briefly at some of the methods involved in producing these types of data – and the threats to validity associated with them. We suggested that, to some degree, the question of which type of data to use is a matter of which is most appropriate for the research question being addressed. And we noted that there is a strong movement today in favour of 'mixing' or combining quantitative and qualitative methods. We ended, however, by noting that there are some deep methodological disputes within the social research community. Some of these treat particular kinds of data and method as superior, reducing others to subordinate status at best. For example, arguments for the role of research in providing a basis for evidence-based practice in medicine, education and other fields tend to prioritise randomised controlled trials and quantitative methods generally. By contrast, many qualitative researchers see the use of experiments and surveys in studying the social world as of very limited value.

These disputes generally involve appeals to philosophical positions and, in the course of this, philosophical terms of various kinds – from 'positivism' through to 'postmodernism' – may be used. These can provide useful means of remembering and relating various kinds of methodological argument – but they also carry dangers, and this is why I have tried to avoid them here. For one thing, their meaning is quite variable across contexts, so that we always need to consider exactly what such terms are intended to mean on any particular occasion. Another danger is that they give the impression that the philosophical issues they highlight are matters that could be immediately resolved if only the 'right' position were adopted. In fact, most of the issues in dispute – including the problem of whether or not understanding other people is possible, and whether or not researchers ought to adopt a detached stance – are complex and difficult ones that can only be dealt with in a practical way in the context of particular pieces of research; and even then rarely in an entirely satisfactory manner. We need to bear these problems in mind, without pretending that they are easily resolvable, but at the same time not allow them to prevent us from addressing the more important substantive issues about childhood.

References

Ansell, N., Barker, J. and Smith, F. (2007) 'UNICEF "Child poverty in perspective" Report: a view from the UK', *Children's Geographies*, vol. 5, no. 3, pp. 325–30.

Bailey, R. (2009) 'Well-being, happiness and education', *British Journal of Sociology of Education*, vol. 30, no. 6, pp. 795–802.

Beaglehole, E. and Beaglehole, P. (1941) *Pangai—Village in Tonga*, Wellington, Polynesian Society.

Bradshaw, J. (2007) 'Some problems in the international comparison of child income poverty', in Wintersberger, H., Alanen, L., Olk, T. and Qvortrup, J. (eds) *Childhood, Generational Order and the Welfare State: Exploring Children's Social and Economic Welfare*, Odense, University Press of Southern Denmark.

Bryman, A. (1994) 'The Mead/Freeman controversy: some implications for qualitative researchers', in Burgess, R. G. (ed) *Studies in Qualitative Methodology: Issues in Qualitative Research*, vol. 4, London, JAI Press.

Bryman, A. (2008) *Social Research Methods*, 3rd edn, Oxford, Oxford University Press.

Cooper, B., Glaesser, J., Gomm, R. and Hammersley, M. (2012) *Challenging the Qualitative–Quantitative Divide: Explorations in Case-Focused Causal Analysis*, London, Continuum.

Croll, P. (2001) *Systematic Classroom Observation*, 2nd edn, London, RoutledgeFalmer.

Freeman, D. (1983) *Margaret Mead and Samoa: The Making and Unmaking of an Anthropological Myth*, Cambridge, MA, Harvard University Press.

Freeman, D. (1999) *The Fateful Hoaxing of Margaret Mead: A Historical Analysis of Her Samoan Research*, Boulder, CO, Westview Press.

George, A. and Bennett, A. (2005) *Case Studies and Theory Development in the Social Sciences*, Cambridge, MA, MIT Press.

Harris, M. (1995) *Cultural Anthropology*, New York, Harper Collins.

Jones, O. (2001) '"Before the dark of reason": some ethical and epistemological considerations on the otherness of childhood', *Ethics, Place and Environment*, vol. 4, no. 2, pp. 173–8.

Kavapalu, H. (1993) 'Dealing with the dark side in the ethnography of childhood: child punishment in Tonga', *Oceania*, vol. 63, no. 4, pp. 313–29.

Matza, D. (1969) *Becoming Deviant*, Chicago, IL, Aldine.

Mead, M. (1928) *Coming of Age in Samoa*, New York, Harper Collins.

Morrow, V. and Mayall, B. (2009) 'What is wrong with children's well-being in the UK? Questions of meaning and measurement', *Journal of Social Welfare and Family Law*, vol. 31, no. 3, pp. 217–29.

Morton, H. (1996) *Becoming Tongan: An Ethnography of Childhood*, Honolulu, University of Hawaii Press.

Nussbaum, M. (2011) *Creating Capabilities: The Human Development Approach*, Cambridge, MA, Harvard University Press.

Roberts, C. (1996) *The Logic of Historical Explanation*, Pennsylvania, The Pennsylvania State University Press.

Scheper-Hughes, N. (ed) (1987) *Child Survival: Anthropological Perspectives on the Treatment and Maltreatment of Children*, Dordrecht, Holland, Reidel.

Shankman, P. (2009) *The Trashing of Margaret Mead: Anatomy of an Anthropological Controversy*, Madison, WI, The University of Wisconsin Press.

Tashakkori, A. and Teddlie, C. (2010) *Handbook of Mixed Methods in Social and Behavioral Research*, 2nd edn, Thousand Oaks, CA, Sage.

UNICEF (2007) *Child Poverty in Perspective: An Overview of Child Well-being in Rich Countries*, Innocenti Report Card 7, Florence, UNICEF Innocenti Research Centre.

Acknowledgements

Every effort has been made to contact copyright holders. If any have been inadvertently overlooked the publishers will be pleased to make the necessary arrangements at the first opportunity.

Grateful acknowledgement is made to the following sources:

Figures

Cover image: *Little Girl with Roses*, 2000 (oil on canvas), © Holzhandler, Dora (Contemporary Artist) / Private Collection / The Bridgeman Art Library; page 5: © istockphoto.com/Naomi Bassitt; page 11: © Mary Jane Kehily; page 14: Thanks to Jim Irving, a contributor to the Remembering the Past, Resourcing the Future Community History Archive for the use of this image; page 21: *Pregnancy & Birth* (2011), Mother & Baby Picture Library, Bauer Media; page 23: © iStockphoto. com/Christopher Futcher; page 25: © Babybond Ltd; page 28: © PSL Images/Alamy; page 56: © The Bodleian Libraries, The University of Oxford, Shelfmark: MS. Douce 276, fol. 110v; page 57: © The National Archives Image Library; page 58: Taken from www.bbc.co.uk/schools/ primaryhistory/victorian_britain/children_in_coal_mines; page 62: Taken from http://www.wikipaintings.org/en/pieter-bruegel-the-elder/ children-s-games-1560; page 70: © DEA/P.Manusardi/Veneranda Biblioteca Ambrosiana/Getty Images; page 70: © Derrick E. Witty/ National Trust Photo Library; page 71: *Many Happy Returns of the Day*, 1856 by Frith, William Powell (1819–1909) Harrogate Museums and Arts, North Yorkshire, UK/© Harrogate Museums and Arts/The Bridgeman Art Library Nationality/copyright status: English/out of copyright; page 74: © istockphoto.com/Duncan Walker; page 76: © *First Stage of Cruelty*, 1751 (engraving), Hogarth, William (1697–1764)/ Private Collection/The Bridgeman Art Library; page 78: NGI 226, *The Village School*, Artist: Jan Steen, Dutch, 17th century, c.1665, Oil on canvas, Unframed: 110.5 x 80.2 cm, Photo © National Gallery of Ireland; page 81: © *A Puritan Family*, from 'The Whole Psalms in Four Parts', 1563 (woodcut) (b/w photo), English School, (16th century)/ Private Collection/The Bridgeman Art Library; page 83: © World History Archive/Alamy; page 85: © Georgios Kollidas/iStockphoto; page 105: Reproduced with permission of Punch Limited; page 113: © English Heritage Photo Library; page 115: Time & Life Pictures/Getty Images; page 118: Reproduced by permission of the Heatherbank

Museum of Social Work; page 119: *The Mothercraft Manual* (1923); page 120: Popperfoto/Getty Images; page 123: © Mary Evans Picture Library; page 127: © Bill Anderson/Science Photo Library; page 133: Adapted from Donaldson. M. (1978) *Children's Minds*, London, Fontana; page 136: © Photomak/Dreamstime.com; page 139: Davey, G. et al. (2004) *Complete Psychology*, Hodder Education. Copyright (c) 2004 Graham Davey, Ian P. Albery, Chris Chandler, Andy Field, Dai Jones, David Messer, Simon Moore and Christopher Sterling. Reproduced by permission of Hodder Education; page 46: © Ryan Cooper; page 165: Courtesy of Queensland State Archives; page 166: © American Philosophical Society; page 167: Courtesy of Library of London School of Economics and Political Science; page 171: Courtesy of David Wilson, Stop Infant Circumcision Society; page 173: © Lonely Planet/Superstock; page 176: Taken from Library of Congress, www.loc.gov; page 179: © Lucian Coman/www.123rf.com; page 180: © Tyagan Miller/Indiana University Research & Creative Activity; page 183: Taken from Library of Congress at http://www.loc.gov/exhibits/mead/; page 186: © Alma Gottlieb, found in *The Afterlife Is Where We Come From: The Culture of Infancy in West Africa*, published by The University of Chicago Press; page 187: © UNICEF Bhutan; page 190: © Jodi Bieber/Save the Children; page 216: © John Chillingworth /Getty Images; page 221: © wavebreakmedia/iStockphoto; page 222: © Bojan Kontrec/iStockphoto; page 226: © Terry Fincher/Getty Images; page 231: © Igor Demchenkov/iStockphoto.com; page 233: © Peter Garbet/iStockphoto.com; page 234: © Goldenkb/Dreamstime.com; page 237: © AFP/Getty Images; page 244: © Lawrence Sawyer/iStockphoto.com; page 246: © David Bukach/istockphoto.com; page 279: Adapted from Brown, R. J., http://en.wikipedia.org/wiki/File:Comparison_standard_deviations.svg; page 279: UNICEF, *Child Poverty in Perspective: An Overview of Child Well-being in Rich Countries*, Innocenti Report Card 7, 2007. UNICEF Innocenti Research Centre, Florence. Copyright © The United Nations Children's Fund, 2007.

Text

Page 32: Geoffrey Pearson, *Hooligan*, published 1983, MacMillan Education Ltd, Hong Kong. Reproduced with permission of Palgrave Macmillan; page 37: *Gender and Consumption*, Emma Casey and Lydia Martens, 2007, Ashgate Publishing; page 44: From *Dream Babies: Childcare Advice from John Locke to Gina Ford* by Christina Hardyment published by Francis Lincoln Ltd, copyright © 2007. Reproduced by

Index